Lincoln and his Cabinet

Biographies of Great Statesmen

Editor: Joe Mieczkowski, Gettysburg Licensed Battlefield Guide

Title: Lincoln and his Cabinet

Subtitle: Biographies of Great Statesmen

Editor: Joe Mieczkowski, Gettysburg Licensed Battlefield Guide

Created on: 2013-09-11 06:45 (UTC)

ISBN: 978-3-86898-002-8

Produced by: PediaPress GmbH, Taunusstrasse 61, Mainz, Germany, http://pediapress.com/

The content within this book was generated collaboratively by volunteers. Please be advised that nothing found here has necessarily been reviewed by people with the expertise required to provide you with complete, accurate or reliable information. Some information in this book may be misleading or simply wrong. PediaPress does not guarantee the validity of the information found here. If you need specific advice (for example, medical, legal, financial, or risk management) please seek a professional who is licensed or knowledgeable in that area.

Sources, licenses and contributors of the articles and images are listed in the section entitled "References". Parts of the books may be licensed under the GNU Free Documentation License. A copy of this license is included in the section entitled "GNU Free Documentation License"

All third-party trademarks used belong to their respective owners.

Create your own custom Wikipedia-Book at http://pediapress.com

collection id:
pdf writer version: 0.10.1 mwlib version: 0.15.8

Contents

Articles	**1**
Preface	1
President	**3**
Abraham Lincoln	3
Vice President	**53**
Hannibal Hamlin	53
Andrew Johnson	60
Secretary of State	**81**
William H. Seward	81
Secretary of War	**99**
Simon Cameron	99
Edwin M. Stanton	104
Secretary of the Treasury	**115**
Salmon P. Chase	115
William P. Fessenden	127
Hugh McCulloch	134
Attorney General	**139**
Edward Bates	139
James Speed	144

Postmaster General   **147**

    Montgomery Blair 147

    William Dennison, Jr. 152

Secretary of the Navy   **157**

    Gideon Welles 157

Secretary of the Interior   **165**

    Caleb Blood Smith 165

    John Palmer Usher 169

Appendix   171

    References 171

    Article Sources and Contributors 185

    Image Sources, Licenses and Contributors 190

Article Licenses   193

Index   195

Preface

Abraham Lincoln began the process of constructing his cabinet on election night in 1860. Lincoln attempted to reach out to every faction of his party with a special emphasis on balancing anti-slavery former Whigs with former free-soil Democrats. It seems clear that his goal was not to create a "War Cabinet" (because he did not expect war), but to create a cabinet that would unite the party.Lincoln's eventual cabinet would include all of his main rivals for the Republican nomination. Lincoln did not shy away from surrounding himself with strong-minded men, even those whose credentials for office appeared to be much more impressive than his own.

Joe Mieczkowski is a Civil War living historian and educator. Having received his Bachelor's Degree from Salem College (WV) and his Master's Degree in Public Administration from Pennsylvania State University, Joe's education provided the foundation to support his 37 year career with the Social Security Administration. He served in a variety of locations and positions, including 16 years as a Manager and Area Director in Washington, D.C. He retired from federal service as the Area Director in Harrisburg, PA. Joe is an Adjunct Professor for local community colleges, teaching courses in various aspects of American History. In addition, Joe teaches management and leadership courses. As a leadership training consultant, Joe works with numerous educational, governmental, and corporate organizations. He is a Licensed Battlefield and Town Guide for the Gettysburg National Military Park, and is a Past President of the Gettysburg Civil War Roundtable.

Joe is a resident of Fairfield, PA, where he lives with his wife, Chris.

President

Abraham Lincoln

	**Abraham Lincoln**

	**16th President of the United States**
	**In office** March 4, 1861 – April 15, 1865
Vice President	Hannibal Hamlin Andrew Johnson
Preceded by	James Buchanan
Succeeded by	Andrew Johnson
	**Member of the U.S. House of Representatives from Illinois's 7th district**
	**In office** March 4, 1847 – March 3, 1849
Preceded by	John Henry
Succeeded by	Thomas Harris
	**Personal details**

Born	February 12, 1809 Hodgenville, Kentucky, U.S.
Died	April 15, 1865 (aged 56) Washington, D.C., U.S.
Political party	Republican Party (1854–1865) National Union Party (1864–1865)
Other political affiliations	Whig Party (Before 1854)
Spouse(s)	Mary Todd
Children	Robert Edward William Tad
Profession	Lawyer
Religion	*See article*
Signature	*Abraham Lincoln*
Military service	
Service/branch	Illinois Militia
Years of service	1832
Battles/wars	Black Hawk War

Abraham Lincoln 🔊 i/ˈeɪbrəhæmˈlɪŋkən/ (February 12, 1809 – April 15, 1865) was the 16th President of the United States, serving from March 1861 until his assassination in 1865. He led the country through a great constitutional, military and moral crisis – the American Civil War – preserving the Union, while ending slavery, and promoting economic and financial modernization. Reared in a poor family on the western frontier, Lincoln was mostly self-educated. He became a country lawyer, an Illinois state legislator, and a one-term member of the United States House of Representatives, but failed in two attempts at a seat in the United States Senate.

After deftly opposing the expansion of slavery in the United States in his campaign debates and speeches,[1] Lincoln secured the Republican nomination and was elected president in 1860. Following declarations of secession by southern slave states, war began in April 1861, and he concentrated on both the military and political dimensions of the war effort, seeking to reunify the nation. He vigorously exercised unprecedented war powers, including the arrest and detention without trial of thousands of suspected secessionists. He prevented British recognition of the Confederacy by skillfully handling the *Trent* affair late in 1861. He issued his Emancipation Proclamation in 1863 and promoted the passage of the Thirteenth Amendment to the United States Constitution, abolishing slavery.

Lincoln closely supervised the war effort, especially the selection of top generals, including commanding general Ulysses S. Grant. He brought leaders of various factions of his party into his cabinet and pressured them to cooperate. Under his leadership, the Union set up a naval blockade that shut down the South's normal trade, took control of the border slave states at the start of the war, gained control communications with gunboats on the southern river systems, and tried repeatedly to capture the Confederate capital at Richmond. Each time a general failed, Lincoln substituted another until finally Grant succeeded in 1865. An exceptionally astute politician deeply involved with power issues in each state, he reached out to War Democrats and managed his own re-election in the 1864 presidential election.

As the leader of the moderate faction of the Republican party, Lincoln came under attack from all sides. Radical Republicans wanted harsher treatment of the South, War Democrats desired more compromise, and Copperheads despised him—not to mention irreconcilable secessionists in reunited areas.[2] Politically, Lincoln fought back with patronage, by pitting his opponents against each other, and by appealing to the American people with his powers of oratory.[3] His Gettysburg Address of 1863 became the most quoted speech in American history.[4] It was an iconic statement of America's dedication to the principles of nationalism, equal rights, liberty, and democracy. At the close of the war, Lincoln held a moderate view of Reconstruction, seeking to speedily reunite the nation through a policy of generous reconciliation in the face of lingering and bitter divisiveness. However, just six days after the surrender of Confederate commanding general Robert E. Lee, Lincoln was shot and killed by Confederate sympathizer John Wilkes Booth at Ford's Theatre in Washington, D.C. His death marked the first assassination of a U.S. president. Lincoln has been consistently ranked by scholars as one of the greatest U.S. presidents.

Family and childhood

Early life

Abraham Lincoln was born February 12, 1809, the second child of Thomas Lincoln and Nancy Lincoln (née Hanks), in a one-room log cabin on the Sinking Spring Farm in Hardin County, Kentucky,[5] (now LaRue County). Lincoln's paternal grandfather and namesake, Abraham, had moved his family from Virginia to Jefferson County, Kentucky,[6,7] where he was ambushed and killed in an Indian raid in 1786, with his children, including Lincoln's father Thomas, looking on.[7] Thomas was left to make his own way on the frontier.[8] Lincoln's mother, Nancy, was the daughter of Lucy Hanks, and was born in what is now Mineral County, West Virginia, then part of Virginia. Lucy moved with Nancy to Kentucky. Nancy Hanks married Thomas, who

Figure 1: *The young Lincoln in sculpture at Senn Park, Chicago*

became a respected citizen. He bought and sold several farms, including the Sinking Spring Farm. The family attended a Separate Baptists church, which had high moral standards and opposed alcohol, dancing, and slavery.[9] Thomas enjoyed considerable status in Kentucky—where he sat on juries, appraised estates, served on country slave patrols, and guarded prisoners. By the time his son Abraham was born, Thomas owned two 600-acre (240 ha) farms, several town lots, livestock, and horses. He was among the richest men in the county.[10,11] However, in 1816, Thomas lost all of his land in court cases because of faulty property titles.[12]

The family moved north across the Ohio River to free (i.e., non-slave) territory and made a new start in Perry County, Indiana. Lincoln later noted that this move was "partly on account of slavery" but mainly due to land title difficulties.[12] In Indiana, when Lincoln was nine, his mother Nancy died of milk sickness in 1818.[13] After the death of Lincoln's mother, his older sister, Sarah, took charge of caring for him until their father remarried in 1819; Sarah later died in her 20s while giving birth to a stillborn son.[14]

Thomas Lincoln's new wife was the widow Sarah Bush Johnston, the mother of three of her own children. Lincoln became very close to his stepmother, and referred to her as "Mother".[15] As a pre-teen, he did not like the hard labor associated with frontier life. Some in his family, and in the neighborhood, for a time considered him to be lazy.[16,17] As he grew into his teens, he willingly took responsibility for all chores expected of him as one of the boys in the household and became an adept axeman in his work building rail fences. He attained a reputation for brawn and audacity after a very competitive wrestling match to which he was challenged by the renowned leader of a group of ruffians, "the Clary's Grove boys".[18] Lincoln also agreed with the customary obligation of a son to give his father all earnings from work done outside the home until age 21.[19] In later years, Lincoln occasionally loaned his father money.[20] Lincoln became increasingly distant from his father, in part because of his father's lack of education. While young Lincoln's formal elementary education consisted approximately of a years worth of classes from several itinerant teachers, he was mostly self-educated and was an avid reader.[21]

In 1830, fearing a milk sickness outbreak along the Ohio River, the Lincoln family moved west, where they settled on public land in Macon County, Illinois, another free, non-slave state.[22] In 1831, Thomas relocated the family to a new homestead in Coles County, Illinois. It was then that as an ambitious 22-year-old, Lincoln decided to seek a better life and struck out on his own. Canoeing down the Sangamon River, Lincoln ended up in the village of New Salem in Sangamon County.[23] In the spring of 1831, hired by New Salem businessman Denton Offutt and accompanied by friends, he took goods by flatboat from New Salem to New Orleans via the Sangamon, Illinois, and Mississippi rivers. After arriving in New Orleans—and witnessing slavery firsthand—he walked back home.[24]

Marriage and children

1864 photo of President Lincoln with youngest son, Tad

Mary Todd Lincoln, wife of Abraham Lincoln, age 28

Lincoln's first romantic interest was Ann Rutledge, whom he met when he first moved to New Salem; by 1835, they were in a relationship but not formally engaged. She died, however, on August 25, most likely of typhoid fever.[25] In the early 1830s, he met Mary Owens from Kentucky when she was visiting her sister. Late in 1836, Lincoln agreed to a match with Mary if she returned to New Salem. Mary did return in November 1836, and Lincoln courted her for a time; however, they both had second thoughts about their relationship. On August 16, 1837, Lincoln wrote Mary a letter suggesting he would not blame her if she ended the relationship. She never replied and the courtship was over.[26]

In 1840, Lincoln became engaged to Mary Todd, who was from a wealthy slave-holding family in Lexington, Kentucky.[27] They met in Springfield, Illinois, in December 1839[28] and were engaged the following December.[29] A wedding set for January 1, 1841 was canceled when the two broke off their engagement at Lincoln's initiative.[28,30] They later met at a party and were married on November 4, 1842, in the Springfield mansion of Mary's married sister.[31] While preparing for the nuptials and feeling reluctance again, Lincoln, when asked where he was going, replied, "To hell, I suppose."[32]

In 1844, the couple bought a house in Springfield near Lincoln's law office.[33] Mary Todd Lincoln worked diligently in their home, assuming full household duties which had previously been performed for her in her own family in Kentucky. She also made efficient use of the limited funds available from her husband's law practice.[34] Robert Todd Lincoln was born in 1843 and Edward Baker Lincoln (Eddie) in 1846. Lincoln "was remarkably fond of children",[35] and the Lincolns were not considered to be strict with their children.[36] Robert was the only child to live to adulthood. Edward died on February 1, 1850, in Springfield, likely of tuberculosis. "Willie" Lincoln was born on December 21, 1850 and died on February 20, 1862. The Lincolns' fourth son, Thomas

"Tad" Lincoln, was born on April 4, 1853 and died of heart failure at the age of 18 on July 16, 1871.[37]

The death of their sons had profound effects on both parents. Later in life, Mary struggled with the stresses of losing her husband and sons, and Robert Lincoln committed her temporarily to a mental health asylum in 1875.[38] Abraham Lincoln suffered from "melancholy", a condition which now may be referred to as clinical depression.[39]

Lincoln's father-in-law was based in Lexington, Kentucky; he and others of the Todd family were either slave owners or slave traders. Lincoln was close to the Todds, and he and his family occasionally visited the Todd estate in Lexington.[40] He was an affectionate, though often absent, husband and father of four children.

Early career and militia service

In 1832, at age 23, Lincoln and a partner bought a small general store on credit in New Salem, Illinois. Although the economy was booming in the region, the business struggled and Lincoln eventually sold his share. That March he began his political career with his first campaign for the Illinois General Assembly. He had attained local popularity and could draw crowds as a natural raconteur in New Salem, though he lacked an education, powerful friends, and money, which may be why he lost. He advocated navigational improvements on the Sangamon River.[41]

Before the election Lincoln served as a captain in the Illinois Militia during the Black Hawk War.[42] Following his return, Lincoln continued his campaign for the August 6 election for the Illinois General Assembly. At 6 feet 4 inches (193 cm),[43] he was tall and "strong enough to intimidate any rival". At his first speech, when he saw a supporter in the crowd being attacked, Lincoln grabbed the assailant by his "neck and the seat of his trousers" and threw him.[44] Lincoln finished eighth out of thirteen candidates (the top four were elected), though he received 277 of the 300 votes cast in the New Salem precinct.[45]

Lincoln served as New Salem's postmaster and later as county surveyor, all the while reading voraciously. He then decided to become a lawyer and began teaching himself law by reading Blackstone's *Commentaries on the Laws of England* and other law books. Of his learning method, Lincoln stated: "I studied with nobody".[46] His second campaign in 1834 was successful. He won election to the state legislature; though he ran as a Whig, many Democrats favored him over a more powerful Whig opponent.[47] Admitted to the bar in 1836,[48] he moved to Springfield, Illinois, and began to practice law under John T. Stuart, Mary Todd's cousin.[49] Lincoln became an able and successful

Figure 2: *A sketch of young Abraham Lincoln*

lawyer with a reputation as a formidable adversary during cross-examinations and closing arguments. He partnered with Stephen T. Logan from 1841 until 1844, when he began his practice with William Herndon, whom Lincoln thought "a studious young man".[50] He served four successive terms in the Illinois House of Representatives as a Whig representative from Sangamon County.[51]

In the 1835–1836 legislative session, he voted to expand suffrage to white males, whether landowners or not.[52] He was known for his "free soil" stance of opposing both slavery and abolitionism. He first articulated this in 1837, saying, "Institution of slavery is founded on both injustice and bad policy, but the promulgation of abolition doctrines tends rather to increase than abate its evils."[53] He closely followed Henry Clay in supporting the American Colonization Society program of making the abolition of slavery practical by helping the freed slaves to settle in Liberia in Africa.[54]

Congressman Lincoln

From the early 1830s, Lincoln was a steadfast Whig and professed to friends in 1861 to be, "an old line Whig, a disciple of Henry Clay".[55] The party, including Lincoln, favored economic modernization in banking, railroads, and internal improvements and espoused urbanization as well as protective tariffs.[56]

In 1846, Lincoln was elected to the U.S. House of Representatives, where he served one two-year term. He was the only Whig in the Illinois delegation, but he showed his party loyalty by participating in almost all votes and making speeches that echoed the party line.[57] Lincoln, in collaboration with abolitionist Congressman Joshua R. Giddings, wrote a bill to abolish slavery in the District of Columbia with compensation for the owners, enforcement to capture fugitive slaves, and a popular vote on the matter. He abandoned the bill when it failed to garner sufficient Whig supporters.[58] On foreign and military policy, Lincoln spoke out against the Mexican–American War, which he attributed to President Polk's desire for "military glory—that attractive rainbow, that rises in showers of blood".[59] Lincoln also supported the Wilmot Proviso, which, if it had been adopted, would have banned slavery in any U.S. territory won from Mexico.[60]

Lincoln emphasized his opposition to Polk by drafting and introducing his Spot Resolutions. The war had begun with a Mexican slaughter of American soldiers in territory disputed by Mexico and the US; Polk insisted that Mexican soldiers had "invaded *our territory* and shed the blood of our fellow-citizens on our *own soil*".[61,62] Lincoln demanded that Polk show Congress the exact spot on which blood had been shed and prove that the spot was on American soil.[62] Congress never enacted the resolution or even debated it, the national papers ignored it, and it resulted in a loss of political support for Lincoln in his district. One Illinois newspaper derisively nicknamed him "spotty Lincoln".[63,64,65] Lincoln later regretted some of his statements, especially his attack on the presidential war-making powers.[66]

Realizing Clay was unlikely to win the presidency, Lincoln, who had pledged in 1846 to serve only one term in the House, supported General Zachary Taylor for the Whig nomination in the 1848 presidential election.[67] Taylor won and Lincoln hoped to be appointed Commissioner of the General Land Office, but that lucrative patronage job went to an Illinois rival, Justin Butterfield, considered by the administration to be a highly skilled lawyer, but in Lincoln's view, an "old fossil".[68] The administration offered him the consolation prize of secretary or governor of the Oregon Territory. This distant territory was a Democratic stronghold, and acceptance of the post would have effectively ended his legal and political career in Illinois, so he declined and resumed his law practice.[69]

Prairie lawyer

Lincoln returned to practicing law in Springfield, handling "every kind of business that could come before a prairie lawyer".[70] Twice a year for sixteen years, ten weeks at a time, he appeared in county seats in the midstate region when the

Figure 3: *Lincoln in his late 30s – photo taken by one of Lincoln's law students around 1846*

county courts were in session.[71] Lincoln handled many transportation cases in the midst of the nation's western expansion, particularly the conflicts arising from the operation of river barges under the many new railroad bridges. As a riverboat man, Lincoln initially favored those interests but ultimately represented whoever hired him.[72] His reputation grew, and he appeared before the Supreme Court of the United States, arguing a case involving a canal boat that sank after hitting a bridge.[73] In 1849, he received a patent for a flotation device for the movement of boats in shallow water. The idea was never commercialized, but Lincoln is the only president to hold a patent.[74,75]

In 1851, he represented Alton & Sangamon Railroad in a dispute with one of its shareholders, James A. Barret, who had refused to pay the balance on his pledge to buy shares in the railroad on the grounds that the company had changed its original train route.[76,77] Lincoln successfully argued that the railroad company was not bound by its original charter in existence at the time of Barret's pledge; the charter was amended in the public interest to provide a newer, superior, and less expensive route, and the corporation retained the right to demand Barret's payment. The decision by the Illinois Supreme Court has been cited by numerous other courts in the nation.[76] Lincoln appeared before the Illinois Supreme Court in 175 cases, in 51 as sole counsel, of which 31 were decided in his favor.[78] From 1853 to 1860, another of Lincoln's largest clients was the Illinois Central Railroad.[79]

Lincoln's most notable criminal trial occurred in 1858 when he defended William "Duff" Armstrong, who was on trial for the murder of James Preston Metzker.[80] The case is famous for Lincoln's use of a fact established by judicial notice in order to challenge the credibility of an eyewitness. After an opposing witness testified seeing the crime in the moonlight, Lincoln produced a Farmers' Almanac showing the moon was at a low angle, drastically reducing visibility. Based on this evidence, Armstrong was acquitted.[80] Lincoln rarely raised objections in the courtroom; but in an 1859 case, where he defended a cousin Peachy Harrison, who was accused of stabbing another to death, Lincoln angrily protested the judge's decision to exclude evidence favorable to his client. Instead of holding Lincoln in contempt of court as was expected, the judge, a Democrat, reversed his ruling, allowing the evidence and acquitting Harrison.[80,81]

Republican politics 1854–1860

Slavery and a "House Divided"

By the 1850s, slavery was still legal in the southern United States but had been generally outlawed in the northern states, such as Illinois.[82] Lincoln disapproved of slavery, and the spread of slavery to new U.S. territory in the west.[83] He returned to politics to oppose the pro-slavery Kansas–Nebraska Act (1854); this law repealed the slavery-restricting Missouri Compromise (1820). Senior Senator Stephen A. Douglas of Illinois had incorporated popular sovereignty into the Act. Douglas' provision, which Lincoln opposed, specified settlers had the right to determine locally whether to allow slavery in new U.S. territory, rather than have such a decision restricted by the national Congress.[84] Foner (2010) contrasts the abolitionists and anti-slavery Radical Republicans of the Northeast who saw slavery as a sin, with the conservative Republicans who thought it was bad because it hurt white people and blocked progress. Foner argues that Lincoln was a moderate in the middle, opposing slavery primarily because it violated the republicanism principles of the Founding Fathers, especially the equality of all men and democratic self-government as expressed in the Declaration of Independence.[85]

On October 16, 1854, in his "Peoria Speech", Lincoln declared his opposition to slavery, which he repeated en route to the presidency.[86] Speaking in his Kentucky accent, with a very powerful voice,[87] he said the Kansas Act had a "*declared* indifference, but as I must think, a covert *real* zeal for the spread of slavery. I cannot but hate it. I hate it because of the monstrous injustice of

Figure 4: *Portrait of Dred Scott. Lincoln denounced the Supreme Court decision in Dred Scott v. Sandford as a conspiracy.*

slavery itself. I hate it because it deprives our republican example of its just influence in the world..."[88]

In late 1854, Lincoln ran as a Whig for the U.S. Senate seat from Illinois. At that time, senators were elected by the state legislature.[89] After leading in the first six rounds of voting in the Illinois assembly, his support began to dwindle, and Lincoln instructed his backers to vote for Lyman Trumbull, who defeated opponent Joel Aldrich Matteson.[90] The Whigs had been irreparably split by the Kansas–Nebraska Act. Lincoln wrote, "I think I am a Whig, but others say there are no Whigs, and that I am an abolitionist, even though I do no more than oppose the *extension* of slavery." Drawing on remnants of the old Whig party, and on disenchanted Free Soil, Liberty, and Democratic party members, he was instrumental in forging the shape of the new Republican Party.[91] At the Republican convention in 1856, Lincoln placed second in the contest to become the party's candidate for vice president.[92]

In 1857–58, Douglas broke with President James Buchanan, leading to a fight for control of the Democratic Party. Some eastern Republicans even favored the reelection of Douglas for the Senate in 1858, since he had led the opposition to the Lecompton Constitution, which would have admitted Kansas as a slave state.[93] In March 1857, the Supreme Court issued its decision in

Figure 5: *A. Helser photographed Lincoln in 1860.*

Dred Scott v. Sandford; Chief Justice Roger B. Taney opined that blacks were not citizens, and derived no rights from the Constitution. Lincoln denounced the decision, alleging it was the product of a conspiracy of Democrats to support the Slave Power[94] Lincoln argued, "The authors of the Declaration of Independence never intended 'to say all were equal in color, size, intellect, moral developments, or social capacity', but they 'did consider all men created equal—equal in certain inalienable rights, among which are life, liberty, and the pursuit of happiness'."[95]

After the state Republican party convention nominated him for the U.S. Senate in 1858, Lincoln delivered his House Divided Speech, drawing on Mark's gospel from the Bible: "A house divided against itself cannot stand. I believe this government cannot endure permanently half slave and half free. I do not expect the Union to be dissolved—I do not expect the house to fall—but I do expect it will cease to be divided. It will become all one thing, or all the other."[96] The speech created an evocative image of the danger of disunion caused by the slavery debate, and rallied Republicans across the North.[97] The stage was then set for the campaign for statewide election of the Illinois legislature which would, in turn, select Lincoln or Douglas as its U.S. senator.[98]

Lincoln–Douglas debates and Cooper Union speech

The 1858 senate campaign featured the seven Lincoln–Douglas debates of 1858, the most famous political debates in American history.[99] The principals stood in stark contrast both physically and politically. Lincoln warned that "The Slave Power" was threatening the values of republicanism, and accused Douglas of distorting the values of the Founding Fathers that all men are created equal, while Douglas emphasized his Freeport Doctrine, that local settlers were free to choose whether to allow slavery or not, and accused Lincoln of having joined the abolitionists.[100] The debates had an atmosphere of a prize fight and drew crowds in the thousands. Lincoln stated Douglas's popular sovereignty theory was a threat to the nation's morality and that Douglas represented a conspiracy to extend slavery to free states. Douglas said that Lincoln was defying the authority of the U.S. Supreme Court and the *Dred Scott* decision.[101]

Though the Republican legislative candidates won more popular votes, the Democrats won more seats, and the legislature re-elected Douglas to the Senate. Despite the bitterness of the defeat for Lincoln, his articulation of the issues gave him a national political reputation.[102] In May 1859, Lincoln purchased the *Illinois Staats-Anzeiger,* a German-language newspaper which was consistently supportive; most of the state's 130,000 German Americans voted Democratic but there was Republican support that a German-language paper could mobilize.[103]

On February 27, 1860, New York party leaders invited Lincoln to give a speech at Cooper Union to a group of powerful Republicans. Lincoln argued that the Founding Fathers had little use for popular sovereignty and had repeatedly sought to restrict slavery. Lincoln insisted the moral foundation of the Republicans required opposition to slavery, and rejected any "groping for some middle ground between the right and the wrong".[104] Despite his inelegant appearance—many in the audience thought him awkward and even ugly[105]—Lincoln demonstrated an intellectual leadership that brought him into the front ranks of the party and into contention for the Republican presidential nomination. Journalist Noah Brooks reported, "No man ever before made such an impression on his first appeal to a New York audience."[106,107] Donald described the speech as a "superb political move for an unannounced candidate, to appear in one rival's (William H. Seward) own state at an event sponsored by the second rival's (Salmon P. Chase) loyalists, while not mentioning either by name during its delivery."[108] In response to an inquiry about his presidential intentions, Lincoln said, "The taste *is* in my mouth a little."[109]

Figure 6: *"The Rail Candidate"*—Lincoln's 1860 candidacy is depicted as held up by the slavery issue—a slave on the left and party organization on the right.

1860 Presidential nomination and campaign

On May 9–10, 1860, the Illinois Republican State Convention was held in Decatur.[110] Lincoln's followers organized a campaign team led by David Davis, Norman Judd, Leonard Swett, and Jesse DuBois, and Lincoln received his first endorsement to run for the presidency.[111] Exploiting the embellished legend of his frontier days with his father, Lincoln's supporters adopted the label of "The Rail Candidate".[112] On May 18, at the Republican National Convention in Chicago, Lincoln's friends promised and manipulated and won the nomination on the third ballot, beating candidates such as William H. Seward and Salmon P. Chase. A former Democrat Hannibal Hamlin of Maine was nominated for Vice President to balance the ticket. Lincoln's success depended on his reputation as a moderate on the slavery issue, and his strong support for Whiggish programs of internal improvements and the protective tariff.[113] On the third ballot Pennsylvania put him over the top. Pennsylvania iron interests were reassured by his support for protective tariffs.[114] Lincoln's managers had been adroitly focused on this delegation as well as the others, while following Lincoln's strong dictate to "Make no contracts that bind me".[115]

Most Republicans agreed with Lincoln that the North was the aggrieved party, as the Slave Power tightened its grasp on the national government with the *Dred*

Scott decision and the presidency of James Buchanan. Throughout the 1850s, Lincoln doubted the prospects of civil war, and his supporters rejected claims that his election would incite secession.[116] Meanwhile, Douglas was selected as the candidate of the Northern Democrats, with Herschel Vespasian Johnson as the vice-presidential candidate. Delegates from 11 slave states walked out of the Democratic convention, disagreeing with Douglas's position on popular sovereignty, and ultimately selected John C. Breckinridge as their candidate.[117]

As Douglas and the other candidates went through with their campaigns, Lincoln was the only one of them who gave no speeches. Instead, he monitored the campaign closely and relied on the enthusiasm of the Republican Party. The party did the leg work that produced majorities across the North, and produced an abundance of campaign posters, leaflets, and newspaper editorials. There were thousands of Republican speakers who focused first on the party platform, and second on Lincoln's life story, emphasizing his childhood poverty. The goal was to demonstrate the superior power of "free labor", whereby a common farm boy could work his way to the top by his own efforts.[118] The Republican Party's production of campaign literature dwarfed the combined opposition; a *Chicago Tribune* writer produced a pamphlet that detailed Lincoln's life, and sold 100,000 to 200,000 copies.[119]

Presidency

1860 election and secession

On November 6, 1860, Lincoln was elected the sixteenth president of the United States, beating Democrat Stephen A. Douglas, John C. Breckinridge of the Southern Democrats, and John Bell of the new Constitutional Union Party. He was the first president from the Republican Party. Winning entirely on the strength of his support in the North and West, no ballots were cast for him in ten of the fifteen Southern slave states, and he won only two of 996 counties in all the Southern states.[120] Lincoln received 1,866,452 votes, Douglas 1,376,957 votes, Breckinridge 849,781 votes, and Bell 588,789 votes. Turnout was 82.2 percent, with Lincoln winning the free Northern states, as well as California and Oregon. Douglas won Missouri, and split New Jersey with Lincoln.[121] Bell won Virginia, Tennessee, and Kentucky, and Breckinridge won the rest of the South.[122] The States' Electoral votes were decisive: Lincoln had 180 and his opponents added together had only 123. There were fusion tickets in which all of Lincoln's opponents combined to support the same slate of Electors in New York, New Jersey, and Rhode Island, but even if the anti-Lincoln vote had been combined in every state, Lincoln still would have won a majority in the Electoral College.[123]

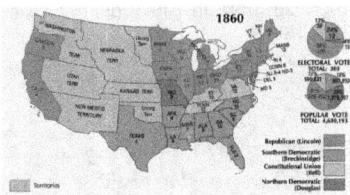

In 1860, northern and western electoral votes (shown in red) put Lincoln into the White House.

1861 inaugural at Capitol still under construction

As Lincoln's election became evident, secessionists made clear their intent to leave the Union before he took office the next March.[124] On December 20, 1860, South Carolina took the lead by adopting an ordinance of secession; by February 1, 1861, Florida, Mississippi, Alabama, Georgia, Louisiana, and Texas followed.[125,126] Six of these states then adopted a constitution and declared themselves to be a sovereign nation, the Confederate States of America.[125] The upper South and border states (Delaware, Maryland, Virginia, North Carolina, Tennessee, Kentucky, Missouri, and Arkansas) listened to, but initially rejected, the secessionist appeal.[127] President Buchanan and President-elect Lincoln refused to recognize the Confederacy, declaring secession illegal.[128] The Confederacy selected Jefferson Davis as their provisional President on February 9, 1861.[129]

There were attempts at compromise. The Crittenden Compromise would have extended the Missouri Compromise line of 1820, dividing the territories into slave and free, contrary to the Republican Party's free-soil platform.[130] Lincoln rejected the idea, saying, "I will suffer death before I consent ... to any concession or compromise which looks like buying the privilege to take possession of this government to which we have a constitutional right."[131] Lincoln, however, did support the Corwin Amendment to the Constitution, which had passed in Congress and protected slavery in those states where it already existed.[132] A few weeks before the war, he went so far as to pen a letter to every governor asking for their support in ratifying the Corwin Amendment as a means to avoid secession.[133]

En route to his inauguration by train, Lincoln addressed crowds and legislatures across the North.[134] The president-elect then evaded possible assassins in Baltimore, who were uncovered by Lincoln's head of security, Allan Pinkerton. On February 23, 1861, he arrived in disguise in Washington, D.C., which was placed under substantial military guard.[135] Lincoln directed his inaugural address to the South, proclaiming once again that he had no intention, or inclination, to abolish slavery in the Southern states:

> *Apprehension seems to exist among the people of the Southern States that by the accession of a Republican Administration their property and their peace and personal security are to be endangered. There has never been any reasonable cause for such apprehension. Indeed, the most ample evidence to the contrary has all the while existed and been open to their inspection. It is found in nearly all the published speeches of him who now addresses you. I do but quote from one of those speeches when I declare that "I have no purpose, directly or indirectly, to interfere with the institution of slavery in the States where it exists. I believe I have no lawful right to do so, and I have no inclination to do so."*
>
> —*First inaugural address, 4 March 1861*[136]

The President ended his address with an appeal to the people of the South: "We are not enemies, but friends. We must not be enemies ... The mystic chords of memory, stretching from every battlefield, and patriot grave, to every living heart and hearthstone, all over this broad land, will yet swell the chorus of the Union, when again touched, as surely they will be, by the better angels of our nature."[137] The failure of the Peace Conference of 1861 signaled that legislative compromise was implausible. By March 1861, no leaders of the insurrection had proposed rejoining the Union on any terms. Meanwhile, Lincoln and nearly every Republican leader agreed that the dismantling of the Union could not be tolerated.[138]

War begins

The commander of Fort Sumter, South Carolina, Major Robert Anderson sent a request for provisions to Washington, and the execution of Lincoln's order to meet that request was seen by the secessionists as an act of war. On April 12, 1861, Confederate forces fired on Union troops at Fort Sumter, forcing them to surrender, and began the war.[139] Historian Allan Nevins argued that the newly inaugurated Lincoln miscalculated in believing that he could preserve the Union,[140] and William Tecumseh Sherman, then a civilian, visited Lincoln in the White House during inauguration week and was "sadly disappointed"

Figure 7: *Major Anderson, Ft. Sumter commander*

at Lincoln's seeming failure to realize that "the country was sleeping on a volcano" and that the South was preparing for war.[141] Donald concludes that, "His repeated efforts to avoid collision in the months between inauguration and the firing on Ft. Sumter showed he adhered to his vow not to be the first to shed fraternal blood. But he also vowed not to surrender the forts. The only resolution of these contradictory positions was for the confederates to fire the first shot; they did just that."[142]

On April 15, Lincoln called on the states to send detachments totaling 75,000 troops to recapture forts, protect Washington, D.C., and "preserve the Union", which, in his view, still existed intact despite the actions of the seceding states. This call forced the states to choose sides. Virginia declared its secession and was rewarded with the Confederate capital, despite the exposed position of Richmond so close to Union lines. North Carolina, Tennessee, and Arkansas also voted for secession over the next two months. Secession sentiment was strong in Missouri and Maryland, but did not prevail; Kentucky tried to be neutral.[143]

Troops headed south towards Washington, to protect the capital in response to Lincoln's call. On April 19, secessionist mobs in Baltimore that controlled the rail links attacked Union troops traveling to the capital. George William Brown, the Mayor of Baltimore, and other suspect Maryland politicians were arrested and imprisoned, without a warrant, as Lincoln suspended the writ of *habeas corpus*.[144] John Merryman, a leader in the secessionist group in Maryland, petitioned Chief Justice Roger Taney to issue a writ of habeas corpus, saying Lincoln's action of holding Merryman without a hearing was unlawful. Taney issued the writ, thereby ordering Merryman's release, but Lincoln ignored it.[145] Throughout the war Lincoln came under heavy, often vituperative attack from most Northern Democrats, called Copperheads,[146] not to mention the Confederates who saw him as the embodiment of the Yankee threat.[147]

Assuming command for the Union in the war

After the fall of Fort Sumter, Lincoln realized the importance of taking immediate executive control of the war and making an overall strategy to put down the rebellion. Lincoln encountered an unprecedented political and military crisis, and he responded as commander-in-chief, using unprecedented powers. He expanded his war powers, and imposed a blockade on all the Confederate shipping ports, disbursed funds before appropriation by Congress, and after suspending *habeas corpus*, arrested and imprisoned thousands of suspected Confederate sympathizers. Lincoln was supported by Congress and the northern public for these actions. In addition, Lincoln had to contend with reinforcing strong Union sympathies in the border slave states and keeping the war from becoming an international conflict.[148]

The war effort was the source of continued disparagement of Lincoln, and dominated his time and attention. From the start, it was clear that bipartisan support would be essential to success in the war effort, and any manner of compromise alienated factions on both sides of the aisle, such as the appointment of Republicans and Democrats to command positions in the Union Army.[149] Copperheads and other opponents of the war criticized Lincoln for refusing to compromise on the slavery issue. Conversely, the Radical Republicans criticized him for moving too slowly in abolishing slavery.[150] On August 6, 1861, Lincoln signed the Confiscation Act that authorized judiciary proceedings to confiscate and free slaves who were used to support the Confederate war effort.[151]

In late August 1861, General John C. Frémont created controversy on the Republican side when he issued, without consulting Lincoln, a proclamation of martial law in Missouri. He declared that any citizen found bearing arms could be court-martialed and shot, and that slaves of persons aiding the rebellion would be freed. Charges of negligence in his command of the Department of the West were compounded with allegations of fraud and corruption. Lincoln overruled Frémont's proclamation and he was given another command in November. This decision, in part, prevented the secession of Kentucky, however, the Northern press criticized Lincoln for not supporting Fremont's

Figure 8: *"Running the 'Machine' ": An 1864 political cartoon takes a swing at Lincoln's administration—featuring William Fessenden, Edwin Stanton, William Seward, Gideon Welles, Lincoln and others.*

emancipation. Lincoln believed that Fremont's emancipation was political; neither militarily necessary nor legal.[152] Union enlistments from Maryland, Kentucky, and Missouri increased by over 40,000 troops.[153]

The Trent Affair of late 1861 threatened war with Great Britain. The U.S. Navy illegally intercepted a British merchant ship the *Trent* on the high seas and seized two Confederate envoys; Britain protested vehemently while the U.S. cheered. Lincoln resolved the issue by releasing the two men and war was successfully averted with Britain.[154] Lincoln's foreign policy approach had been initially hands off, due to his inexperience; he left most diplomacy appointments and other foreign policy matters to his Secretary of State, William Seward. Seward's initial reaction to the *Trent* affair, however, was too bellicose, so Lincoln also turned to Senator Charles Sumner, the chairman of the Senate Foreign Relations Committee and an expert in British diplomacy.[155]

To learn technical military terms, Lincoln borrowed and studied Henry Halleck's book, *Elements of Military Art and Science* from the Library of Congress.[156] Lincoln painstakingly monitored the telegraphic reports coming into the War Department in Washington D.C. He kept close tabs on all phases of the military effort, consulted with governors, and selected generals based on their past success (as well as their state and party). In January 1862, after many complaints of inefficiency and profiteering in the War Department, Lincoln replaced Cameron with Edwin Stanton as Secretary. Stanton was one of many conservative Democrats (he supported Breckenridge in the 1860 election) who became anti-slavery Republicans under Lincoln's leadership.[157] In terms of war strategy, Lincoln articulated two priorities: to ensure that Washington was well-defended, and to conduct an aggressive war effort that would satisfy the demand in the North for prompt, decisive victory; major Northern newspaper editors expected victory within 90 days.[158] Twice a week, Lincoln would meet with his cabinet in the afternoon, and occasionally Mary Lincoln would force him to take a carriage ride because she was concerned he was working too hard.[159] Lincoln learned from his chief of staff General Henry Halleck–a student of the European strategist Jomini–of the critical need control strategic points, such as the Mississippi River;[160] and he also knew well the importance of Vicksburg, and understood the necessity of defeating the enemy's army, rather than simply capturing territory.[161]

General McClellan

After the Union defeat at the First Battle of Bull Run and the retirement of the aged Winfield Scott in late 1861, Lincoln appointed Major General George B. McClellan general-in-chief of all the Union armies.[162] McClellan, a young West Point graduate, railroad executive, and Pennsylvania Democrat, took several months to plan and attempt his Peninsula Campaign, longer than Lincoln wanted. The campaign's objective was to capture Richmond by moving the Army of the Potomac by boat to the peninsula and then overland to the Confederate capital. McClellan's repeated delays frustrated Lincoln and Congress, as did his position that no troops were needed to defend Washington. Lincoln insisted on holding some of McClellan's troops in defense of the capital; McClellan, who consistently overestimated the strength of Confederate troops, blamed this decision for the ultimate failure of the Peninsula Campaign.[163]

Lincoln removed McClellan as general-in-chief and appointed Henry Wager Halleck in March 1862, after McClellan's "Harrison's Landing Letter", in which he offered unsolicited political advice to Lincoln urging caution in the war effort.[164] McClellan's letter incensed Radical Republicans, who successfully pressured Lincoln to appoint John Pope, a Republican, as head of the new Army of Virginia. Pope complied with Lincoln's strategic desire to move toward Richmond from the north, thus protecting the capital from attack. However, lacking requested reinforcements from McClellan, now commanding the Army of the Potomac, Pope was soundly defeated at the Second Battle of Bull

Figure 9: *Lincoln and McClellan after the Battle of Antietam*

Run in the summer of 1862, forcing the Army of the Potomac to defend Washington for a second time.[165] The war also expanded with naval operations in 1862 when the CSS *Virginia*, formerly the USS *Merrimack*, damaged or destroyed three Union vessels in Norfolk, Virginia, before being engaged and damaged by the USS *Monitor*. Lincoln closely reviewed the dispatches and interrogated naval officers during their clash in the Battle of Hampton Roads.[166]

Despite his dissatisfaction with McClellan's failure to reinforce Pope, Lincoln was desperate, and restored him to command of all forces around Washington, to the dismay of all in his cabinet but Seward.[167] Two days after McClellan's return to command, General Robert E. Lee's forces crossed the Potomac River into Maryland, leading to the Battle of Antietam in September 1862.[168] The ensuing Union victory was among the bloodiest in American history, but it enabled Lincoln to announce that he would issue an Emancipation Proclamation in January. Having composed the Proclamation some time earlier, Lincoln had waited for a military victory to publish it to avoid it being perceived as the product of desperation.[169] McClellan then resisted the President's demand that he pursue Lee's retreating and exposed army, while his counterpart General Don Carlos Buell likewise refused orders to move the Army of the Ohio against rebel forces in eastern Tennessee. As a result, Lincoln replaced Buell with William Rosecrans; and, after the 1862 midterm elections, he replaced McClellan with Republican Ambrose Burnside. Both of these replacements were political moderates and prospectively more supportive of the Commander in Chief.[170]

Burnside, against the advice of the president, prematurely launched an offensive across the Rappahannock River and was stunningly defeated by Lee at Fredericksburg in December. Not only had Burnside been defeated on the battlefield, but his soldiers were disgruntled and undisciplined. Desertions during 1863 were in the thousands and they increased after Fredericksburg.[171] Lincoln brought in Joseph Hooker, despite his history of loose talk about a military dictatorship.[172]

The mid-term elections in 1862 brought the Republicans severe losses due to sharp disfavor with the administration over its failure to deliver a speedy end to the war, as well as rising inflation, new high taxes, rumors of corruption, the suspension of habeas corpus, the military draft law, and fears that freed slaves would undermine the labor market. The Emancipation Proclamation announced in September gained votes for the Republicans in the rural areas of New England and the upper Midwest, but it lost votes in the cities and the lower Midwest. While Republicans were discouraged, Democrats were energized and did especially well in Pennsylvania, Ohio, Indiana, and New York. The Republicans did maintain their majorities in Congress and in the major states, except New York. The Cincinnati *Gazette* contended that the voters were "depressed by the interminable nature of this war, as so far conducted, and by the rapid exhaustion of the national resources without progress".[173]

In the spring of 1863, Lincoln was optimistic about a group of upcoming battle plans, to the point of thinking the end of the war could be near if a string of victories could be put together; these plans included Hooker's attack on Lee north of Richmond, Rosecrans' on Chattanooga, Grant's on Vicksburg, and a naval assault on Charleston. Lincoln became despondent when none of these plans, at least initially, succeeded.[174]

Hooker was routed by Lee at the Battle of Chancellorsville in May,[175] but continued to command his troops for some weeks. He ignored Lincoln's order to divide his troops, and possibly force Lee to do the same in Harper's Ferry, and tendered his resignation, which Lincoln accepted. He was replaced by George Meade, who followed Lee into Pennsylvania for the Gettysburg Campaign, which was a victory for the Union, though Lee's army avoided capture. At the same time, after initial setbacks, Grant laid siege to Vicksburg and the Union navy attained some success in Charleston harbor.[176] After the Battle of Gettysburg, Lincoln clearly understood that his military decisions would be more effectively carried out by conveying his orders through his War Secretary or his general-in-chief on to his generals, who resented his civilian interference with their own plans. Even so, he often continued to give detailed directions to his generals as Commander in Chief.[177]

Figure 10: *Lincoln presents the first draft of the Emancipation Proclamation to his cabinet. Painted by Francis Bicknell Carpenter in 1864*

Emancipation Proclamation

Lincoln understood that the Federal government's power to end slavery was limited by the Constitution, which before 1865, committed the issue to individual states. He argued before and during his election that the eventual extinction of slavery would result from preventing its expansion into new U.S. territory. At the beginning of the war, he also sought to persuade the states to accept compensated emancipation in return for their prohibition of slavery (an offer that took effect only in Washington, D.C., in April 1862). Lincoln believed that curtailing slavery in these ways would economically expunge it, as envisioned by the Founding Fathers, under the constitution.[178] President Lincoln rejected two geographically limited emancipation attempts by Major General John C. Frémont in August 1861 and by Major General David Hunter in May 1862, on the grounds that it was not within their power, and it would upset the border states loyal to the Union.[179]

On June 19, 1862, Congress passed an act banning slavery on all federal territory, and in July 1862 passed the Second Confiscation Act, which set up court procedures that could free the slaves of anyone convicted of aiding the rebellion. Although Lincoln believed it was not within Congress's power to free the slaves within the states, he approved the bill in deference to the legislature. He felt such action could only be taken by the commander-in-chief using war powers granted to the president by the Constitution, and Lincoln was planning to take that action. In that month, Lincoln discussed a draft of the Emancipation Proclamation with his cabinet. In it, he stated that "as a fit and necessary military measure, on January 1, 1863, all persons held as slaves in the Confederate states will thenceforward, and forever, be free."[180]

Privately, Lincoln concluded at this point that the war could not be won without freeing the slaves. However Confederate and anti-war propagandists had success spreading the theme that emancipation was a stumbling block to peace and reunification. Republican editor Horace Greeley of the highly influential *New York Tribune* fell for the ploy.[181] and Lincoln refuted it directly in a shrewd letter of August 22, 1862. The President said the primary goal of his actions as president (he used the first person pronoun and explicitly refers to his "official duty") was preserving the Union:

> *My paramount object in this struggle is to save the Union, and is not either to save or to destroy slavery. If I could save the Union without freeing any slave I would do it, and if I could save it by freeing all the slaves I would do it; and if I could save it by freeing some and leaving others alone I would also do that. What I do about slavery, and the colored race, I do because I believe it helps to save the Union; and what I forbear, I forbear because I do not believe it would help to save the Union. . . .* [¶] *I have here stated my purpose according to my view of official duty; and I intend no modification of my oft-expressed personal wish that all men everywhere could be free.*[182]

Lincoln had over and over again made clear that he wanted the states to emancipate the slaves (which they officially did in 1865 by ratifying the Thirteenth Amendment). His role in leading the national army would be to save the union, using every tool available, including complete or partial emancipation (he employed partial emancipation). As for the Confederates, they would return only at the point of a bayonet.[183]

The Emancipation Proclamation, issued on September 22, 1862, and put into effect on January 1, 1863, declared free the slaves in ten states not then under Union control, with exemptions specified for areas already under Union control in two states.[184] Once the abolition of slavery in the rebel states became a military objective, as Union armies advanced south, more slaves were liberated until over three million of them in Confederate territory were freed. Lincoln's comment on the signing of the Proclamation was: "I never, in my life, felt more certain that I was doing right, than I do in signing this paper."[185] For some time, Lincoln continued earlier plans to set up colonies for the newly freed slaves. He commented favorably on colonization in the Emancipation Proclamation, but all attempts at such a massive undertaking failed.[186] A few days after Emancipation was announced, 13 Republican governors met at the War Governors' Conference; they supported the president's Proclamation, but suggested the removal of General George B. McClellan as commander of the Union Army.[187]

Using former slaves in the military was official government policy after the issuance of the Emancipation Proclamation. At first, Lincoln was reluctant to fully implement this program, but by the spring of 1863, he was ready to initiate "a massive recruitment of Negro troops". In a letter to Andrew Johnson, the military governor of Tennessee, encouraging him to lead the way in raising black troops, Lincoln wrote, "The bare sight of 50,000 armed and drilled black soldiers on the banks of the Mississippi would end the rebellion at once".[188] By the end of 1863, at Lincoln's direction, General Lorenzo Thomas had recruited 20 regiments of blacks from the Mississippi Valley.[189] Frederick Douglass once observed of Lincoln: "In his company, I was never reminded of my humble origin, or of my unpopular color".[190]

Gettysburg Address

With the great Union victory at the Battle of Gettysburg in July 1863, and the defeat of the Copperheads in the Ohio election in the fall, Lincoln maintained a strong base of party support and was in a strong position to redefine the war effort, despite the New York City draft riots. The stage was set for his address at the Gettysburg battlefield cemetery.[191] Defying Lincoln's prediction that "the world will little note, nor long remember what we say here," the Address became the most quoted speech in American history.[4]

The Gettysburg Address was delivered at the dedication of the Soldiers' National Cemetery in Gettysburg, Pennsylvania, on the afternoon of Thursday, November 19, 1863. In 272 words, and three minutes, Lincoln asserted the nation was born, not in 1789, but in 1776, "conceived in Liberty, and dedicated to the proposition that all men are created equal." He defined the war as an effort dedicated to these principles of liberty and equality for all. The emancipation of slaves was now part of the national war effort. He declared that the deaths of so many brave soldiers would not be in vain, that slavery would end as a result of the losses, and the future of democracy would be assured, that "government of the people, by the people, for the people, shall not perish from the earth." Lincoln concluded that the Civil War had a profound objective—a new birth of freedom in the nation.[192,193]

General Grant

Meade's failure to capture Lee's army as it retreated from Gettysburg, and the continued passivity of the Army of the Potomac, persuaded Lincoln that a change in command was needed. General Ulysses S. Grant's victories at the Battle of Shiloh and in the Vicksburg campaign impressed Lincoln and

Figure 11: *President Lincoln (center right) with, from left, Generals Sherman, Grant and Admiral Porter – 1868 painting of events aboard the River Queen in March, 1865*

made Grant a strong candidate to head the Union Army. Responding to criticism of Grant after Shiloh, Lincoln had said, "I can't spare this man. He fights."[194] With Grant in command, Lincoln felt the Union Army could relentlessly pursue a series of coordinated offensives in multiple theaters, and have a top commander who agreed on the use of black troops.[195]

Nevertheless, Lincoln was concerned that Grant might be considering a candidacy for President in 1864, as McClellan was. Lincoln arranged for an intermediary to make inquiry into Grant's political intentions, and being assured that he had none, submitted to the Senate Grant's promotion to commander of the Union Army. He obtained Congress's consent to reinstate for Grant the rank of Lieutenant General, which no officer had held since George Washington.[196]

Grant waged his bloody Overland Campaign in 1864. This is often characterized as a war of attrition, given high Union losses at battles such as the Battle of the Wilderness and Cold Harbor. Even though they had the advantage of fighting on the defensive, the Confederate forces had "almost as high a percentage of casualties as the Union forces".[197] The high casualty figures of the Union alarmed the North; Grant had lost a third of his army, and Lincoln asked what

Grant's plans were, to which the general replied, "I propose to fight it out on this line if it takes all summer."[198]

The Confederacy lacked reinforcements, so Lee's army shrank with every battle, forcing it back to trenches outside Petersburg, Virginia, where Grant began a siege. Lincoln then made an extended visit to Grant's headquarters at City Point, Virginia. This allowed the president to confer in person with Grant and William Tecumseh Sherman about the hostilities, as Sherman coincidentally managed a hasty visit to Grant from his position in North Carolina.[199] Lincoln and the Republican party mobilized support for the draft throughout the North, and replaced his losses.[200]

Lincoln authorized Grant to target the Confederate infrastructure—such as plantations, railroads, and bridges—hoping to destroy the South's morale and weaken its economic ability to continue fighting. Grant's move to Petersburg resulted in the obstruction of three railroads between Richmond and the South. This strategy allowed Generals Sherman and Philip Sheridan to destroy plantations and towns in Virginia's Shenandoah Valley. The damage caused by Sherman's March to the Sea through Georgia in 1864 was limited to a 60-mile (97 km) swath but neither Lincoln nor his commanders saw destruction as the main goal, but rather defeat of the Confederate armies. As Neely (2004) concludes, there was no effort to engage in "total war" against civilians, as in World War II.[201]

Confederate general Jubal Anderson Early began a series of assaults in the North that threatened the Capital. During his raid on Washington, D.C. in 1864, Lincoln was watching the combat from an exposed position; Captain Oliver Wendell Holmes shouted at him, "Get down, you damn fool, before you get shot!"[202] After repeated calls on Grant to defend Washington, Sheridan was appointed and the threat from Early was dispatched.[203]

As Grant continued to wear down Lee's forces, efforts to discuss peace began. Confederate Vice President Stephens led a group to meet with Lincoln, Seward, and others at Hampton Roads. Lincoln refused to allow any negotiation with the Confederacy as a coequal; his sole objective was an agreement to end the fighting and the meetings produced no results.[204] On April 1, 1865, Grant successfully outflanked Lee's forces in the Battle of Five Forks and nearly encircled Petersburg, and the Confederate government evacuated Richmond. Days later, when that city fell, Lincoln visited the vanquished Confederate capital; as he walked through the city, white Southerners were stone-faced, but freedmen greeted him as a hero. On April 9, Lee surrendered to Grant at Appomattox and the war was effectively over.[205]

1864 re-election

Lincoln was a master politician, bringing together—and holding together—all the main factions of the Republican Party, and bringing in War Democrats such as Edwin M. Stanton and Andrew Johnson as well. Lincoln spent many hours a week talking to politicians from across the land and using his patronage powers—greatly expanded over peacetime—to hold the factions of his party together, build support for his own policies, and fend off efforts by Radicals to drop him from the 1864 ticket.[206,207] At its 1864 convention, the Republican Party selected Andrew Johnson, a War Democrat from the Southern state of Tennessee, as his running mate. To broaden his coalition to include War Democrats as well as Republicans, Lincoln ran under the label of the new Union Party.[208]

When Grant's spring campaigns turned into bloody stalemates and Union casualties mounted, the lack of military success wore heavily on the President's re-election prospects, and many Republicans across the country feared that Lincoln would be defeated. Sharing this fear, Lincoln wrote and signed a pledge that, if he should lose the election, he would still defeat the Confederacy before turning over the White House:[209]

> *This morning, as for some days past, it seems exceedingly probable that this Administration will not be re-elected. Then it will be my duty to so cooperate with the President elect, as to save the Union between the election and the inauguration; as he will have secured his election on such ground that he cannot possibly save it afterward.*[210]

Lincoln did not show the pledge to his cabinet, but asked them to sign the sealed envelope.

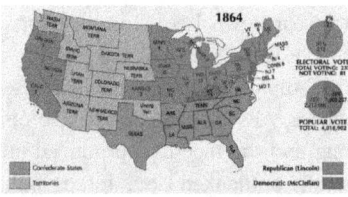

An electoral landslide (in red) for Lincoln in the 1864 election, southern states (brown) and territories (light brown) not in play

Lincoln's second inaugural address in 1865 at the almost completed Capitol building

While the Democratic platform followed the Peace wing of the party and called the war a "failure", their candidate, General George B. McClellan, supported the war and repudiated the platform. Lincoln provided Grant with more troops and mobilized his party to renew its support of Grant in the war effort. Sherman's capture of Atlanta in September and David Farragut's capture of Mobile ended defeatist jitters;[211] the Democratic Party was deeply split, with some leaders and most soldiers openly for Lincoln. By contrast, the National Union Party was united and energized as Lincoln made emancipation the central issue, and state Republican parties stressed the perfidy of the Copperheads.[212] Lincoln was re-elected in a landslide, carrying all but three states, and receiving 78 percent of the Union soldiers' vote.[213]

On March 4, 1865, Lincoln delivered his second inaugural address. In it, he deemed the high casualties on both sides to be God's will. Historian Mark Noll concludes it ranks "among the small handful of semi-sacred texts by which Americans conceive their place in the world".[214] Lincoln said:

> *Fondly do we hope—fervently do we pray—that this mighty scourge of war may speedily pass away. Yet, if God wills that it continue, until all the wealth piled by the bond-man's 250 years of unrequited toil shall be sunk, and until every drop of blood drawn with the lash, shall be paid by another drawn with the sword, as was said 3,000 years ago, so still it must be said, "the judgments of the Lord, are true and righteous altogether". With malice toward none; with charity for all; with firmness in the right, as God gives us to see the right, let us strive on to finish the work we are in; to bind up the nation's wounds; to care for him who shall have borne the battle, and for his widow, and his orphan—to do all which may achieve and cherish a just and lasting peace, among ourselves, and with all nations.*[215]

Figure 12: *A political cartoon of Andrew Johnson and Abraham Lincoln, 1865, entitled "The Rail Splitter At Work Repairing the Union." The caption reads (Johnson): Take it quietly Uncle Abe and I will draw it closer than ever. (Lincoln): A few more stitches Andy and the good old Union will be mended.*

Reconstruction

Reconstruction began during the war, as Lincoln and his associates anticipated questions of how to reintegrate the conquered southern states, and how to determine the fates of Confederate leaders and freed slaves. Shortly after Lee's surrender, a general had asked Lincoln how the defeated Confederates should be treated, and Lincoln replied, "Let 'em up easy."[216] In keeping with that sentiment, Lincoln led the moderates regarding Reconstruction policy, and was opposed by the Radical Republicans, under Rep. Thaddeus Stevens, Sen. Charles Sumner and Sen. Benjamin Wade, political allies of the president on other issues. Determined to find a course that would reunite the nation and not alienate the South, Lincoln urged that speedy elections under generous terms be held throughout the war. His Amnesty Proclamation of December 8, 1863, offered pardons to those who had not held a Confederate civil office, had not mistreated Union prisoners, and would sign an oath of allegiance.[217]

As Southern states were subdued, critical decisions had to be made as to their leadership while their administrations were re-formed. Of special importance were Tennessee and Arkansas, where Lincoln appointed Generals

Andrew Johnson and Frederick Steele as military governors, respectively. In Louisiana, Lincoln ordered General Nathaniel P. Banks to promote a plan that would restore statehood when 10 percent of the voters agreed to it. Lincoln's Democratic opponents seized on these appointments to accuse him of using the military to ensure his and the Republicans' political aspirations. On the other hand, the Radicals denounced his policy as too lenient, and passed their own plan, the Wade-Davis Bill, in 1864. When Lincoln vetoed the bill, the Radicals retaliated by refusing to seat representatives elected from Louisiana, Arkansas, and Tennessee.[218]

Lincoln's appointments were designed to keep both the moderate and Radical factions in harness. To fill the late Chief Justice Taney's seat on the Supreme Court, he named the choice of the Radicals, Salmon P. Chase, who Lincoln believed would uphold the emancipation and paper money policies.[219]

After implementing the Emancipation Proclamation, which did not apply to every state, Lincoln increased pressure on Congress to outlaw slavery throughout the entire nation with a constitutional amendment. Lincoln declared that such an amendment would "clinch the whole matter".[220] By December 1863 a proposed constitutional amendment that would outlaw slavery absolutely was brought to Congress for passage. This first attempt at an amendment failed to pass, falling short of the required two-thirds majority on June 15, 1864, in the House of Representatives. After a long debate in the House, a second attempt passed Congress on January 13, 1865, and was sent to the state legislatures for ratification.[221] Upon ratification, it became the Thirteenth Amendment to the United States Constitution on December 6, 1865.[222]

As the war drew to a close, Lincoln's presidential Reconstruction for the South was in flux; having believed the federal government had limited responsibility to the millions of freedmen. He signed into law Senator Charles Sumner's Freedman's Bureau bill that set up a temporary federal agency designed to meet the immediate material needs of former slaves. The law assigned land for a lease of three years with the ability to purchase title for the freedmen. Lincoln stated that his Louisiana plan did not apply to all states under Reconstruction. Shortly before his assassination Lincoln announced he had a new plan for southern Reconstruction. Discussions with his cabinet revealed Lincoln planned short term military control over southern states, until readmission under the control of southern Unionists.[223]

Redefining the republic and republicanism

The successful reunification of the states had consequences for the name of the country. The term "the United States" has historically been used, sometimes in the plural ("these United States"), and other times in the singular, without

Figure 13: *The last high-quality photograph of Lincoln was taken March 1865.*

any particular grammatical consistency. The Civil War was a significant force in the eventual dominance of the singular usage by the end of the nineteenth century.[224]

In recent years, historians have stressed Lincoln's redefinition of republican values. As early as the 1850s, a time when most political rhetoric focused on the sanctity of the Constitution, Lincoln redirected emphasis to the Declaration of Independence as the foundation of American political values—what he called the "sheet anchor" of republicanism.[225] The Declaration's emphasis on freedom and equality for all, in contrast to the Constitution's tolerance of slavery, shifted the debate. As Diggins concludes regarding the highly influential Cooper Union speech of early 1860, "Lincoln presented Americans a theory of history that offers a profound contribution to the theory and destiny of republicanism itself."[226] His position gained strength because he highlighted the moral basis of republicanism, rather than its legalisms.[227] Nevertheless, in 1861, Lincoln justified the war in terms of legalisms (the Constitution was a contract, and for one party to get out of a contract all the other parties had to agree), and then in terms of the national duty to guarantee a republican form of government in every state.[228]

In March 1861, in his First Inaugural Address, Lincoln explored the nature of democracy. He denounced secession as anarchy, and explained that majority rule had to be balanced by constitutional restraints in the American system. He said "A majority held in restraint by constitutional checks and limitations, and always changing easily with deliberate changes of popular opinions and sentiments, is the only true sovereign of a free people."[229]

Other enactments

Lincoln adhered to the Whig theory of the presidency, which gave Congress primary responsibility for writing the laws while the Executive enforced them. Lincoln only vetoed four bills passed by Congress; the only important one was the Wade-Davis Bill with its harsh program of Reconstruction.[230] He signed the Homestead Act in 1862, making millions of acres of government-held land in the West available for purchase at very low cost. The Morrill Land-Grant Colleges Act, also signed in 1862, provided government grants for agricultural colleges in each state. The Pacific Railway Acts of 1862 and 1864 granted federal support for the construction of the United States' First Transcontinental Railroad, which was completed in 1869.[231] The passage of the Homestead Act and the Pacific Railway Acts was made possible by the absence of Southern congressmen and senators who had opposed the measures in the 1850s.[232]

The Lincoln Cabinet[233]		
Office	Name	Term
President	Abraham Lincoln	1861–1865
Vice President	Hannibal Hamlin	1861–1865
	Andrew Johnson	1865
State	William H. Seward	1861–1865
War	Simon Cameron	1861–1862
	Edwin M. Stanton	1862–1865
Treasury	Salmon P. Chase	1861–1864
	William P. Fessenden	1864–1865
	Hugh McCulloch	1865
Justice	Edward Bates	1861–1864
	James Speed	1864–1865
Post	Montgomery Blair	1861–1864
	William Dennison, Jr.	1864–1865
Navy	Gideon Welles	1861–1865
Interior	Caleb B. Smith	1861–1862
	John P. Usher	1863–1865

Other important legislation involved two measures to raise revenues for the Federal government: tariffs (a policy with long precedent), and a new Federal income tax. In 1861, Lincoln signed the second and third Morrill Tariff, the first having become law under James Buchanan. In 1861, Lincoln signed the Revenue Act of 1861, creating the first U.S. income tax.[234] This created a flat tax of 3 percent on incomes above $800, which was later changed by the Revenue Act of 1862 to a progressive rate structure.[235]

Lincoln also presided over the expansion of the federal government's economic influence in several other areas. The creation of the system of national banks by the National Banking Act provided a strong financial network in the country. It also established a national currency. In 1862, Congress created, with Lincoln's approval, the Department of Agriculture.[236] In 1862, Lincoln sent a senior general, John Pope, to put down the "Sioux Uprising" in Minnesota. Presented with 303 execution warrants for convicted Santee Dakota who were accused of killing innocent farmers, Lincoln conducted his own personal review of each of these warrants, eventually approving 39 for execution (one was later reprieved).[237] President Lincoln had planned to reform federal Indian policy.[238]

In the wake of Grant's casualties in his campaign against Lee, Lincoln had considered yet another executive call for a military draft, but it was never issued. In response to rumors of one, however, the editors of the *New York World* and the *Journal of Commerce* published a false draft proclamation which created an opportunity for the editors and others employed at the publications to corner the gold market. Lincoln's reaction was to send the strongest of messages to the media about such behavior; he ordered the military to seize the two papers. The seizure lasted for two days.[239]

Lincoln is largely responsible for the institution of the Thanksgiving holiday in the United States.[240] Before Lincoln's presidency, Thanksgiving, while a regional holiday in New England since the 17th century, had only been proclaimed by the federal government sporadically, and on irregular dates. The last such proclamation had been during James Madison's presidency 50 years before. In 1863, Lincoln declared the final Thursday in November of that year to be a day of Thanksgiving.[240] In June 1864, Lincoln approved the Yosemite Grant enacted by Congress, which provided unprecedented federal protection for the area now known as Yosemite National Park.[241]

Administration, cabinet and Supreme Court appointments 1861–1865

Lincoln's declared philosophy on court nominations was that "we cannot ask a man what he will do, and if we should, and he should answer us, we should despise him for it. Therefore we must take a man whose opinions are known."[240] Lincoln made five appointments to the United States Supreme Court. Noah Haynes Swayne, nominated January 21, 1862 and appointed January 24, 1862, was chosen as an anti-slavery lawyer who was committed to the Union. Samuel Freeman Miller, nominated and appointed on July 16, 1862, supported Lincoln in the 1860 election and was an avowed abolitionist. David Davis, Lincoln's campaign manager in 1860, nominated December 1, 1862 and appointed December 8, 1862, had also served as a judge in Lincoln's Illinois court circuit. Stephen Johnson Field, a previous California Supreme Court justice, was nominated March 6, 1863 and appointed March 10, 1863, and provided geographic balance, as well as political balance to the court as a Democrat. Finally, Lincoln's Treasury Secretary, Salmon P. Chase, was nominated as Chief Justice, and appointed the same day, on December 6, 1864. Lincoln believed Chase was an able jurist, would support Reconstruction legislation, and that his appointment united the Republican Party.[242]

States admitted to the Union

West Virginia, admitted to the Union June 20, 1863, contained the former north-westernmost counties of Virginia that seceded from Virginia after that commonwealth declared its secession from the Union. Nevada, which became the third State in the far-west of the continent, was admitted October 31, 1864. Lincoln recognized both of these state governments when formed locally, but was not otherwise involved prior to their admission by Congress.[243]

Assassination

John Wilkes Booth was a well-known actor and a Confederate spy from Maryland; though he never joined the Confederate army, he had contacts with the Confederate secret service.[244] In 1864, Booth formulated a plan (very similar to one of Thomas N. Conrad previously authorized by the Confederacy[245]) to kidnap Lincoln in exchange for the release of Confederate prisoners.

After attending an April 11, 1865, speech in which Lincoln promoted voting rights for blacks, an incensed Booth changed his plans and became determined to assassinate the president.[246] Learning that the President, First Lady, and head Union general Ulysses S. Grant would be attending Ford's Theatre, Booth formulated a plan with co-conspirators to assassinate Vice President Andrew

Figure 14: *Shown in the presidential booth of Ford's Theatre, from left to right, are Henry Rathbone, Clara Harris, Mary Todd Lincoln, Abraham Lincoln, and his assassin John Wilkes Booth.*

Johnson, Secretary of State William H. Seward and General Grant. Without his main bodyguard, Ward Hill Lamon, Lincoln left to attend the play *Our American Cousin* on April 14. Grant along with his wife chose at the last minute to travel to Philadelphia instead of attending the play.[247]

Lincoln's bodyguard, John Parker, left Ford's Theater during intermission to join Lincoln's coachman for drinks in the Star Saloon next door. The now unguarded President sat in his state box in the balcony. Seizing the opportunity, Booth crept up from behind and at about 10:13 pm, aimed at the back of Lincoln's head and fired at point-blank range, mortally wounding the President. Major Henry Rathbone momentarily grappled with Booth but Booth stabbed him and escaped.[248,249]

After being on the run for ten days, Booth was tracked down and found on a farm in Virginia, some 30 miles (48 km) south of Washington D.C. After a brief fight, Booth was killed by Union soldiers on April 26.[250]

An Army surgeon, Doctor Charles Leale, assessed Lincoln's wound as mortal. The dying man was taken across the street to Petersen House. After being in a coma for nine hours, Lincoln died at 7:22 am on April 15. Presbyterian minister Phineas Densmore Gurley, then present, was asked to offer a prayer,

Figure 15: *Lincoln: painting by George Peter Alexander Healy in 1869*

after which Secretary of War Stanton saluted and said, "Now he belongs to the ages."[251]

Lincoln's flag-enfolded body was then escorted in the rain to the White House by bareheaded Union officers, while the city's church bells rang. Vice President Johnson was sworn in as President at 10:00 am the day after the assassination. Lincoln lay in state in the East Room, and then in the Capitol Rotunda from April 19 – April 21. For three weeks his funeral train brought the body to cities across the North for large-scale memorials attended by hundreds of thousands, as well as many people who gathered in informal trackside tributes with bands, bonfires and hymn singing.[252,253]

Religious and philosophical beliefs

Scholars have extensively written on topics concerning Lincoln's beliefs and philosophy; e.g. whether Lincoln's frequent use of religious imagery and language reflected his own personal beliefs or was a device to appeal to his audiences, who were mostly evangelical Protestants.[254] Though he never joined a church, Lincoln was familiar with the Bible, quoted it and praised it.[255]

In the 1840s Lincoln subscribed to the *Doctrine of Necessity*, a belief that asserted the human mind was controlled by some higher power.[256] Some scholars maintain that in the 1850s, Lincoln acknowledged "providence" in a general way, and rarely used the language or imagery of the evangelicals; instead, they argue, he regarded the republicanism of the Founding Fathers with an almost religious reverence. Some historians also conclude that when he suffered the death of his son Edward, Lincoln more frequently acknowledged his own need to depend on God.[257]

As Lincoln grew older, it maybe the idea of a divine will somehow interacting with human affairs increasingly influenced his beliefs and public expressions. On a personal level, the death of his son Willie in February 1862 may have caused Lincoln to look towards religion for answers and solace.[258] After Willie's death, in the summer or early fall of 1862, Lincoln apparently attempted to put on paper his private thoughts on why, from a divine standpoint, the severity of the war was necessary. He wrote at this time that God "could have either saved or destroyed the Union without a human contest. Yet the contest began. And having begun He could give the final victory to either side any day. Yet the contest proceeds."[259] In April 1864, discussing Emancipation, Lincoln wrote, "I claim not to have controlled events, but confess plainly that events have controlled me. Now, at the end of three years struggle the nation's condition is not what either party, or any man devised, or expected. God alone can claim it."[260]

Historical reputation

In surveys of scholars ranking Presidents, Lincoln is ranked in the top three, often #1. A 2004 study found that scholars in the fields of history and politics ranked Lincoln number one, while legal scholars placed him second after Washington.[261]

President Lincoln's assassination made him a national martyr and endowed him with a recognition of mythic proportion. Lincoln was viewed by abolitionists as a champion for human liberty. Republicans linked Lincoln's name to their party. Many, though not all, in the South considered Lincoln as a man of outstanding ability.[262]

Schwartz argues that Lincoln's reputation grew slowly in the late 19th century until the Progressive Era (1900-1920s) when he emerged as one of the most venerated heroes in American history, with even white Southerners in agreement. The high point came in 1922 with the dedication of the Lincoln Memorial on the Mall in Washington.[263] In the New Deal era liberals honored Lincoln not so much as the self-made man or the great war president, but as the advocate of the common man who doubtless would have supported the welfare state. In the Cold War years, Lincoln's image shifted to emphasize the symbol of freedom who brought hope to those oppressed by communist regimes.[264]

Figure 16: *The Abraham Lincoln Presidential Library and Museum focuses on Lincoln scholarship and popular interpretation*

In recent decades, Lincoln became a hero to political conservatives (apart from neo-Confederates) for his intense nationalism, support for business, his insistence on stopping the spread of un-freedom (slavery), his acting in terms of Lockean and Burkean principles, and his devotion to the principles of the Founding Fathers.[265,266,267] As a Whig activist, Lincoln was a spokesman for business interests, favoring high tariffs, banks, internal improvements, and railroads in opposition to the agrarian Democrats.[268] William C. Harris found that Lincoln's "reverence for the Founding Fathers, the Constitution, the laws under it, and the preservation of the Republic and its institutions undergirded and strengthened his conservatism.".[269] James G. Randall emphasizes his tolerance and his especially his moderation "in his preference for orderly progress, his distrust of dangerous agitation, and his reluctance toward ill digested schemes of reform." Randall concludes that, "he was conservative in his complete avoidance of that type of so-called 'radicalism' which involved abuse of the South, hatred for the slaveholder, thirst for vengeance, partisan plotting, and ungenerous demands that Southern institutions be transformed overnight by outsiders."[270]

By the late 1960s liberals were having second thoughts, especially regarding Lincoln's views on racial issues.[271,272] Black historian Lerone Bennett won wide attention when he called Lincoln a white supremacist in 1968.[273] Critics

Figure 17: *Lincoln Memorial in Washington, D.C.*

complained that Lincoln used ethnic slurs, told jokes that ridiculed blacks, insisted he opposed social equality, and proposed sending freed slaves to another country. Defenders retorted that he was not as bad as most politicians;[274] and that he was a "moral visionary" who deftly advanced the abolitionist cause, as fast as politically possible.[275] The emphasis shifted away from Lincoln-the-emancipator to an argument that blacks had freed themselves from slavery, or at least were responsible for pressuring the government on emancipation.[276,277] Historian Barry Schwartz wrote in 2009 that Lincoln's image suffered "erosion, fading prestige, benign ridicule," in the late 20th century.[278] Whereas, Donald in his 1996 biography opined that Lincoln was distinctly endowed with the personality trait of negative capability, defined by the poet John Keats and attributed to extraordinary leaders who were "content in the midst of uncertainties and doubts, and not compelled toward fact or reason."[279]

Memorials

Lincoln has been memorialized in many town, city, and county names,[280] including the capital of Nebraska. The first public monument to Abraham Lincoln was a statue erected in front of the District of Columbia City Hall in 1868, three years after his assassination.[281] Lincoln's name and image appear in numerous other places, such as the Lincoln Memorial in Washington, D.C. and Lincoln's sculpture on Mount Rushmore.[282] Abraham Lincoln Birthplace National Historical Park in Hodgenville, Kentucky,[283] Lincoln Boyhood National

Memorial in Lincoln City, Indiana,[284] Lincoln's New Salem, Illinois,[285] and Lincoln Home National Historic Site in Springfield, Illinois[286] commemorate the president.[287] Ford's Theatre and Petersen House (where he died) are maintained as museums, as is the Abraham Lincoln Presidential Library and Museum, located in Springfield.[288,289] The Lincoln Tomb in Oak Ridge Cemetery in Springfield, Illinois, contains his remains and those of his wife Mary and three of his four sons, Edward, William, and Thomas.[290]

Within a year of this death, his image began to be disseminated throughout the world on stamps,[291] and he is the only U.S. President to appear on a U.S. airmail stamp.[292] Currency honoring the president includes the United States five-dollar bill and the Lincoln cent, which represents the first regularly circulating U.S. coin to feature an actual person.[293]

Abraham Lincoln's birthday, February 12, was never a national holiday, but it was at one time observed by as many as 30 states.[280] In 1971, Presidents Day became a national holiday, combining Lincoln's and Washington's birthdays and replacing most states' celebration of his birthday.[294] The Abraham Lincoln Association was formed in 1908 to commemorate the centennial of Lincoln's birth.[295] In 2000, Congress established the Abraham Lincoln Bicentennial Commission to commemorate his 200th birthday in February 2009.[296]

Lincoln sites remain popular tourist attractions, but crowds have thinned. In the late 1960s, 650,000 people a year visited the home in Springfield, slipping to 393,000 in 2000–2003. Likewise visits to New Salem fell by half, probably because of the enormous draw of the new museum in Springfield. Visits to the Lincoln Memorial in Washington peaked at 4.3 million in 1987 and have since declined. However crowds at Ford's Theatre in Washington have grown sharply.[297]

Bibliography

Cited in footnotes

- Adams, Charles F. (April 1912). "The Trent Affair". *The American Historical Review* (The University of Chicago Press) **17** (3): 540–562. JSTOR 1834388.
- Ambrose, Stephen E. (1962). *Halleck: Lincoln's Chief of Staff*. Louisiana State University Press. OCLC 1178496.
- Baker, Jean H. (1989). *Mary Todd Lincoln: A Biography*. W. W. Norton & Company. ISBN 9780393305869.
- Basler, Roy Prentice, ed (1946). *Abraham Lincoln: his speeches and writings*. World Publishing. OCLC 518824.

- Belz, Herman (1998). *Abraham Lincoln, Constitutionalism, and Equal Rights in the Civil War Era*. Fordham University Press. ISBN 9780823217694.
- Belz, Herman (2006). "Lincoln, Abraham". In Frohnen, Bruce; Beer, Jeremy; Nelson, Jeffrey O.. *American Conservatism: An Encyclopedia*. ISI Books. ISBN 9781932236439.
- Bennett Jr, Lerone (February 1968). "Was Abe Lincoln a White Supremacist?"[298]. *Ebony* (Johnson Publishing) **23** (4). ISSN 0012-9011.
- Blue, Frederick J. (1987). *Salmon P. Chase: a life in politics*. The Kent State University Press. ISBN 0873383400.
- Boritt, Gabor (1994) [1978]. *Lincoln and the Economics of the American Dream*. University of Illinois Press. ISBN 0252064453.
- Bulla, David W.; Gregory A. Borchard (2010). *Journalism in the Civil War Era*. Peter Lang Publishing Inc.. ISBN 1433107228.
- Carwardine, Richard J. (Winter 1997). "Lincoln, Evangelical Religion, and American Political Culture in the Era of the Civil War"[299]. *Journal of the Abraham Lincoln Association* (Abraham Lincoln Association) **18** (1): 27–55.
- Carwardine, Richard (2003). *Lincoln*. Pearson Education Ltd. ISBN 9780582032798.
- Cashin, Joan E. (2002). *The War Was You and Me: Civilians in The American Civil War*. Princeton University Press. ISBN 9780691091730.
- Chesebrough, David B. (1994). *No Sorrow Like Our Sorrow*. Kent State University Press. ISBN 9780873384919.
- Cox, Hank H. (2005). *Lincoln And The Sioux Uprising of 1862*. Cumberland House Publisher. ISBN 9781581824575.
- Cummings, William W.; James B. Hatcher (1982). *Scott Specialized Catalogue of United States Stamps*. Scott Publishing Company,. p. 284. ISBN 0894870424.
- Dennis, Matthew (2002). *Red, White, and Blue Letter Days: an American Calendar*. Cornell University Press. ISBN 9780801472688.
- Diggins, John P. (1986). *The Lost Soul of American Politics: Virtue, Self-Interest, and the Foundations of Liberalism*. University of Chicago Press. ISBN 0226148777.
- Dirck, Brian R. (2007). *Lincoln Emancipated: The President and the Politics of Race*. Northern Illinois University Press. ISBN 9780875803593.
- Dirck, Brian (2008). *Lincoln the Lawyer*. University of Illinois Press. ISBN 9780252076145.
- Donald, David Herbert (1948). *Lincoln's Herndon*. A. A. Knopf.
- Donald, David Herbert (1996) [1995]. *Lincoln*. Simon and Schuster. ISBN 9780684825359.

- Donald, David Herbert (2001). *Lincoln Reconsidered*. Knopf Doubleday Publishing Group. ISBN 9780375725326.
- Douglass, Frederick (2008). *The Life and Times of Frederick Douglass*. Cosimo Classics. ISBN 1605203998.
- Edgar, Walter B. (1998). *South Carolina: A History*. University of South Carolina Press. ISBN 9781570032554.
- Fish, Carl Russell (October 1902). "Lincoln and the Patronage". *American Historical Review* (American Historical Association) **8** (1): 53–69. JSTOR 1832574.
- Foner, Eric (1995) [1970]. *Free Soil, Free Labor, Free Men: The Ideology of the Republican Party before the Civil War*. Oxford University Press. ISBN 9780195094978.
- Foner, Eric (2010). *The Fiery Trial: Abraham Lincoln and American Slavery*. W.W. Norton. ISBN 9780393066180.
- Goodwin, Doris Kearns (2005). *Team of Rivals: The Political Genius of Abraham Lincoln*. Simon & Schuster. ISBN 0684824906.
- Goodrich, Thomas (2005). *The Darkest Dawn: Lincoln, Booth, and the Great American Tragedy*. Indiana University Press. OCLC 501324387.
- Graebner, Norman (1959). "Abraham Lincoln: Conservative Statesman". *The Enduring Lincoln: Lincoln Sesquicentennial Lectures at the University of Illinois*. University of Illinois Press. OCLC 428674.
- Grimsley, Mark (2001). *The Collapse of the Confederacy*. University of Nebraska Press. ISBN 0803221703.
- Guelzo, Allen C. (1999). *Abraham Lincoln: Redeemer President*. W.B. Eerdmans Pub. Co. ISBN 0-8028-3872-3.
- Guelzo, Allen C. (2004). *Lincoln's Emancipation Proclamation: The End of Slavery in America*. Simon & Schuster. ISBN 9780743221825.
- Guelzo, Allen C. (2009). *Lincoln: A Very Short Introduction*. Oxford University Press. ISBN 0195367804.
- Handy, James S. (1917). *Book Review: Abraham Lincoln, the Lawyer-Statesman*. Northwestern University Law Publication Association.
- Harrison, J. Houston (1935). *Settlers by the Long Grey Trail*. J.K. Reubush.
- Harrison, Lowell Hayes (2000). *Lincoln of Kentucky*. University Press of Kentucky. ISBN 0813121566.
- Harris, William C. (2007). *Lincoln's Rise to the Presidency*. University Press of Kansas. ISBN 9780700615209.
- Heidler, David S.; Jeanne T. Heidler, ed (2000). *Encyclopedia of the American Civil War: A Political, Social, and Military History*. W. W. Norton & Company, Inc. ISBN 9780393047585.
- Heidler, David Stephen (2006). *The Mexican War*. Greenwood Publishing Group. ISBN 9780313327926.

- Hofstadter, Richard (October 1938). "The Tariff Issue on the Eve of the Civil War". *American Historical Review* (American Historical Association) **44** (1): 50–55. JSTOR 1840850.
- Holzer, Harold (2004). *Lincoln at Cooper Union: The Speech That Made Abraham Lincoln President*. Simon & Schuster. ISBN 9780743299640.
- Jaffa, Harry V. (2000). *A New Birth of Freedom: Abraham Lincoln and the Coming of the Civil War*. Rowman & Littlefield. ISBN 0-8476-9952-8.
- Lamb, Brian; Susan Swain, ed (2008). *Abraham Lincoln: Great American Historians on Our Sixteenth President*. PublicAffairs. ISBN 9781586486761.
- Kelley, Robin D. G.; Lewis, Earl (2005). *To Make Our World Anew: Volume I: A History of African Americans to 1880*. Oxford University Press. ISBN 9780198040064.
- Lupton, John A. (September–October 2006). "Abraham Lincoln and the Corwin Amendment"[300]. *Illinois Heritage* (The Illinois State Historical Society) **9** (5): 34.
- Luthin, Reinhard H. (1944). *The First Lincoln Campaign*. Harvard University Press. ISBN 9780844612928.
- Luthin, Reinhard H. (July 1994). "Abraham Lincoln and the Tariff". *American Historical Review* (American Historical Association) **49** (4): 609–629. JSTOR 1850218.
- Mansch, Larry D. (2005). *Abraham Lincoln, President-Elect: The Four Critical Months from Election to Inauguration*. McFarland. ISBN 078642026X.
- McGovern, George S. (2008). *Abraham Lincoln*. Macmillan. ISBN 9780805083453.
- McPherson, James M. (1992). *Abraham Lincoln and the Second American Revolution*. Oxford University Press. ISBN 9780195076066.
- McPherson, James M. (1993). *Battle Cry of Freedom: the Civil War Era*. Oxford University Press. ISBN 9780195168952.
- McPherson, James M. (2009). *Abraham Lincoln*. Oxford University Press. ISBN 9780195374520.
- Miller, William Lee (2002). *Lincoln's Virtues: An Ethical Biography*. Alfred A. Knopf. ISBN 0-375-40158-X.
- Neely, Mark E. (1992). *The Fate of Liberty: Abraham Lincoln and Civil Liberties*. Oxford University Press. ISBN 9780195080322.
- Neely Jr., Mark E. (December 2004). "Was the Civil War a Total War?"[301]. *Civil War History* (The Kent State University Press) **50** (4): 434–458.
- Nevins, Allan (1947). *Ordeal of the Union; 2 vol*. Scribner's. ISBN 9780684104164.

- Nevins, Allan (1950). *The Emergence of Lincoln: Prologue to Civil War, 1857–1861 2 vol.* Scribner's. ISBN 9780684104164., also published as vol 3–4 of *Ordeal of the Union*
- Nevins, Allan (1960–1971). *The War for the Union; 4 vol 1861–1865.* Scribner's. ISBN 9781568522975.; also published as vol 5–8 of *Ordeal of the Union*
- Nichols, David A. (2010). Richard W. Etulain. ed. *Lincoln Looks West: From the Mississippi to the Pacific.* Southern Illinois University. ISBN 0809329611.
- Noll, Mark (2000). *America's God: From Jonathan Edwards to Abraham Lincoln.* Oxford University Press. ISBN 0195151119.
- Oates, Stephen B. (1993). *With Malice Toward None: a Life of Abraham Lincoln.* HarperCollins. ISBN 9780060924713.
- Paludan, Phillip Shaw (1994). *The Presidency of Abraham Lincoln.* University Press of Kansas. ISBN 9780700606719.
- Parrillo, Nicholas (September 2000). "Lincoln's Calvinist Transformation: Emancipation and War". *Civil War History* (Kent State University Press) **46** (3): 227–253.
- Pessen, Edward (1984). *The Log Cabin Myth: The Social Backgrounds of American Presidents.* Yale University Press. ISBN 0300031661.
- Peterson, Merrill D. (1995). *Lincoln in American Memory.* Oxford University Press. ISBN 9780195096453.
- Potter, David M.; Don Edward Fehrenbacher (1976). *The impending crisis, 1848–1861.* HarperCollins. ISBN 9780061319297.
- Prokopowicz, Gerald J. (2008). *Did Lincoln Own Slaves?.* Vintage Books. ISBN 9780307279293.
- Randall, James G. (1947). *Lincoln, the Liberal Statesman.* Dodd, Mead.
- Randall, J.G.; Current, Richard Nelson (1955). *Lincoln the President: Last Full Measure.* Dodd, Mead.
- Reinhart, Mark S. (2008). *Abraham Lincoln on Screen.* McFarland. ISBN 9780786435364.
- Sandburg, Carl. (1926). *Abraham Lincoln: The Prairie Years.* ISBN 1402742886.
- Sandburg, Carl (2002). "Chapter 18, Lincoln Takes the Oath as President". *Abraham Lincoln: The Prairie Years and the War Years.* Houghton Mifflin Harcourt. p. 212. ISBN 0156027526.
- Schwartz, Barry (2000). *Abraham Lincoln and the Forge of National Memory.* University Of Chicago Press. ISBN 978-0226741970.
- Schwartz, Barry (2009). *Abraham Lincoln in the Post-Heroic Era: History and Memory in Late Twentieth-Century America.* University of Chicago Press. ISBN 9780226741888.
- Scott, Kenneth (September 1948). "Press Opposition to Lincoln in New

Hampshire". *The New England Quarterly* (The New England Quarterly, Inc.) **21** (3): 326–341. JSTOR 361094.
- Scott (2005). *Scott 2006 Classic Specialized Catalogue*. Scott Pub. Co.. ISBN 089487358X.
- Sherman, William T. (1990). *Memoirs of General W.T. Sherman*. BiblioBazaar. ISBN 1174631724.
- Simon, Paul (1990). *Lincoln's Preparation for Greatness: The Illinois Legislative Years*. University of Illinois. ISBN 0252002032.
- Smith, Robert C. (2010). *Conservatism and Racism, and Why in America They Are the Same*. State University of New York Press. ISBN 978-1438432335.
- Steers, Edward (2010). *The Lincoln Assassination Encyclopedia*. Harper Collins. ISBN 0061787752.
- Striner, Richard (2006). *Father Abraham: Lincoln's Relentless Struggle to End Slavery*. Oxford University Press. ISBN 978-0195183061.
- Tagg, Larry (2009). *The Unpopular Mr. Lincoln*. Casemate Publishers. ISBN 9781932714616.
- Taranto, James; Leonard Leo (2004). *Presidential Leadership: Rating the Best and the Worst in the White House*. Simon and Schuster. ISBN 9780743254335.
- Tegeder, Vincent G. (June 1948). "Lincoln and the Territorial Patronage: The Ascendancy of the Radicals in the West". *Mississippi Valley Historical Review* (Organization of American Historians) **35** (1): 77–90. JSTOR 1895140.
- Thomas, Emory M. (2007). Gordon, Lesley J.; Inscoe, John C.. eds. *Inside the Confederate Nation: Essays in Honor of Emory M. Thomas*. Louisiana State University Press. ISBN 9780807132319.
- Thomas, Benjamin P. (2008). *Abraham Lincoln: A Biography*. Southern Illinois University. ISBN 9780809328871.
- Trostel, Scott D. (2002). *The Lincoln Funeral Train: The Final Journey and National Funeral for Abraham Lincoln*. Cam-Tech Publishing. ISBN 9780925436214.
- Vorenberg, Michael (2001). *Final Freedom: the Civil War, the Abolition of Slavery, and the Thirteenth Amendment*. Cambridge University Press. ISBN 9780521652674.
- White, Jr., Ronald C. (2009). *A. Lincoln: A Biography*. Random House, Inc. ISBN 9781400064991.
- Wills, Garry (1993). *Lincoln at Gettysburg: The Words That Remade America*. Simon & Schuster. ISBN 0671867423.
- Wilson, Douglas L. (1999). *Honor's Voice: The Transformation of Abraham Lincoln*. Knopf Publishing Group. ISBN 9780375703966.

- Winkle, Kenneth J. (2001). *The young eagle: the rise of Abraham Lincoln*. Taylor Trade Publications. ISBN 9780878332557.
- Zarefsky, David S. (1993). *Lincoln, Douglas, and Slavery: In the Crucible of Public Debate*. University of Chicago Press. ISBN 9780226978765.
- Zilversmit, Arthur (1980). "Lincoln and the Problem of Race: A Decade of Interpretations"[302]. *Journal of the Abraham Lincoln Association* (Abraham Lincoln Association) **2** (11): 22–24.</ref>

Additional references

- Burkhimer, Michael (2003). *One Hundred Essential Lincoln Books*. Turner Publishing Co. ISBN 158182369X, guide to historiography
- Burlingame, Michael. (2008) *Abraham Lincoln: A Life* (2 vol. The Johns Hopkins University Press) 2024 pp; the most detailed biography
- Cox, LaWanda. (1981) *Lincoln and Black Freedom: A Study in Presidential Leadership* (Columbia: U of SC Press) ISBN 0872494004
- Foner, Eric, ed. (2008) *Our Lincoln: New Perspectives on Lincoln and His World* (W.W. Norton), essays on diverse topics by scholars
- McPherson, James M. (2008). *Tried by War: Abraham Lincoln as Commander in Chief*. Penguin Press. ISBN 9781594201912.
- Neely, Mark E (1984). *The Abraham Lincoln Encyclopedia*. Da Capo Press. ISBN 9780306802096.
- Neely, Mark E (1994). *The Last Best Hope of Earth: Abraham Lincoln and the promise of America*. Harvard University Press. ISBN 9780674511255.
- Randall, James G. (1953) *Lincoln the President* (3 vol), a famous scholarly biography; vol 4 by Randall and Current is *Lincoln the president. Vol. IV: Last full measure* (1955)

External links

- The Collected Works of Abraham Lincoln[303]
- Works by or about Abraham Lincoln[304] in libraries (WorldCat catalog)
- Mr. Lincoln's Virtual Library[305]
- Poetry written by Abraham Lincoln[306]
- The Abraham Lincoln Presidential Library and Museum[307] Springfield, Illinois
- The Papers of Abraham Lincoln[308] documentary editing project
- US PAT No. 6,469[309]—*Manner of Buoying Vessels*—A. Lincoln—1849
- National Endowment for the Humanities Spotlight – Abraham Lincoln[310]
- The Abraham Lincoln Bicentennial Commission[311]

- Lincoln/Net: Abraham Lincoln Historical Digitization Project, Northern Illinois University Libraries[312]
- Abraham Lincoln: A Resource Guide from the Library of Congress[313]

Vice President

Hannibal Hamlin

	**Hannibal Hamlin**

	15th Vice President of the United States
	In office March 4, 1861 – March 4, 1865
President	Abraham Lincoln
Preceded by	John C. Breckinridge
Succeeded by	Andrew Johnson
	Member of the U.S. House of Representatives from Maine's 6th district
	In office March 4, 1843 – March 3, 1847
Preceded by	Alfred Marshall
Succeeded by	James S. Wiley
	United States Senator from Maine
	In office June 8, 1848 – January 7, 1857 March 4, 1857 – January 17, 1861 March 4, 1869 – March 3, 1881

Preceded by	Wyman B. S. Moor Amos Nourse Lot M. Morrill
Succeeded by	Amos Nourse Lot M. Morrill Eugene Hale
	**26th Governor of Maine**
	**In office** January 8, 1857 – February 25, 1857
Preceded by	Samuel Wells
Succeeded by	Joseph H. Williams
	**Personal details**
Born	August 27, 1809 Paris, Maine
Died	July 4, 1891 (aged 81) Bangor, Maine
Political party	Democrat, Republican
Spouse(s)	Sarah Jane Emery (m. 1833–1855), her death Ellen Vesta Emery Hamlin (m. 1856–1891), his death
Religion	Unitarian
Signature	*H. Hamlin*

Hannibal Hamlin (August 27, 1809 – July 4, 1891) was the 15th Vice President of the United States (1861-1865), serving under President Abraham Lincoln during the American Civil War. He was the first Vice President from the Republican Party.

Prior to his election in 1860, Hamlin served in the United States Senate, the House of Representatives, and, briefly, as the 26th Governor of Maine.

Early life

Hamlin was born to Cyrus Hamlin and Anna Livermore in Paris, Maine. He was a descendant in the sixth generation of James Hamlin who had settled in the Massachusetts Bay Colony in 1639. Hamlin was a great nephew of U.S. Senator Samuel Livermore II of New Hampshire, and a grandson of Stephen Emery, Maine's Attorney General in 1839–40.

Hamlin attended the district schools and Hebron Academy and later managed his father's farm. For the next few years he worked at several jobs: schoolmaster, cook, woodcutter, surveyor, manager of a weekly newspaper in Paris, and a compositor at a printer's office. He studied law and was admitted to the bar in 1833. He began practicing in Hampden, a suburb of Bangor, where he lived until 1848.

Figure 18: *Hamlin in his younger years*

Hamlin married Sarah Jane Emery of Paris Hill in 1833. After Sarah died in 1855, he married her half-sister, Ellen Vesta Emery in 1856. He had four children with Sarah: George, Charles, Cyrus and Sarah. And he had two children, Hannibal E. and Frank, with Ellen. Ellen Hamlin died in 1925.[314]

Political beginnings

Hamlin's political career began in 1836, when he began a term in the Maine House of Representatives after being elected the year before. He served in the bloodless Aroostook War, which took place in 1839. Hamlin unsuccessfully ran for the United States House of Representatives in 1840 and left the State House in 1841. He later served two terms in the United States House of Representatives, from 1843–1847. He was elected to fill a U.S. Senate vacancy in 1848, and to a full term in 1851. A Democrat at the beginning of his career, Hamlin supported the candidacy of Franklin Pierce in 1852.

From the very beginning of his service in Congress, he was prominent as an opponent of the extension of slavery. He was a conspicuous supporter of the Wilmot Proviso and spoke against the Compromise Measures of 1850. In 1854, he strongly opposed the passage of the Kansas-Nebraska Act, which repealed the Missouri Compromise. After the Democratic Party endorsed that repeal at the 1856 Democratic National Convention, on June 12, 1856, he

Figure 19: *1860 election campaign button for Abraham Lincoln and Hannibal Hamlin. The other side of the button has Lincoln's portrait.*

withdrew from the Democratic Party and joined the newly organized Republican Party, causing a national sensation.

The Republicans nominated him for Governor of Maine in the same year. He carried the election by a large majority and was inaugurated on January 8, 1857. In the latter part of February 1857, however, he resigned the governorship, and was again a member of the United States Senate from 1857 to January 1861.

Vice presidency

In 1861, Hamlin became Vice President under Abraham Lincoln, whom he did not meet until after the election. Maine was the first state in the Northeast to embrace the Republican Party, and the Lincoln-Hamlin ticket thus made sense in terms of regional balance. Hamlin was also a strong orator, and a known opponent of slavery. While serving as Vice President, Hamlin had little authority in the Lincoln Administration, although he urged both the Emancipation Proclamation and the arming of Black Americans. He strongly supported Joseph Hooker's appointment as commander of the Army of the Potomac, which was a dismal failure. In June 1864, the Republicans and War Democrats joined to form the National Union Party. Although Lincoln was renominated,

War Democrat Andrew Johnson of Tennessee was named to replace Hamlin as Lincoln's running mate. Lincoln was seeking to broaden his base support and was also looking ahead to Southern Reconstruction, at which Johnson had proven himself adept as war governor of occupied Tennessee. Hamlin, by contrast, was an ally of Northern radicals (who would later impeach Johnson). Lincoln and Johnson were elected in November 1864, and Hamlin's term expired on March 4, 1865.

Hamlin and Lincoln were not close personally, but had a good working relationship. As with the time, White House etiquette did not require the Vice President to regularly attend cabinet meetings; thus, Hamlin did not regularly visit the White House. It was said that Mary Todd Lincoln and Hamlin disliked each other. For his part, Hamlin complained, "I am only a fifth wheel of a coach and can do little for my friends."[315]

Although Hamlin narrowly missed becoming President, his vice presidency would usher in a half-century of sustained national influence for the Maine Republican Party. In the period 1861–1911, Maine Republicans occupied the offices of Vice President, Secretary of the Treasury (twice), Secretary of State, President pro tempore of the United States Senate, Speaker of the United States House of Representatives (twice), and would field a national presidential candidate in James G. Blaine, a level of influence in national politics seldom matched by subsequent Maine political delegations.

Later life and death

Not content with private life, Hamlin returned to the U.S. Senate in 1868 to serve two more terms before declining to run for re-election in 1880 because of a weak heart. His last duty as a public servant came in 1881, when Secretary of State James G. Blaine—a Mainer—convinced James Garfield to name Hamlin minister to Spain, nominating him for the post of ambassador to Spain. Hamlin held the position for two years, then retired to Bangor, Maine. He continued, however, to be a behind-the-scenes influence in the local and state Republican Party.

Upon returning from Spain, Hamlin retired from public life to his home in Bangor, where he had bought an Italianate mansion in 1851 at 15 Fifth St., on the west side of the city. On July 4, 1891, while playing cards at the Tarratine Club (which he founded) in downtown Bangor, Hannibal Hamlin died on the club's couch. He was 81. Hamlin was buried with honors in the Hamlin Family plot at Mount Hope Cemetery, in Bangor, Maine.

Figure 20: *Hamlin in his elder years*

Family

Hamlin had three sons who grew to adulthood: Charles Hamlin, Cyrus Hamlin, and Hannibal Emery Hamlin. Charles and Cyrus served in the Union forces during the Civil War, both becoming generals, Charles by brevet. Cyrus was among the first Union officers to argue for the enlistment of black troops, and himself commanded a brigade of freemen in the Mississippi River campaign. Charles and sister Sarah were present at Ford's Theater the night of Lincoln's assassination. Hannibal Emery Hamlin was Maine Attorney General from 1905 to 1908. Hannibal Hamlin's great-granddaughter Sally Hamlin was a child actor who made many spoken word recordings for the Victor Talking Machine Company in the early years of the 20th century.

Hannibal's older brother, Elijah Livermore Hamlin, was president of the Mutual Fire Insurance Co. of Bangor, and the Bangor Institution for Savings.[316] He was twice an unsuccessful candidate for Governor of Maine in the late 1840s, though he did serve as Mayor of Bangor in 1851–52. The brothers were members of different political parties (Hannibal a Democrat, and Elijah a Whig) before both becoming Republican in the later 1850s.[317] Hannibal's nephew (Elijah's son) Augustus Choate Hamlin was a physician, artist, mineralogist, author, and historian. He was also Mayor of Bangor in 1877–78, and a founding member of the Bangor Historical Society.[318] Augustus served as surgeon in the 2nd Maine Volunteer Infantry Regiment during the Civil War, eventually becoming a U.S. Army Medical Inspector, and later the Surgeon General of Maine. He wrote books about Andersonville Prison and the Battle of Chancellorsville.[319]

Hannibal's first cousin Cyrus Hamlin, who was a graduate of the Bangor Theological Seminary, became a missionary in Turkey, where he founded Robert College. He later became president of Middlebury College in Vermont. His son, A.D.F. Hamlin, Hannibal's first cousin once removed, became a professor of architecture at Columbia University and a noted architectural historian.

There are biographies of Hamlin by his grandson Charles E. Hamlin (published 1899, reprinted 1971) and by H. Draper Hunt (published 1969).

Monuments and memorials

Hannibal Hamlin is buried at Mount Hope Cemetery in Bangor.

Hamlin County, South Dakota, is named in his honor, as is Hamlin, New York, and Hamlin Lake, Mason Co., Michigan. There are statues in Hamlin's likeness in the United States Capitol and in a public park (Norumbega Mall) in Bangor. There is also a building on the University of Maine Campus, in Orono, named Hannibal Hamlin Hall. This burned down in 1945, in a fire that killed two students, but was subsequently rebuilt. Hannibal Hamlin Memorial Library is next to his birthplace in Paris Maine.

Hamlin's house in Bangor subsequently housed the Presidents of the adjacent Bangor Theological Seminary. It is listed on the National Register of Historic Places.

Hamlin's house in Paris is listed on the National Register of Historic Places.

Biographies

- Harry Draper Hunt (1969). *Hannibal Hamlin of Maine, Lincoln's first Vice-President*. Syracuse University Press. ISBN 9780815621423. OCLC 24587.
- Charles Eugene Hamlin (1899). *The Life and Times of Hannibal Hamlin*[320]. Syracuse University Press. OCLC 1559174.

External links

- Hannibal Hamlin[321] at the *Biographical Directory of the United States Congress*
- Biography at Mr. Lincoln's White House[322]
- *The life and times of Hannibal Hamlin* by Charles Eugene Hamlin[323]
- Bangor in Focus: Hannibal Hamlin[324]
- Ted Widmer (November 22, 2010). "Lincoln Speaks"[325]. *NY Times*.

Andrew Johnson

Andrew Johnson	
17th President of the United States	
In office April 15, 1865 – March 4, 1869	
Preceded by	Abraham Lincoln
Succeeded by	Ulysses Grant
16th Vice President of the United States	
In office March 4, 1865 – April 15, 1865	
President	Abraham Lincoln
Preceded by	Hannibal Hamlin
Succeeded by	Schuyler Colfax
United States Senator from Tennessee	
In office March 4, 1875 – July 31, 1875	
Preceded by	William Brownlow

Succeeded by	David Key
In office October 8, 1857 – March 4, 1862	
Preceded by	James Jones
Succeeded by	David Patterson
17th and 19th Governor of Tennessee	
In office October 17, 1853 – November 3, 1857	
Preceded by	William B. Campbell
Succeeded by	Isham Harris
In office March 12, 1862 – March 4, 1865	
Preceded by	Isham Harris
Succeeded by	William Brownlow
Member of the U.S. House of Representatives from Tennessee's 1st district	
In office March 4, 1843 – March 3, 1853	
Preceded by	Thomas Arnold
Succeeded by	Brookins Campbell
Personal details	
Born	December 29, 1808 Raleigh, North Carolina, U.S.
Died	July 31, 1875 (aged 66) Elizabethton, Tennessee, U.S.
Political party	Democratic Party National Union Party (1864–1868)
Spouse(s)	Eliza McCardle
Children	Martha Charles Mary Robert Andrew
Profession	Tailor
Religion	Irreligion / Non-denominational Christianity[326,327]
Signature	*Andrew Johnson*

Andrew Johnson (December 29, 1808 – July 31, 1875) was the 17th President of the United States (1865–1869). Following the assassination of President Abraham Lincoln, Johnson presided over the Reconstruction era of the United States in the four years after the American Civil War. His tenure was controversial as his positions hostile to the Freedmen came under heavy political attack from Republicans.

When Tennessee seceded in 1861, Johnson was a U.S. Senator from Greeneville in East Tennessee. A Unionist, he was the only Southern senator not to resign. He became the most prominent War Democrat from the South and supported Lincoln's military policies during the American Civil War of 1861–1865. In 1862, Lincoln appointed Johnson military governor of occupied Tennessee, where he was energetic and effective in fighting the rebellion and beginning the transition to Reconstruction.

Johnson was nominated as the vice presidential candidate in 1864 on the National Union Party ticket. He and Lincoln were elected in November 1864 and inaugurated on March 4, 1865. Johnson succeeded to the presidency upon Lincoln's assassination on April 15, 1865.

As president, he took charge of Presidential Reconstruction – the first phase of Reconstruction – which lasted until the Radical Republicans gained control of Congress in the 1866 elections. His conciliatory policies towards the South, his hurry to reincorporate the former Confederate states back into the union, and his vetoes of civil rights bills embroiled him in a bitter dispute with Radical Republicans.[328] The Radicals in the House of Representatives impeached him in 1868, charging him with violating the law (specifically the Tenure of Office Act), but the Senate acquitted him by a single vote.

Johnson's party status was ambiguous during his presidency. As president, he did not identify with the two main parties – though he did try for the Democratic presidential nomination in 1868. While President he attempted to build a party of loyalists under the National Union label. Asked in 1868 why he did not become a Democrat, he said, "It is true I am asked why don't I join the Democratic Party. Why don't they join me ... if I have administered the office of president so well?"[329] His failure to make the National Union brand an actual party made Johnson effectively an independent during his presidency, though he was supported by Democrats and later rejoined the party as a Democratic Senator from Tennessee from 1875 until his death.[330] Johnson was the first U.S. President to undergo an impeachment trial. He is commonly ranked by historians as being among the worst U.S. presidents.

Early life

Andrew Johnson was born in Raleigh, North Carolina, to Jacob Johnson (1778–1812) and Mary McDonough (1783–1856). Jacob died when Andrew was around three years old, leaving his family in poverty. Johnson's mother then took in work spinning and weaving to support her family, and she later remarried. She bound Andrew as an apprentice tailor. In the 1820s, he worked

Figure 21: *Johnson's boyhood home in North Carolina, located at the Mordecai Historic Park in Raleigh, North Carolina.*

as a tailor in Laurens, South Carolina. Johnson had no formal education and taught himself how to read and write.[331]

At age 16 or 17, Johnson left his apprenticeship and ran away with his brother to Greeneville, Tennessee, where he found work as a tailor. His master used legal procedures to force him to return but failed, and Johnson was on his own.[332] At the age of 18, Johnson married 16 year-old Eliza McCardle in 1827; she was the daughter of a local shoemaker. Between 1828 and 1852, the couple had five children: Martha (1828), Charles (1830), Mary (1832), Robert (1834), and Andrew Jr. (1852). Eliza taught Johnson arithmetic up to basic algebra and tutored him to improve his literacy, reading, and writing skills.[333]

Early political career

Johnson participated in debates at the local academy at Greeneville, Tennessee[334] and later organized a worker's party that elected him as alderman in 1829. He served in this position until he was elected mayor in 1833. In 1835, he was elected to the Tennessee House of Representatives where, after serving a single term, he was defeated for re-election.

Johnson was attracted to the states rights Democratic Party of Andrew Jackson. He became a spokesman for the numerous yeomen farmers and mountaineers against the wealthier, but fewer, planter elite families that had held political control in the state and nationally.[335] In 1839, Johnson was elected

Figure 22: *Pre-Civil War photo of Johnson.*

to a second, non-consecutive term in the Tennessee House, and was elected to the Tennessee Senate in 1841, where he served one two-year term.[336] In 1843, he became the first Democrat to win election as the U.S. representative from Tennessee's 1st congressional district. Among his activities for the common man's interests as a member of the House of Representatives and the Senate, Johnson advocated "a free farm for the poor" bill that would give land to farmers. Johnson was a U.S. representative for five terms until 1853, when he was elected Governor of Tennessee.[337]

Political ascendancy

Johnson was elected governor of Tennessee, serving from 1853 to 1857. He was then elected as a Democrat to the United States Senate, serving from October 8, 1857 – March 4, 1862. He was chairman of the Committee to Audit and Control the Contingent Expense (Thirty-sixth Congress). As a U.S. senator, he continued to push for the Homestead Act. It finally passed in 1862, after the Civil War had begun and Southerners had resigned from Congress.

As the slavery question became more critical, Johnson continued to take a middle course. He opposed the antislavery Republican Party because he believed the Constitution guaranteed the right to own slaves. He supported President Buchanan's administration. He also approved the Lecompton Constitution proposed by proslavery settlers in Kansas. At the same time, he made it clear that his devotion to the Union exceeded his devotion to right to own slaves.

Johnson's stand in favor of both the Union and the right to own slaves might have made him a logical compromise candidate for president. However, he was not nominated in 1856 because of a split within the Tennessee delegation. In 1860, the Tennessee delegation nominated Johnson for president at the Democratic National Convention, but when the convention and the party broke up, he withdrew from the race. In the election, Johnson reluctantly supported Vice President John C. Breckinridge of Kentucky, the candidate of most Southern Democrats.[338]

Before Tennessee voted on secession, Johnson, based in Unionist East Tennessee, toured the state speaking in opposition to the act, which he said was unconstitutional. Johnson was an aggressive stump speaker and often responded to hecklers, even those in the Senate. When Tennessee seceded, Johnson was the only Senator from the seceded states to continue participation in Congress. His explanation for this decision was, "Damn the negroes, I am fighting those traitorous aristocrats, their masters."[339]

Lincoln appointed Johnson military governor of occupied Tennessee in March 1862 with the rank of brigadier general.[340] During his three years in this office, he "moved resolutely to eradicate all pro-Confederate influences in the state." This "unwavering commitment to the Union" was a significant factor in his choice as vice president by Lincoln.[341] Johnson vigorously suppressed the Confederates, telling his subordinates: "Whenever you hear a man prating about the Constitution, spot him as a traitor."[342] He later spoke out for black suffrage, arguing, "The better class of them will go to work and sustain themselves, and that class ought to be allowed to vote, on the ground that a loyal negro is more worthy than a disloyal white man."[343] The Confederacy seized his slaves.[344]

Vice presidency

As a leading War Democrat and pro-Union southerner, Johnson was an ideal candidate for the Republicans in 1864 as they enlarged their base to include War Democrats. They changed the party name to the National Union Party to reflect this expansion. During the election, Johnson replaced Hannibal Hamlin as Lincoln's running mate. He was elected vice president of the United States and was inaugurated March 4, 1865. At the ceremony, Johnson, who had been drinking to offset the pain of typhoid fever (as he claimed later), gave a rambling speech and appeared intoxicated to many. According to Senator Zachariah Chandler, he "disgraced himself and the Senate by making a

Figure 23: *Currier and Ives print of the National Union Party presidential and vice presidential candidates, 1864. Lithograph and watercolor.*

drunken foolish speech."[345] In early 1865, Johnson talked harshly of hanging traitors like Jefferson Davis, which endeared him to radicals.[346]

On April 14, 1865, Abraham Lincoln was shot and mortally wounded by John Wilkes Booth, a Confederate sympathizer, while the president was attending a play at Ford's Theater. Booth's plan was to destroy the administration by ordering conspirators to assassinate Johnson, lieutenant general of the Union army Ulysses S. Grant, and Secretary of State William H. Seward that night. Grant survived when he failed to attend the theater with Lincoln as planned, Seward narrowly survived his wounds, while Johnson escaped attack as his would-be assassin, George Atzerodt, failed to go through with the plan.

Presidency 1865–1869

On April 15, 1865, following Lincoln's death that morning, Johnson was sworn in as President of the United States by the newly appointed Chief Justice Salmon P. Chase. Johnson was the first vice president to succeed to the presidency upon the assassination of a president and the third vice president to become a president upon the death of a sitting president.[334,347]

Figure 24: *Engraving of Johnson*

Reconstruction

Northern anger over the assassination of Lincoln and the immense human cost of the war led to demands for harsh policies. Vice President Andrew Johnson had taken a hard line and had spoken of hanging rebel Confederates. In late April 1865, he was noted telling an Indiana delegation that, "Treason must be made odious ... traitors must be punished and impoverished ... their social power must be destroyed." However, when he succeeded Lincoln as president, Johnson took a much softer line, commenting, "I say, as to the leaders, punishment. I also say leniency, reconciliation and amnesty to the thousands whom they have misled and deceived,"[348] and ended up pardoning many Confederate leaders.[349]

His class-based resentment of the rich appeared in a May 1865 statement to W.H. Holden, the man he appointed governor of North Carolina: "I intend to confiscate the lands of these rich men whom I have excluded from pardon by my proclamation, and divide the proceeds thereof among the families of the wool hat boys, the Confederate soldiers, whom these men forced into battle to protect their property in slaves."[350] In practice, Johnson was seemingly not harsh toward the Confederate leaders. He allowed the Southern states to hold elections in 1865. Subsequently, prominent former Confederate leaders were elected to the U.S. Congress, which, however, refused to seat them. Congress

Figure 25: *A political cartoon of Andrew Johnson and Abraham Lincoln, 1865. The caption reads (Johnson to the former rail-splitter): Take it quietly Uncle Abe and I will draw it closer than ever!! (Lincoln to the former tailor): A few more stitches Andy and the good old Union will be mended!*

and Johnson argued in an increasingly public way about Reconstruction and the way the Southern secessionist states would be readmitted to the Union. Johnson favored a quick restoration, similar to the plan of leniency that Lincoln advocated before his death.

Break with the Republicans: 1866

Johnson-appointed governments all passed Black Codes that gave the freedmen second class status. In response to the Black Codes and worrisome signs of Southern recalcitrance, the Republicans prevented the secessionist states from receiving representation in Congress in fall 1865. Congress also renewed the Freedman's Bureau, but Johnson vetoed it. Senator Lyman Trumbull of Illinois, leader of the moderate Republicans, took affront at the Black Codes. Trumbull proposed the first Civil Rights bill.

Although strongly urged by moderates in Congress to sign the Civil Rights bill, Johnson broke decisively with them by vetoing it on March 27. His veto message objected to the measure because it conferred citizenship on the freedmen at a time when eleven out of thirty-six states were unrepresented and attempted to fix, by federal law, "a perfect equality of the white and black races in every State of the Union." Johnson said it was an invasion by federal authority of the rights of the states; it had no warrant in the Constitution and was contrary to all precedents. It was a "stride toward centralization and the concentration of all legislative power in the national government."[351] Johnson, in a letter to Gov. Thomas C. Fletcher of Missouri, wrote, "This is a country for white men, and by God, as long as I am President, it shall be a government for white men."[352]

The Democratic Party, proclaiming itself the party of white men, North and South, aligned with Johnson.[353] However, the Republicans in Congress overrode his veto and the Civil Rights measure became law.

The last moderate proposal was the Fourteenth Amendment, also written by Trumbull. It was designed to put the key provisions of the Civil Rights Act into the Constitution, but it went further. It extended citizenship to every person born in the United States (except Indians on reservations), penalized states that did not give the vote to freedmen, and most importantly, created new federal civil rights that could be protected by federal courts. It guaranteed the federal war debt and voided all Confederate war debts. Johnson unsuccessfully sought to block ratification of the amendment.

The moderates' effort to compromise with Johnson had failed and an all-out political war broke out between the Republicans (both radical and moderate) on one side, and on the other Johnson and his allies in the Democratic party in the North, and the conservative groupings in the South. The decisive battle was the election of 1866, in which the Southern states were not allowed to vote. Johnson campaigned vigorously, undertaking a public speaking tour of the north that was known as the "Swing Around the Circle"; the tour proved politically disastrous, with Johnson widely ridiculed and occasionally engaging in hostile arguments with his audiences.[354] The Republicans won by a landslide and took full control of Reconstruction.

Historian James Ford Rhodes explained Johnson's inability to engage in serious negotiations:

> "But," as Sumner shrewdly said, "the President himself is his own worst counsellor, as he is his own worst defender." Johnson acted in accordance with his nature. He had intellectual force but it worked in a groove. Obstinate rather than firm it undoubtedly seemed to him that following counsel and making concessions were a display of weakness. At all events from his December message to the veto of the Civil Rights Bill he yielded not a jot to Congress. The moderate senators and representatives (who constituted a majority of the Union party) asked him for only a slight compromise; their action was really an entreaty that he would unite with them to preserve Congress and the country from the policy of the radicals. The two

Figure 26: *Theodore R. Davis' illustration of Johnson's impeachment trial in the United States Senate, published in Harper's Weekly.*

projects which Johnson had most at heart were the speedy admission of the Southern senators and representatives to Congress and the relegation of the question of negro suffrage to the States themselves. Himself shrinking from the imposition on these communities of the franchise for the coloured people, his unyielding disposition in regard to matters involving no vital principle did much to bring it about. His quarrel with Congress prevented the readmission into the Union on generous terms of the members of the late Confederacy....He sacrificed two important objects to petty considerations. His pride of opinion, his desire to beat, blinded him to the real welfare of the South and of the whole country.[355]

Impeachment

First attempt

There were two attempts to remove President Andrew Johnson from office. The first occurred in the fall of 1867. On November 21, 1867, the House Judiciary committee produced a bill of impeachment that consisted of a vast collection of complaints against him. After a furious debate, a formal vote was held in the House of Representatives on December 5, 1867, which failed 57–108.[356]

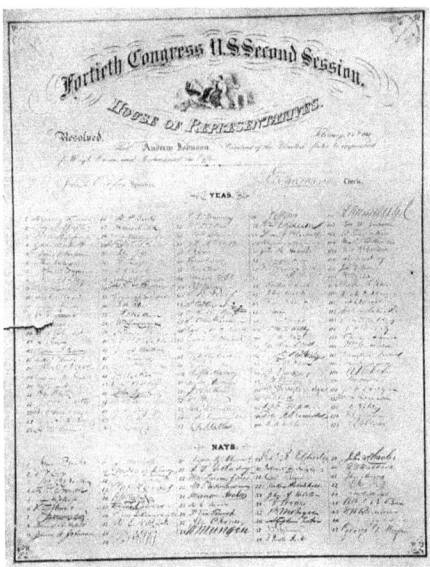

Figure 27: *The 1868 Impeachment Resolution*

Second attempt

Johnson notified Congress that he had removed Edwin Stanton as Secretary of War and was replacing him in the interim with Adjutant-General Lorenzo Thomas. Johnson had originally wanted to replace Stanton with General Ulysses S. Grant, but Grant refused to accept the position. This violated the Tenure of Office Act, a law enacted by Congress in March 1867 over Johnson's veto, specifically designed to protect Stanton.[357] Johnson had vetoed the act, claiming it was unconstitutional. The act said, "...every person holding any civil office, to which he has been appointed by and with the advice and consent of the Senate ... shall be entitled to hold such office until a successor shall have been in like manner appointed and duly qualified," thus removing the president's previous unlimited power to remove any of his cabinet members at will. Years later in the case *Myers v. United States* in 1926, the Supreme Court ruled that such laws were unconstitutional.[358]

The Senate and House debated the act. Thomas attempted to move into the war office, for which Stanton had Thomas arrested. Three days after Stanton's removal, the House impeached Johnson for intentionally violating the Tenure of Office Act.

On March 5, 1868, a court of impeachment to hear charges against the president was constituted in the Senate. William M. Evarts served as his counsel.

Figure 28: *The SituationA Harper's Weekly cartoon gives a humorous breakdown of "the situation". Secretary of War Edwin Stanton aims a cannon labeled "Congress" on the side at President Johnson and Lorenzo Thomas to show how Stanton was using congress to defeat the president and his unsuccessful replacement. He also holds a rammer marked "Tenure of Office Bill" and cannon balls on the floor are marked "Justice". Ulysses S. Grant and an unidentified man stand to Stanton's left.*

Eleven articles were set out in the resolution, and the trial before the Senate lasted almost three months. Johnson's defense was based on a clause in the Tenure of Office Act stating that the then-current secretaries would hold their posts throughout the term of the president who appointed them. Since Lincoln had appointed Stanton, it was claimed, the applicability of the act had already run its course.

There were three votes in the Senate. One came on May 16 for the 11th article of impeachment, which included many of the charges contained in the other articles, and two on May 26 for the second and third articles, after which the trial adjourned. On all three occasions, 35 senators voted "guilty" and 19 "not guilty", thus falling short of the two-thirds majority required for conviction in impeachment trials by a single vote. A decisive role was played by seven Republican senators - William Pitt Fessenden, Joseph S. Fowler, James W. Grimes, John B. Henderson, Lyman Trumbull, Peter G. Van Winkle and Edmund G. Ross of Kansas, who provided the decisive vote;[359] disturbed by how the proceedings had been manipulated to give a one-sided presentation of the evidence, they voted against conviction, in defiance of their party and public opinion.[360] President John F. Kennedy discusses this in further detail in his book, *Profiles In Courage*.

Christmas Day amnesty for Confederates

One of Johnson's last significant acts was granting unconditional amnesty to all Confederates on Christmas Day, December 25, 1868, after the election of Ulysses S. Grant to succeed him, but before Grant took office in March 1869. Earlier amnesties, requiring signed oaths and excluding certain classes of people, had been issued by Lincoln and by Johnson.

Administration and Cabinet

\multicolumn{3}{c}{The A. Johnson Cabinet}		
Office	Name	Term
President	**Andrew Johnson**	1865–1869
Vice President	*None*	1865–1869
Secretary of State	**William H. Seward**	1865–1869
Secretary of Treasury	**Hugh McCulloch**	1865–1869
Secretary of War	**Edwin M. Stanton**	1865–1868 (replaced ad interim by Ulysses Grant, before being reinstated by Congress in Jan. 1868)
	John M. Schofield	1868–1869
Attorney General	**James Speed**	1865–1866
	Henry Stanbery	1866–1868
	William M. Evarts	1868–1869
Postmaster General	**William Dennison**	1865–1866
	Alexander W. Randall	1866–1869
Secretary of the Navy	**Gideon Welles**	1865–1869

Secretary of the Interior	John P. Usher	1865
	James Harlan	1865–1866
	Orville H. Browning	1866–1869

Judicial appointments

Andrew Johnson appointed only nine Article III federal judges during his presidency, all to United States district courts. Johnson is one of only four presidents[361] who did not appoint a justice to serve on the Supreme Court. In April 1866 he nominated Henry Stanbery to fill the vacancy left with the death of John Catron, but the Republican Congress eliminated the seat. Johnson also appointed one judge to the United States Court of Claims, Samuel Milligan, who served from 1868 to 1874.

States admitted to the Union

- Nebraska – March 1, 1867

Foreign policy

Johnson forced the French out of Mexico by sending an army to the border and issuing an ultimatum. The French withdrew in 1867, and the government they supported quickly collapsed. Secretary of State Seward negotiated the purchase of Alaska from Russia on April 9, 1867 for $7.2 million. This is equivalent to $113 million in present day terms.[362] Critics sneered at "Seward's Folly" and "Seward's Icebox" and "Icebergia." Seward also negotiated to purchase the Danish West Indies, but the Senate refused to approve the purchase in 1867 (it eventually happened in 1917). The Senate likewise rejected Seward's arrangement with Britain to arbitrate the *Alabama* Claims.

The U.S. experienced tense relations with Britain and its colonial government in Canada in the aftermath of the war. Lingering resentment over the perception of British sympathy toward the Confederacy resulted in Johnson initially turning a blind eye towards a series of armed incursions by Fenians (Irish-American civil war veterans) into Canada. These small-scale Fenian Raids were easily repulsed by the British. Eventually, Johnson ordered the Fenians disarmed and barred from crossing the border, but the Canadians feared an American takeover and moved toward Canadian Confederation.[363]

Johnson's purchase of Alaska from the Russian Empire in 1867 was his most important foreign policy action. The idea and implementation is credited to Seward as Secretary of State, but Johnson approved the plan.[364]

Figure 29: *The Johnson home in Greeneville, Tennessee, 1886, today restored and known as the Andrew Johnson National Historic Site.*

Post-presidency

Johnson was an unsuccessful candidate for election to the United States Senate from Tennessee in 1868 and to the House of Representatives in 1872. However, in 1874 the Tennessee legislature did elect him to the U.S. Senate. Johnson served from March 4, 1875, until his death from a stroke near Elizabethton, Tennessee, on July 31 that year. In his first speech since returning to the Senate, which was also his last, Johnson spoke about political turmoil in Louisiana.[365] His passion aroused a standing ovation from many of his fellow senators who had once voted to remove him from the presidency.[366] He is the only former president to serve in the Senate.[365]

Johnson was buried just outside Greeneville, Tennessee, with his body wrapped in an American flag and a copy of the U.S. Constitution placed under his head, according to his wishes. The burial ground was dedicated as the Andrew Johnson National Cemetery in 1906, now part of the Andrew Johnson National Historic Site.

Figure 30: *Senator Andrew Johnson in 1875. (age 66)*

Historians' changing views on Andrew Johnson

Views on Johnson changed over time, depending on historians' perception of Reconstruction. The widespread denunciation of Reconstruction after the compromise of 1877 resulted in Johnson being portrayed in a favorable light. By the 1930s a series of favorable biographies enhanced his prestige.[367] Furthermore, a Beardian School (named after Charles Beard and typified by Howard K. Beale) argued that the Republican Party in the 1860s was a tool of corrupt business interests, and that Johnson stood for the people. They rated Johnson "near great", but have since reevaluated and now consider Johnson "a flat failure".[368]

The Civil Rights movement of the 1960s brought a new perspective on Reconstruction, which was increasingly seen as a noble effort to build an interracial nation.[368,369] Beginning with W.E.B. Du Bois' *Black Reconstruction*, first published in 1935, historians noted African American efforts to establish public education and welfare institutions, gave muted praise for Republican efforts to extend suffrage and provide other social institutions, and excoriated Johnson for siding with the opposition to extending basic rights to former slaves.[368] In this vein, Eric Foner denounced Johnson as a "fervent white supremacist" who foiled Reconstruction,[368] whereas Sean Wilentz wrote that Johnson "actively sided with former Confederates" in his attempts to derail it.[370] Accordingly,

Figure 31:
~ *Andrew Johnson* ~
1938 Issue

Johnson is today among those commonly mentioned among the worst presidents in U.S. history.[369]

According to Glenn W. LaFantasie, Professor of Civil War History at Western Kentucky University, "Johnson is a particular favorite for the bottom of the pile because of his impeachment (although he was acquitted in the Senate by one vote in May 1868), his complete mishandling of Reconstruction policy, his inept dealings with his Cabinet and Congress, his drinking problem (he was probably inebriated at his inauguration), his bristling personality, and his enormous sense of self-importance. He once suggested that God saw fit to have Lincoln assassinated so that he could become president. A Northern senator averred that "Andrew Johnson was the queerest character that ever occupied the White House."[371]

Bibliography

- Beale, Howard K., *The Critical Year. A Study of Andrew Johnson and Reconstruction* (1930). ISBN 0-8044-1085-2
- Les Benedict, Michael, *The Impeachment and Trial of Andrew Johnson*[372] (1999). ISBN 0-393-31982-2

- Boulard, Garry, "The Swing Around the Circle—Andrew Johnson and the Train Ride that Destroyed a Presidency" (2008) ISBN 978-1-4401-0239-4
- Castel, Albert E., *The Presidency of Andrew Johnson* (1979). ISBN 0-7006-0190-2
- DeWitt, D. M., *The Impeachment and Trial of Andrew Johnson* (1903).
- Du Bois, W. E. B. 'The Transubstantiation of a Poor White' in *Black Reconstruction: An Essay Toward the History of the Part Which Black People Have Played in the Attempt to Reconstruct Democracy in America, 1860–1880* (1935). ISBN 0-527-25280-8.
- Dunning, W. A., *Essays on the Civil War and Reconstruction*[373] (New York, 1898)
- Dunning, W. A., *Reconstruction, Political and Economic* (New York, 1907) online edition[374]
- Foster, G. Allen, *Impeached: The President who almost lost his job* (New York, 1964).
- Gordon-Reed, Annette *Andrew Johnson: The American Presidents Series: The 17th President, 1865-1869*, ISBN 0-8050-6948-8 .
  - Gordon-Reed, Annette speaking on[375] CSPAN Booktv *Andrew Johnson*
- Hatfield, Mark O., with the Senate Historical Office, Vice Presidents of the United States, 1789–1993.(U.S. Government Printing Office, 1997), p. 219
- Mantell,Martin E. *Johnson, Grant, and the Politics of Reconstruction*[376] (1973)
- McKitrick,Eric L., *Andrew Johnson and Reconstruction* (1961). ISBN 0-19-505707-4
- Means;Howard, *The Avenger Takes His Place: Andrew Johnson and the 45 Days That Changed the Nation* (New York, 2006)
- Milton; George Fort. *The Age of Hate: Andrew Johnson and the Radicals* (1930) online edition[377]
- Patton; James Welch. *Unionism and Reconstruction in Tennessee, 1860–1869* (1934) online edition[378]
- Rhodes; James Ford *History of the United States from the Compromise of 1850 to the McKinley-Bryan Campaign of 1896*[379] Volume: 6. 1920. Pulitzer prize.
- Schouler, James. *History of the United States of America: Under the Constitution vol. 7. 1865–1877. The Reconstruction Period*[380] (1917)
- Sledge, James L. III. "Johnson, Andrew" in *Encyclopedia of the American Civil War.* edited by David S. Heidler and Jeanne T. Heidler. (2000)
- Stewart, David, O. *Impeached: the Trial of President Andrew Johnson and the Fight for Lincoln's Legacy* (2009) Simon and Schuster, New

York, NY. ISBN 978-1-4165-4749-5.
- Stryker, Lloyd P., *Andrew Johnson: A Study in Courage* (1929). ISBN 0-403-01231-7 online edition[381]
- Trefousse, Hans L. *Andrew Johnson: A Biography* (1989). ISBN 0-393-31742-0 online edition[382]
- Winston; Robert W. *Andrew Johnson: Plebeian and Patriot* (1928) online edition[383]

Primary sources

- Ralph W. Haskins, LeRoy P. Graf, and Paul H. Bergeron et al., eds. *The Papers of Andrew Johnson* 16 volumes; University of Tennessee Press, (1967–2000). ISBN 1-57233-091-0. Includes all letters and speeches by Johnson, and many letters written to him. Complete to 1875.
- Newspaper clippings, 1865–1869[384]
- Series of *Harper's Weekly* articles covering the impeachment controversy and trial[385]
- Johnson's obituary, from the *New York Times*[386]

External links

- The Impeachment trial of President Johnson as reported in Harper's Monthly Magazine April 1868[387]
- Obituary, NY Times, August 1, 1875, *Andrew Johnson Dead*[388]
- Articles of Impeachment[389]
- White House Biography[390]
- Vice Presidential biography. From the Senate Historical Office.[391]
- Mr. Lincoln's White House: Andrew Johnson[392]
- Andrew Johnson Cleveland Speech (September 3, 1866)[393]
- *Congressional Globe* transcript of Johnsons inaugural address[394]
- *Speeches of Andrew Johnson : President of the United States* 1866 collection at archive.org[395]
- Andrew Johnson's 200th Birthday Celebration site at Discover-Greeneville.com[396]
- Andrew Johnson: A Resource Guide from the Library of Congress[397]
- Tennessee State Library & Archives, Andrew Johnson Papers, 1846-1875[398]
- Tennessee State Library & Archives, Papers of Governor Andrew Johnson, 1853-1857[399]
- Tennessee State Library & Archives, Papers of (Military) Governor Andrew Johnson, 1862-1865[400]
- Andrew Johnson[401] at the *Biographical Directory of the United States Congress* Retrieved on 2009-03-02

- Essay on Andrew Johnson and shorter essays on each member of his cabinet and First Lady from the Miller Center of Public Affairs[402]
- Paper comparing the impeachments of Andrew Johnson and Bill Clinton[403]

Secretary of State

William H. Seward

	**The Honorable** **William Henry Seward**
	**24th United States Secretary of State**
	**In office** March 5, 1861 – March 4, 1869
President	Abraham Lincoln Andrew Johnson
Preceded by	Jeremiah S. Black
Succeeded by	Elihu B. Washburne
	**12th Governor of New York**
	**In office** January 1, 1839 – December 31, 1842
Lieutenant	Luther Bradish
Preceded by	William L. Marcy
Succeeded by	William C. Bouck
	**United States Senator** **from New York**

\multicolumn{2}{c}{**In office**}
\multicolumn{2}{c}{March 4, 1849 – March 4, 1861}
Preceded by	John A. Dix
Succeeded by	Ira Harris
\multicolumn{2}{c}{**Personal details**}
Born	May 16, 1801 Florida, New York
Died	October 10, 1872 (aged 71) Auburn, New York
Political party	Whig, Republican
Spouse(s)	Frances Adeline Seward
Children	Augustus Henry Seward Frederick William Seward Cornelia Seward William Henry Seward, Jr. Frances Adeline Seward Olive Risley Seward (adopted)
Alma mater	Union College
Profession	Lawyer, Land Agent, Politician
Religion	Episcopalian
Signature	*William H Seward.*

William Henry Seward, Sr. (May 16, 1801 – October 10, 1872) was the 12th Governor of New York, United States Senator and the United States Secretary of State under Abraham Lincoln and Andrew Johnson. A drastic encounter with the spread of slavery in the years leading up to the American Civil War, he was a dominant figure in the Republican Party in its formative years, and was widely regarded as the leading contender for the party's presidential nomination in 1860 – yet his very outspokenness may have cost him the nomination. Despite his loss, he became a loyal member of Lincoln's wartime cabinet, and played a role in preventing foreign intervention early in the war.[404] On the night of Lincoln's assassination, he survived an attempt on his life in the conspirators' effort to decapitate the Union government. As Johnson's Secretary of State, he engineered the purchase of Alaska from Russia in an act that was ridiculed at the time as "Seward's Folly", but which somehow exemplified his character. His contemporary Carl Schurz described Seward as "one of those spirits who sometimes will go ahead of public opinion instead of tamely following its footprints."[405]

Early life and career

Seward was born in Florida, New York, on May 16, 1801, one of five children of Samuel Sweezy Seward and his wife Mary Jennings Seward. Samuel Seward, described as "a prosperous, domineering doctor and businessman,"[406] was the founder of the S. S. Seward Institute, today a secondary school in the Florida Union Free School District[407].[408]

Seward served as president of the S.S. Seward Institute after the death of his father, even while serving as Secretary of State during the Lincoln and Johnson administrations.

Seward studied law at Union College, graduating in 1820 with highest honors, and as a member of Phi Beta Kappa.[409] He was admitted to the New York State Bar in 1821.[410] In that same year, he met Frances Adeline Miller, a classmate of his sister Cornelia at Emma Willard's Troy Female Seminary and the daughter of Judge Elijah Miller of Auburn, New York. In 1823, he moved to Auburn where he entered into law partnership with Judge Miller, and married Frances Miller on October 20, 1824. They raised five children:

- Augustus Henry Seward (1826–1876)
- Frederick William Seward (1830–1915)
- Cornelia Seward (1836–1837)
- William Henry Seward, Jr. (1839–1920)
- Frances Adeline "Fanny" Seward (1844–1866)
- Olive Risley Seward (1841–1908), adopted

Seward entered politics with the help of his friend Thurlow Weed, whom he had met by chance after a stagecoach accident.[411] In 1830, Seward was elected to the state senate as an Anti-Masonic candidate, and served for four years. In 1834, the 33-year-old Seward was named the Whig party candidate for Governor of New York, but lost to incumbent Democrat William Marcy who won 52% of the vote to Seward's 48%.

From 1836 to 1838, Seward served as agent for a group of investors who had purchased the over 3-million-acre (12,000 km^2) western New York holdings of the Holland Land Company. He moved the land office from Mayville, NY to Westfield, New York, where he was successful in easing tensions between the investors and local landowners. On July 16, 1837, he delivered to the students and faculty of the newly formed Westfield Academy a *Discourse on Education*, in which he advocated for universal education.[412]

In 1838, Seward again challenged Marcy, and was elected Governor of New York by a majority of 51.4% to Marcy's 48.6%. He was narrowly re-elected to a second two-year term in 1840. As a state senator and governor, Seward promoted progressive political policies including prison reform and increased

Figure 32: *Seward's wife Frances Adeline Seward.*

spending on education. He supported state funding for schools for immigrants operated by their own clergy and taught in their native language. This support, which included Catholic parochial schools, came back to haunt him in the 1850s, when anti-Catholic feelings were high, especially among ex-Whigs in the Republican Party.

Seward developed his views about slavery while still a boy. His parents, like other Hudson Valley residents of the early 19th century, owned several slaves. (Slavery was slowly abolished in New York from 1797 to 1827 through a gradual mandated process.) Seward recalled his preference as a child for the company and conversation of the slaves in his father's kitchen to the 'severe decorum' in his family's front parlor. He discerned very quickly the inequality between races, writing in later years "I early came to the conclusion that something was wrong...and [that] determined me...to be an abolitionist." This belief would stay with Seward through his life and permeate his career.[413]

Seward's wife Frances was deeply committed to the abolitionist movement. In the 1850s, the Seward family opened their Auburn home as a safehouse to fugitive slaves. Seward's frequent travel and political work suggest that it was Frances who played the more active role in Auburn abolitionist activities. In the excitement following the rescue and safe transport of fugitive slave William "Jerry" Henry in Syracuse on October 1, 1851, Frances wrote to her husband, "two fugitives have gone to Canada—one of them our acquaintance John."[414] Another time she wrote, "A man by the name of William Johnson will apply to you for assistance to purchase the freedom of his daughter. You will see that I have given him something by his book. I told him I thought you would give him more."[415]

In 1846 Seward became the center of controversy in his hometown when he defended, in separate cases, two convicts accused of murder. Henry Wyatt, a white man, was charged in the stabbing death of a fellow prison inmate; William Freeman, of African American and Native American ancestry, was accused of breaking into a home and stabbing four people to death. In both cases the defendants were mentally ill and had been severely abused while in prison. Seward, having long been an advocate of prison reform and better treatment for the insane, sought to prevent both men from being executed by using a relatively new defense of insanity. In a case involving mental illness with heavy racial overtones Seward argued, "The color of the prisoner's skin, and the form of his features, are not impressed upon the spiritual immortal mind which works beneath. In spite of human pride, he is still your brother, and mine, in form and color accepted and approved by his Father, and yours, and mine, and bears equally with us the proudest inheritance of our race—the image of our Maker. Hold him then to be a Man."[416]

Later, Seward quoted Freeman's brother-in-law, praising his eloquence: "They have made William Freeman what he is, a brute beast; they don't make anything else of any of our people but brute beasts; but when we violate their laws, then they want to punish us as if we were men."[417] In the end both men were convicted. Although Wyatt was executed, Freeman, whose conviction was reversed on Seward's successful appeal to the New York Supreme Court, died in his cell of tuberculosis.

United States Senator and Presidential Candidate

Seward supported the Whig candidate, General Zachary Taylor, in the presidential election of 1848. He said of Taylor, "He is the most gentle-looking and amiable of men." Taylor was a slaveholding plantation owner, but was friendly to Seward anyway.

William Seward was elected a U.S. Senator from New York as a Whig in 1849, and emerged as the leader of the anti-slavery "Conscience Whigs". Seward opposed the Compromise of 1850, and was thought to have encouraged Taylor in his supposed opposition. More recent scholarship suggests that Taylor was not under Seward's influence and would have accepted the Compromise if he had not died. Seward believed that slavery was morally wrong, and said so many times, outraging Southerners. He acknowledged that slavery was legal under the Constitution, but denied that the Constitution recognized or protected slavery. He famously remarked in 1850 that "there is a higher law than

Figure 33: *William H. Seward (c. 1850)*

the Constitution". He continued to argue this point of view over the next ten years. He presented himself as the leading enemy of the Slave Power – that is, the perceived conspiracy of southern slaveowners to seize the government and defeat the progress of liberty.

Seward was an opponent of the Fugitive Slave Act, and he defended runaway slaves in court. He supported personal liberty laws.

In February 1855, he was re-elected as a Whig to the U.S. Senate, and joined the Republican Party when the New York Whigs merged with the Anti-Nebraskans later the same year. Seward did not seriously compete for the presidential nomination (won by John C. Frémont) in 1856, but sought and was expected to receive the nomination in 1860. In October 1858, he delivered a famous speech in which he argued that the political and economic systems of North and South were incompatible, and that, due to this "irrepressible conflict," the inevitable "collision" of the two systems would eventually result in the nation becoming "either entirely a slaveholding nation, or entirely a free-labor nation."[418] Like Lincoln, he believed slavery could and should be extinguished by long-run historical forces rather than by coercion or war.[419]

In 1859, confident of gaining the presidential nomination and advised by his political ally and friend Thurlow Weed that he would be better off avoiding political gatherings where his words might be misinterpreted by one faction

Figure 34: *Lincoln met with his Cabinet for the first reading of the Emancipation Proclamation draft on July 22, 1862.*

or another, Seward left the country for an eight-month tour of Europe that included a visit to Syria, where Ayub Beg Tarabulsy gave him several Arabian horses.[420] During that hiatus, his lesser-known rival Abraham Lincoln worked diligently to line up support in case Seward failed to win on the first ballot. After returning to the United States, Seward gave a conciliatory, pro-Union Senate speech that reassured moderates but alienated some radical Republicans. (Observing events from Europe, Karl Marx, who was ideologically sympathetic to Frémont, contemptuously regarded Seward as a "Republican Richelieu" and the "Demosthenes of the Republican Party" who had sabotaged Frémont's presidential ambitions.) Around the same time, his friend Horace Greeley turned against him, opposing Seward on the grounds that his radical reputation made him unelectable. When Lincoln won the nomination, Seward loyally supported him and made a long speaking tour of the West in the autumn of 1860.

Secretary of State

"Our population is destined to roll its resistless waves to the icy barriers of the north, and to encounter oriental civilization on the shores of the Pacific."
—William H. Seward, 1846[421]

Abraham Lincoln appointed Seward his Secretary of State in 1861. Seward played an integral role in resolving the Trent Affair and in negotiating the ensuing Lyons-Seward Treaty of 1862, which set forth strong measures by which

Figure 35: *Running The "Machine"*
An 1864 cartoon mocking Lincoln's cabinet depicts Seward, William Fessenden, Lincoln, Edwin Stanton, Gideon Welles and other members.

the United States and Great Britain agreed to enforce an end to the Atlantic slave trade.

Seward pursued his vision of American expansion. "Give me only this assurance, that there never be an unlawful resistance by an armed force to the ... United States, and give me fifty, forty, thirty more years of life, and I will engage to give you the possession of the American continent and the control of the world."[422] Having argued for taking American possession of vulnerable but useful places such as the Danish West Indies, Samaná, Panama, and Hawaii, Seward oversaw the annexation of only one, that of the Brook Islands in 1867. Despite minimal Congressional support, though, he developed American influence in the Hawaiian Islands, as well as in Japan and China to some extent.

Despite his endorsement of expansionist policies, Seward also strongly advocated non-interventionism. After Tsar Alexander II put down the 1863 January Uprising in Poland, French Emperor Napoleon III asked the United States to "join in a protest to the Tsar."[423] Seward declined, "defending 'our policy of non-intervention — straight, absolute, and peculiar as it may seem to other nations,'" and insisted that "[t]he American people must be content to recommend the cause of human progress by the wisdom with which they should

Figure 36: *Lewis Powell attacking Frederick Seward after attempting to shoot him.*

exercise the powers of self-government, forbearing at all times, and in every way, from foreign alliances, intervention, and interference."[423]

Assassination attempt

On April 14, 1865, Lewis Powell, an associate of John Wilkes Booth, attempted to assassinate Seward, the same night that Abraham Lincoln was shot. Powell gained access to Seward's home by telling a servant, William H. Bell, that he was delivering medicine for Seward, who was recovering from a recent carriage accident on April 5, 1865. Powell started up the stairs when then confronted by one of Seward's sons, Frederick. He told the intruder that his father was asleep and Powell began to start down the stairs, but suddenly swung around and pointed a gun at Frederick's head. After the gun jammed, Powell panicked, then repeatedly struck Frederick over the head with the pistol, leaving Frederick in critical condition on the floor.

Powell then burst into William Seward's bedroom with a knife and stabbed him several times in the face and neck. Powell also attacked and injured another son (Augustus), a soldier and nurse (Sgt. George Robinson) who had been assigned to stay with Seward, and a messenger (Emerick Hansell) who arrived just as Powell was escaping.[424] Luckily all five men that were injured that night survived, although Seward Sr. would carry the facial scars from the attack through his remaining life. The events of that night took their toll on his wife, Frances, who died June 1865. His daughter Fanny died of tuberculosis in October 1866.

Powell was captured the next day and was executed on July 7, 1865, along with David Herold, George Atzerodt, and Mary Surratt, the three others convicted as conspirators in the Lincoln assassination.

Although it took Seward several months to recover from his wounds, he emerged as a major force in the administration of the new president, Andrew Johnson, frequently defending his more moderate reconciliation policies towards the South, to the point of enraging Radical Republicans who had once regarded Seward as their ally.

In the fall of 1866, Seward joined Johnson, as well as Ulysses S. Grant and the young General George Armstrong Custer, along with several other administration figures, on the president's ill-fated "Swing Around the Circle" campaign trip.

At one point Seward became so ill, probably from cholera, that he was sent back to Washington in a special car. Both Johnson and Grant, as well as several members of the Seward family, thought the Secretary was near death. But as with his April 1865 stabbing, Seward surprised many by making a good recovery.

The purchase of Alaska

Seward's most famous achievement as Secretary of State was his successful acquisition of Alaska from Russia. On March 30, 1867, he completed negotiations for the territory, which involved the purchase of 586,412 square miles (1,518,800 km²) of territory (more than twice the area of Texas) for $7,200,000, or approximately 2 cents per acre (equivalent to US$95 million in 2005). The purchase of this frontier land was variously mocked by the public as Seward's Folly, "Seward's Icebox," and Andrew Johnson's "polar bear garden." Alaska celebrates the purchase on Seward's Day, the last Monday of March. When asked what he considered to be his greatest achievement as Secretary of State, Seward replied "The purchase of Alaska—but it will take the people a generation to find it out".[425]

Figure 37: *The signing of the Alaska Treaty of Cessation on March 30, 1867.*

Later life

Seward retired as Secretary of State after Ulysses S. Grant took office as president. During his last years, Seward traveled and wrote prolifically. Most notably, he traveled around the world in fourteen months and two days from August, 1870 to October, 1871. On October 10, 1872, Seward died in his office in his home in Auburn, New York, after having difficulty breathing. His last words were to his children saying, "Love one another." He was buried in Fort Hill Cemetery in Auburn, New York, with his wife and two children, Cornelia and Fanny. His headstone reads, *"He was faithful."*

His son, Frederick, edited and published his memoirs in three volumes.

In 1967, a century after the Alaska Purchase, the actor, Joseph Cotten, portrayed Seward in "The Freeman Story", a part of his NBC anthology series, *The Joseph Cotten Show*. Virginia Gregg played Fanny Seward. Popular actor, Richard Mulligan, portrayed William Seward in the 1988 Lincoln mini-series, "Random Letters".

Figure 38: *Statue of Seward in Madison Square Park in New York City*

Seward's homes in Auburn and Florida, New York

Seward and his family owned a home in Auburn, New York which is now a museum; it was built in 1816 by Seward's father-in-law, Judge Elijah Miller. Seward married the Judge's daughter, Frances, in 1824 on the condition that they would live with Miller in his Auburn home. Seward made many changes to the home, adding an addition in the late 1840s and another one in 1866. When he died, Seward left the home to his son, William Seward, Jr.; it passed on to his grandson, William Henry Seward III, in 1920. At his death in 1951, it became a museum that opened to the public in 1955. Four generations of the family's artifacts are contained within the museum, located at 33 South Street in Auburn. The museum is open Tuesday through Saturday from 10am to 5pm.

Meanwhile, Seward's birthplace in Florida, New York was bought by the village in 2010, with the purpose of refurbishing it. (The property actually contains two houses: one in back—Seward's actual birthplace—which was converted into a barn; and one in front, built in the 1890s, used by the family that lived there for many years.) The property (after spending an estimated $200,000, to be raised by private donations) is expected to be turned into a museum and opened to the public by 2013.

Figure 39: *Southern patio of the Seward House Museum located in Auburn, NY*

Legacy

- The purchase of Alaska.
- The Guano Islands Act of 1856
- The $50-dollar Treasury note, also called the Coin note, of the Series 1891, features a portrait of Seward on the obverse. Examples of this note are very rare and would likely sell for about $50,000 at auction.
- His house in Auburn, New York is open as a public museum.
- The house in which he lived in Westfield, New York is now home to a bed and breakfast.
- He was a name partner of the law firm of Blatchford, Seward & Griswold, today known as Cravath, Swaine & Moore.
- Was famous in his lifetime for his red hair and energetic way of walking. Henry Adams described him as "wonderfully resembling" a parrot in "manner and profile".[426]

Memorials

- Seward Avenue in Auburn. Also in Auburn, Frances Street, Augustus Street, and Frederick Street are named for members of his family. The four streets form a block.

Figure 40: *Statue of William H. Seward in New York City*

Figure 41: *Statue of Seward in Volunteer Park, Seattle, Washington.*

Figure 42: *Bust depicting William H. Seward in Seward, Alaska*

- Seward Elementary School in Auburn.
- Seward Place in Schenectady, New York, on the west side of the Union College campus.
- Seward Park in Auburn, New York.
- Seward Park in the Lower East Side of Manhattan.
- Seward Park in Seattle, Washington.
- Seward Square park in Washington, D.C..
- The Seward Peninsula in Alaska.
- City of Seward[427], on Alaska's Kenai Peninsula
- Seward, Illinois; Seward, Kansas; Seward, New York; Seward, Nebraska; and Seward, Alaska.
- A hamburger is called "Seward's Folly" at West Rib Deli & Pub in Talkeetna, Alaska is named for him.
- Seward County, Nebraska
- Seward's Success, Alaska, an unbuilt community to be enclosed by a dome.
- The Seward neighborhood of Minneapolis, Minnesota
- Seward Mountain (4,361 feet, 1,329 m), one of the Adirondack High Peaks, the highest point in Franklin County.
- At Union College, the campus bus is known as Seward's Trolley, a pun on Seward's Folly.

- Seward High School in his hometown of Florida is named for his father, Dr. Samuel Seward.
- Statues of him in Seward Park in Auburn, in Madison Square Park in New York City, on the grounds of the Z. J. Loussac Public Library in Anchorage, Alaska, and in Volunteer Park in Seattle (not facing towards Alaska).
- The William Henry Seward Memorial in Florida, with a bust sculpted by Daniel Chester French.
- Seward Park Housing Corporation, a housing cooperative in the Lower East Side of Manhattan
- Seward Mansion in Mount Olive, NJ
- The Auburn Doubledays minor league baseball team gave away William Seward bobble-head dolls as a promotion in 2010.

Works

- Frederick William Seward. *Autobiography of William H. Seward from 1801 to 1834: With a memoir of his life, and selections from his letters from 1831 to 1840*[428] (1877)
- *Life and Public Services of John Quincy Adams, Sixth President of the United States* (1849)
- *Commerce in the Pacific ocean. Speech of William H. Seward, in the Senate of the United States, July 29, 1852* (1852; Digitized page images & text[429])
- *The continental rights and relations of our country. Speech of William Henry Seward, in Senate of the United States, January 26, 1853* (1853; Digitized page images & text[430])
- *The destiny of America. Speech of William H. Seward, at the dedication of Capital University, at Columbus, Ohio, September 14, 1853* (1853; Digitized page images & text[431])
- *Certificate of Exchange* (1867; Digitized page images & text[432])
- *Alaska. Speech of William H. Seward at Sitka, August 12, 1869* (1869; Digitized page images & text[433])
- *The Works of William H. Seward*. Edited by George E. Baker. Volume I of III (1853) online edition[434]
- *The Works of William H. Seward*. Edited by George E. Baker. Volume II of III (1853) online edition[435]
- *The Works of William H. Seward: Vol. 5: The diplomatic history of the war for the union.*. Edited by George E. Baker. Volume 5 (1890)[436]

Further reading

- Bancroft, Frederic (1900). *The Life of William H. Seward* 2 vol.
- Boulard, Garry (2008). *The Swing Around the Circle: Andrew Johnson and the Train Ride that Destroyed a Presidency.* New York: iUniverse. ISBN 9781440102394.
- Donald, David Herbert (2003). *We Are Lincoln Men: Abraham Lincoln and His Friends.* New York: Simon & Schuster. pp. 140–176. ISBN 0743254686.
- Goodwin, Doris Kearns (2005). *Team of Rivals: The Political Genius of Abraham Lincoln.* New York: Simon & Schuster. ISBN 0684824906.
- Hendrick, Burton (1946). *Lincoln's War Cabinet.* Boston: Little, Brown.
- Neely, Mark E., Jr. (1991). *The Fate of Liberty: Abraham Lincoln and Civil Liberties.* New York: Oxford University Press. ISBN 0195064968.
- Taylor, John M. (1991). *William Henry Seward: Lincoln's Right Hand.* New York: HarperCollins. ISBN 0060163070.
- Van Deusen, Glyndon (1967). *William Henry Seward.* New York: Oxford University Press.
- Marx, Karl (November 26, 1861). "The Dismissal of Frémont". *Die Presse* **325**.
- Swanson, James L. (2006). *Manhunt: The 12-Day Chase for Lincoln's Killer.* New York: HarperCollins. pp. 58–59.
- Hamilton, Holman (1951). *Zachary Taylor: Soldier in the White House.* Indianapolis: Bobbs-Merrill.
- Lattimer, John (1980). *Kennedy and Lincoln, Medical & Ballistic Comparisons of Their Assassinations.* New York: Harcourt Brace Jovanovich. ISBN 0151522812. [information about Seward's accident and jaw splint, in particular]

External links

- William H. Seward[437] at the *Biographical Directory of the United States Congress* Retrieved on 2009-04-30
- Seward House, Auburn, NY[438]
- Brief Seward biography[439]
- Mr. Lincoln and Friends: William H. Seward[440]
- Mr. Lincoln and New York: William H. Seward[441]
- Mr. Lincoln's White House: William H. Seward[442]
- Works by William H. Seward[443] at Project Gutenberg
- Pictures of US Treasury Notes featuring William Seward, provided by the Federal Reserve Bank of San Francisco.[444]

- William Henry Seward, the Virginia controversy, and the anti-slavery movement, 1839-1841[445]
- Chisholm, Hugh, ed (1911). "Seward, William Henry". *Encyclopædia Britannica* (11th ed.). Cambridge University Press.

Secretary of War

Simon Cameron

Simon Cameron	

26th United States Secretary of War	
In office March 5, 1861 – January 14, 1862	
President	Abraham Lincoln
Preceded by	Joseph Holt
Succeeded by	Edwin M. Stanton
Personal details	
Born	March 8, 1799 Maytown, Pennsylvania, U.S.
Died	June 26, 1889 (aged 90) Maytown, Pennsylvania, U.S.
Political party	Whig, Democratic, Republican
Spouse(s)	Margaret Brua Cameron
Profession	Politician, Journalist, Editor

| Signature | *Simon Cameron* |

Simon Cameron (March 8, 1799 – June 26, 1889) was an American politician who served as United States Secretary of War for Abraham Lincoln at the start of the American Civil War. After making his fortune in railways and banking, he turned to a life of politics. He became a U.S. senator in 1845 for the state of Pennsylvania, succeeding James Buchanan. Originally a Democrat, he failed to secure a nomination for senator from the Know-Nothing party, and joined the People's Party, the Pennsylvania branch of what became the Republican Party. He won the Senate seat in 1857, and became one of the candidates for the Republican nomination in the presidential election of 1860.

Cameron gave his support to Abraham Lincoln, and became his Secretary of War. He only served a year before resigning amidst corruption. Cameron became the minister to Russia during the Civil War, but was overseas for less than a year. He again served in the Senate, eventually being succeeded by his son, J. Donald Cameron, and only resigned from the Senate upon confirmation that his son would succeed him.

Early life

Cameron was born in Maytown, Pennsylvania, to Charles Cameron and Marth Pfoutz. He was orphaned at nine and later apprenticed to a printer, Andrew Kennedy, editor of the Northumberland *Gazette* before entering the field of journalism. He was editor of the *Bucks County Messenger* in 1821. A year later, he moved to Washington, D.C., and studied political movements while working for the printing firm of Gales and Seaton. He married Margaret Brua and returned to Harrisburg, Pennsylvania where he purchased and ran the *Republican* in 1824.

Cameron served as state printer of Pennsylvania from 1825 until 1827 and was state adjutant general in 1826. He constructed several rail lines and merged them into the Northern Central Railway. He founded the Bank of Middletown in 1832 and engaged in other business enterprises. In 1838, he was appointed as commissioner to settle claims of the Winnebago Indians.

Politics

Cameron became a Whig Party member, and later a member of the Democratic Party, before being elected to replace James Buchanan in the Senate in 1844. He switched to the Republican Party and was nominated for President, but gave his support to Abraham Lincoln at the 1860 Republican National

Figure 43: *Portrait of Simon Cameron by Freeman Thorp.*

Figure 44: *Cameron as a senator favoring greenbacks, Harper's Weekly, June 6, 1874*

Figure 45: *Simon Cameron*

Convention. Lincoln, as part of a political bargain, named Cameron Secretary of War. Because of allegations of corruption, however, he was forced to resign early in 1862. His corruption was so notorious that a Pennsylvania congressman, Thaddeus Stevens, when discussing Cameron's honesty with Lincoln, told Lincoln that "I don't think that he would steal a red hot stove". When Cameron demanded Stevens retract this statement, Stevens told Lincoln "I believe I told you he would not steal a red-hot stove. I will now take that back." He was succeeded by Edwin M. Stanton, who had been serving as a legal advisor to the War Secretary. Cameron then served as United States Minister to Russia.

In 1866, Cameron was again elected to the Senate and served there until 1877, when on assurances from the Pennsylvania General Assembly that his son, James Donald Cameron, would be the successor to his seat, he resigned. His son had already been named as Secretary of War in 1876.

Later life

Cameron retired to his farm at *Donegal Springs Cameron Estate* near Maytown, Pennsylvania where he died on June 26, 1889. He is buried in the Harrisburg Cemetery in Harrisburg, Pennsylvania. Cameron County, Pennsylvania and Cameron Parish, Louisiana are named in his honor.

Quotes

- "An honest politician is one who, when he is bought, will stay bought."[446]
- "I am tired of all this sort of thing called science here... We have spent millions in that sort of thing for the last few years, and it is time it should be stopped." (on the Smithsonian Institution, 1861)[447]

Further reading

- Bradley, Edwin Stanley. *Simon Cameron, Lincoln's Secretary of War; a political biography.* (1966)

External links

- Simon Cameron biography[448] in *Secretaries of War and Secretaries of the Army* a publication of the United States Army Center of Military History
- Spartacus Educational: Simon Cameron[449]
- Mathew Brady Studio: Simon Cameron[450]
- biographic sketch at U.S. Congress website[451]
- Biography at Lincoln Institute[452]
- Mr. Lincoln and Friends: Simon Cameron[453]
- Simon Cameron[454] at Find a Grave
- The John Harris-Simon Cameron Mansion[455]

Edwin M. Stanton

**Edwin McMasters Stanton**	

25th United States Attorney General	
In office December 20, 1860 – March 4, 1861	
President	James Buchanan
Preceded by	Jeremiah S. Black
Succeeded by	Edward Bates
27th United States Secretary of War	
In office January 20, 1862 – May 28, 1868	
President	Abraham Lincoln (1862–1865) Andrew Johnson (1865–1868)
Preceded by	Simon Cameron
Succeeded by	John M. Schofield
Personal details	
Born	December 19, 1814 Steubenville, Ohio, U.S.
Died	December 24, 1869 (aged 55) Washington, D.C., U.S.
Political party	Democratic/Republican
Spouse(s)	Mary Lamson Stanton Ellen Hutchison Stanton
Alma mater	Kenyon College
Profession	Lawyer, Politician
Religion	Methodist
Signature	Edwin M Stanton

Figure 46: *Stanton between 1852 and 1855, with his son, Edwin Lamson Stanton (1842–1877).*

Edwin McMasters Stanton (December 19, 1814 – December 24, 1869) was an American lawyer and politician who served as Secretary of War under the Lincoln Administration during the American Civil War from 1862–1865. Stanton's effective management helped organize the massive military resources of the North and guide the Union to victory.

After Lincoln's assassination, Stanton remained as the Secretary of War under the new President Andrew Johnson during the first years of Reconstruction. He opposed the lenient policies of Johnson towards the former Confederate States. Johnson's attempt to dismiss Stanton led the House of Representatives to impeach him.[456,457,458,459]

Early life and career

Stanton was born in Steubenville, Ohio, the eldest of four children to David and Lucy Norman Stanton. Throughout his childhood and adult life Stanton suffered from asthma. His mother ran a general store in Steubenville.[458] His father was a physician of Quaker stock. Stanton's father died in 1827 when Edwin was only thirteen. Stanton was forced to leave school to help support his mother. Stanton began his political life as a lawyer in Ohio and an antislavery

Democrat. After leaving Kenyon College he returned to Steubenville in 1833 to get a job to support his family. He began studying law and was admitted to the Ohio bar in 1836. At the age of twenty one Stanton argued his first case before the court.[457] Stanton built a house in the small town of Cadiz, Ohio, and practiced law there until 1847, when he moved to Pittsburgh, Pennsylvania. He resided at one point in Richmond, Ohio, in what is now Everhart Bove Funeral Home.

Law and politics

Stanton's legal career would bring him to practice in Ohio, then Pittsburgh, and finally in Washington, D.C. In 1856, Stanton moved to Washington, D.C., where he had a large practice before the Supreme Court. In 1859, Stanton was the defense attorney in the sensational trial of Daniel E. Sickles, a politician and later a Union general, who was tried on a charge of murdering his wife's lover, Philip Barton Key II (son of Francis Scott Key), but was acquitted after Stanton invoked one of the first uses of the insanity defense in U.S. history. In 1860 Stanton gave up a successful law practice and was appointed Attorney General in the lame-duck presidential administration of James Buchanan[458,459]

Stanton was sent to California in 1858 by the US Attorney General as special Federal agent for the settlement of land claims, where he succeeded in breaking up a conspiracy to defraud the US government of vast tracts of land of considerable value.[460]

Attorney general

In 1860, Stanton was appointed Attorney General by President James Buchanan. He strongly opposed secession, and is credited by historians for changing Buchanan's governmental position away from tolerating secession to denouncing it as unconstitutional and illegal. He also was thought to have said, "I love this country more than myself."

Time of war

Civil War

Stanton was Lincoln's closest adviser during the American Civil War but was divided over the issue he supported arming freed slaves to fight in the Union Army.[457] After Lincoln was elected president, Stanton agreed to work as a legal adviser to the inefficient Secretary of War, Simon Cameron who was dismissed by Lincoln for including in his yearly report the call of freed slaves to be armed and used against the Confederate Army. Cameron was replaced

Figure 47: *First Reading of the Emancipation Proclamation of President Lincoln by Francis Bicknell Carpenter<ref> Reference[461]. Lincoln met with his cabinet on July 22, 1862 for the first reading of a draft of the Emancipation Proclamation. Sight measurement. Height: 108 inches (274.32 cm) Width: 180 inches (457.2 cm)</ref> Use your cursor to see who is who*

by Stanton on January 15, 1862. Lincoln, who was unaware of Stanton's role in the report, appointed him as his new Secretary of War.[459] He accepted the position only to "help save the country." He was very effective in administering the huge War Department, but devoted considerable amounts of his energy to the persecution of Union officers whom he suspected of having traitorous sympathies for the South, the most famous of these being Maj. Gen. Fitz John Porter. Stanton used his power as Secretary to ensure every general who sat on the court-martial would vote for conviction or else be unable to obtain career advancement.

On August 8, 1862 Stanton issued an order to "arrest and imprison any person or persons who may be engaged, by act, speech or writing, in discouraging volunteer enlistments, or in any way giving aid and comfort to the enemy, or in any other disloyal practice against the United States."

The president recognized Stanton's ability, but whenever necessary Lincoln managed to "plow around him." Stanton once tried to fire the Chief of the War Department Telegraph Office, Thomas Eckert. Lincoln prevented this by praising Eckert to Stanton. Yet, when pressure was exerted to remove the unpopular secretary from office, Lincoln refused. His high opinion of Stanton can be seen from the following quote:

> He is the rock on the beach of our national ocean against which the breakers dash and roar, dash and roar without ceasing. He fights back the angry waters and prevents them from undermining and overwhelming the land. Gentlemen, I do not see how he survives, why he is not crushed and torn to pieces. Without him I should be destroyed.
>
> —President Abraham Lincoln[462], on Secretary of War Edwin M. Stanton

Stanton became a Republican and apparently changed his opinion of Lincoln.

After Lincoln was assassinated, Stanton strongly disagreed with Andrew Johnson's plan to readmit the seceded states to the Union without guarantees of civil rights for freed slaves. In 1867 President Johnson attempted to force Stanton from office and replace him with Ulysses S. Grant. Stanton refused to go and was supported by the Senate. After the Civil War Stanton remained as Secretary of War but found it difficult to perform his duties under the new president, Andrew Johnson.[459]

Lincoln's assassination

When Stanton came to the Peterson House, he took charge of the scene. Mary Lincoln was so unhinged by the experience of the assassination that Stanton had her ordered from the room by shouting, "Take that woman out and do not let her in again!" At Lincoln's death Stanton uttered what became a memorable quote, "Now he belongs to the ages," and lamented,[458] "There lies the most perfect ruler of men the world has ever seen." He vigorously pursued the apprehension and prosecution of the conspirators involved in Lincoln's assassination. These proceedings were not handled by the civil courts, but by a military tribunal, and therefore under Stanton's tutelage. Stanton has subsequently been accused of witness tampering, most notably of Louis J. Weichmann, and of other activities that skewed the outcome of the trials.

Though, from the start, Booth was known to be the murderer, in the search for his conspirators, scores of suspected accomplices, probably some innocent ones, were arrested and thrown into prison. The suspects were finally winnowed to the eight prisoners, seven men and a woman, on whom there was enough evidence to try in court: Samuel Arnold, George Atzerodt, David Herold, Samuel Mudd, Michael O'Laughlen, Lewis Powell, Edmund Spangler, and Mary Surratt.[463]

Stanton ordered an unusual form of isolation for the eight suspects. He ordered eight heavy canvas hoods made, padded one-inch thick with cotton, with one small hole for eating, no opening for eyes or ears. Stanton ordered that the bags be worn by the seven men day and night to prevent conversation. Hood number eight was never used on Mrs. Surratt, the owner of the boarding house where the conspirators had laid their plans. A ball of extra cotton padding covered the

Figure 48: *The Running Machine*
An 1864 cartoon featuring Stanton, William Fessenden, Abraham Lincoln, William Seward and Gideon Welles takes a swing at the Lincoln administration.

eyes so that there was painful pressure on the closed lids. No baths or washing of any kind were allowed, and during the hot breathless weeks of the trial the prisoners' faces became more swollen and bloated by the day. The prison doctor began to fear for the conspirators' sanity, but Stanton would not allow them, nor the rigid wrist irons and anklets, each connected to a ball weighing seventy-five pounds, to be removed.[463]

Andrew Johnson's administration

Stanton continued to hold the position of secretary of war under President Andrew Johnson until 1868. The two clashed over implementation of Reconstruction policy, so Johnson removed Stanton from the Cabinet and replaced him with Ulysses S. Grant. However, this was overruled by the Senate, and Stanton barricaded himself in his office when Johnson tried again to replace Stanton with General Thomas, while radical Republicans initiated impeachment proceedings against Johnson on the grounds that Johnson's removal of Stanton without Senate approval violated the Tenure of Office Act. Stanton played a central role in the attempt to impeach President Andrew Johnson. Johnson escaped conviction by a single vote in the Senate.[458]

U.S. Supreme Court moment

After this, Stanton resigned and returned to the practice of law. The next year he was appointed by President Grant to the Supreme Court, but he died four days after he was confirmed by the Senate. He died in Washington, DC, and is buried there in Oak Hill Cemetery. Stanton did not take the necessary oath of office, according to the Supreme Court's official list of justices[464], which notes that:

> "The acceptance of the appointment and commission by the appointee, as evidenced by the taking of the prescribed oaths, is here implied; otherwise the individual is not carried on this list of the Members of the Court. Examples: ..... Edwin M. Stanton who died before he could take the necessary steps toward becoming a Member of the Court."

Marriage and Family

On May 31, 1836, Edwin Stanton married Mary Lamson, and they had two children: Lucy Lamson Stanton (b. March 11, 1837) and Edwin Lamson Stanton (b. August 1842). They built a house in the small town of Cadiz, Ohio, and he practiced law there. Fifteen-month-old daughter Lucy died in 1841.

Mary Lamson Stanton died on March 13, 1844. The loss of his beloved wife sent Stanton spiraling into a deep depression. Then, in 1846, Stanton's brother Darwin cut his own throat - "The blood spouted up to the ceiling," a doctor recalled.

So many losses in so short a time changed Stanton, replacing a hearty good humor with a brusque, even rude, intensity. He moved to Pittsburgh, lost himself in legal work, and turned into a ferocious litigator.

Stanton on US Postage

Edwin Stanton was the second American other than a US President to appear on a US Postage issue, the first being Benjamin Franklin, who appeared on a stamp in 1847. The first and only Stanton stamp was issued March 6, 1871. This was also the only stamp issued by the post office that year. The Stanton 7-cent stamp paid the single rate postage for letters sent from the U.S. to various countries in Europe.[465,466]

Figure 49: *The 1st Stanton postage stamp, issue of 1871.*

Legacy

A distinctive engraved portrait of Stanton appeared on U.S. paper money in 1890 and 1891. The bills are called "treasury notes" or "coin notes" and are widely collected today. These rare notes are considered by many to be among the finest examples of detailed engraving ever to appear on banknotes. The $1 Stanton "fancyback" note of 1890, with an estimated 900–1,300 in existence relative to the millions printed, ranks as number 83 in the "100 Greatest American Currency Notes" compiled by Bowers and Sundman (2006). Stanton also appears on the fourth issue of Fractional Currency, in the amount of 50 cents. Stanton Park, four blocks from the United States Capitol in Washington, D.C., is named for him, as is Stanton College Preparatory School in Jacksonville, Florida. A steam engine, built in 1862, was named the "E. M. Stanton" in honor of the new Secretary of War. Stanton County, Nebraska is named for him. Stanton Middle School in Hammondsville, Ohio is named after him.

In popular media

- In the 1930s, a book written by Otto Eisenschiml accused Stanton of arranging the assassination of Lincoln. Although these charges remain largely unsubstantiated, Eisenschim's book inspired considerable debate and the 1977 book and movie, *The Lincoln Conspiracy*.

Figure 50: "The Situation," a Harper's Weekly cartoon gives a humorous breakdown of "the situation". Stanton aims a cannon labeled "Congress" on the side at President Andrew Johnson and Lorenzo Thomas to show how he was using Congress to defeat the president and his unsuccessful replacement. He also holds a ramrod marked "Tenure of Office Bill" and cannon balls on the floor are marked "Justice". Ulysses S. Grant and an unidentified man stand to Stanton's left.

- In 1930, Stanton was portrayed by Oscar Apfel in the movie *Abraham Lincoln*.
- In 1972, Stanton appears in Philip K. Dick's *We Can Build You* in the form of a self-aware, cybernetic automaton.
- In 1980, Stanton was portrayed by Richard A. Dysart in the TV movie *The Ordeal of Dr. Mudd*.
- Stanton appears prominently in the alternate history Civil War trilogy by Newt Gingrich and William R. Forstchen.
- Stanton Davis Kirkham was named after Stanton by his father, Murray S. Davis, one-time confidential military aide to Stanton during his period as Secretary of War. (Source: "Olden Times in Colorado" by Carlyle Channing Davis.)
- In the Clive Cussler thriller novel, *Sahara*, Stanton is described as being behind a cover-up of Lincoln's kidnapping and later death, in Confederate custody, aboard the ironclad *CSS Texas*. Lincoln's body is later recovered by Dirk Pitt and given a state funeral in the Lincoln memorial.
- In 2011, Stanton was portrayed by Kevin Kline in the Robert Redford film *The Conspirator*.

- Stanton will be played by Bruce McGill in Steven Spielberg's upcoming film Lincoln.[467]

Bibliography

- Bowers, Q.D., and Sundman, D.M., 2006, *100 Greatest American Currency Notes*, Whitman Pub., Atlanta, GA, 134 p.
- Bissland, James. "Blood, Tears, and Glory". Wilmington, Ohio: Orange Frazer Press, 2007. Explains Stanton's key role in winning the Civil War.
- Goodwin, Doris Kearns. *Team of Rivals: The Political Genius of Abraham Lincoln* (2005) on Lincoln's cabinet.
- Harold M. Hyman, "Johnson, Stanton, and Grant: A Reconsideration of the Army's Role in the Events Leading to Impeachment," *American Historical Review* 66 (October 1960): 85–96, online in JSTOR.
- Hendrick, Burton J. *Lincoln's War Cabinet* (1946).
- Kunhardt, Dorothy Meserve, and Kunhardt Jr., Phillip B. *Twenty Days*. Castle Books, 1965. ISBN 1-55521-975-6
- Meneely, A. Howard, "Stanton, Edwin McMasters," in *Dictionary of American Biography,* Volume 9 (1935)
- Pratt, Fletcher. *Stanton: Lincoln's Secretary of War* (1953).
- Simpson, Brooks D. *Let Us Have Peace: Ulysses S. Grant and the Politics of War and Reconstruction, 1861–1868* (1991)
- Skelton, William B. . "Stanton, Edwin McMasters"; *American National Biography Online* 2000.[468]
- Stanton, Edwin (Edited by: Ben Ames Williams Jr.) *Mr. Secretary* (1940), partial autobiography.
- Thomas, Benjamin P., and Hyman, Harold M. *Stanton: The Life and Times of Lincoln's Secretary of War*[469] (1962), the standard scholarly biography.
- William Hanchett *The Lincoln Murder Conspiracies* (1983); demolishes the allegation that Stanton was the center of the plot to assassinate Lincoln.

External links

- Biography from "Impeach Andrew Johnson".[470]
- Mr. Lincoln and Friends: Edwin M. Stanton Biography.[471]
- Mr. Lincoln's White House: Edwin M. Stanton Biography.[472]
- Pictures of Fractional Currency featuring Edwin Stanton, provided by the Federal Reserve Bank of San Francisco.[473]
- Pictures of US Treasury Notes featuring Edwin Stanton, provided by the Federal Reserve Bank of San Francisco.[474]

- Spartacus Educational: Edwin M. Stanton.[475]
- Stanton biography in Columbia Electronic Encyclopedia, 6th ed.[476]

Secretary of the Treasury

Salmon P. Chase

Salmon Portland Chase	
6th Chief Justice of the United States	
In office December 6, 1864[477] – May 7, 1873	
Nominated by	Abraham Lincoln
Preceded by	Roger B. Taney
Succeeded by	Morrison R. Waite
25th United States Secretary of the Treasury	
In office March 7, 1861 – June 30, 1864	
President	Abraham Lincoln
Preceded by	John A. Dix
Succeeded by	William P. Fessenden
23rd Governor of Ohio	
In office January 14, 1856 – January 9, 1860	

Lieutenant	Thomas H. Ford (1856–1858) Martin Welker (1858–1860)
Preceded by	William Medill
Succeeded by	William Dennison Jr.
United States Senator from Ohio	
In office March 4, 1849 – March 3, 1855	
Preceded by	William Allen
Succeeded by	George E. Pugh
In office March 4 – March 7, 1861	
Preceded by	George E. Pugh
Succeeded by	John Sherman
Personal details	
Born	January 13, 1808 Cornish, New Hampshire, U.S.
Died	May 7, 1873 (aged 65) New York City, New York, U.S.
Political party	Free Soil, Liberty, Republican, Democrat
Spouse(s)	i) Katherine Jane Garmiss ii) Eliza Ann Smith iii) Sarah Bella Dunlop Ludlow[478]
Alma mater	Cincinnati College Dartmouth College
Profession	Politician, Lawyer, Judge
Religion	Episcopalian
Signature	

Salmon Portland Chase (January 13, 1808 – May 7, 1873) was an American politician and jurist who served as U.S. Senator from Ohio and the 23rd Governor of Ohio; as U.S. Treasury Secretary under President Abraham Lincoln; and as the sixth Chief Justice of the United States Supreme Court.

Chase was one of the most prominent members of the new Republican Party before becoming Chief Justice. Chase articulated the "Slave Power conspiracy" thesis well before Lincoln. He coined the slogan of the Free Soil Party, "Free Soil, Free Labor, Free Men." He devoted his energies to the destruction of what he considered the Slave Power – the conspiracy of Southern slave owners to seize control of the federal government and block the progress of liberty.

Early life and education

Chase was born in Cornish, New Hampshire to Ithamar Chase and his wife Janet Ralston. His father died when the boy was nine years old. Janet Chase was left a widow with "a small amount of property and ten surviving children". Salmon was raised by his uncle, Philander Chase, an Episcopal bishop.[479]

He studied in the common schools of Windsor, Vermont and Worthington, Ohio, and at Cincinnati College before entering the junior class at Dartmouth College. He was a member of the Alpha Delta Phi Fraternity and Phi Beta Kappa, and graduated from Dartmouth in 1826. While at Dartmouth, he taught at the Royalton Academy in Royalton, Vermont.

Chase moved to the District of Columbia, where he studied law under U.S. Attorney General William Wirt and continued to teach. He was admitted to the bar in 1829.

Entrance into politics

In 1830, Chase moved to Cincinnati, Ohio, where he quickly gained a position of prominence at the bar. He published an annotated edition of the laws of Ohio which was long considered a standard. The death of his first wife in 1835 triggered Chase's spiritual reawakening and devotion to causes more aligned with his faith, including abolition.

He worked initially with the American Sunday School Union and began defending fugitive slaves. At a time when public opinion in Cincinnati was dominated by Southern business connections, Chase, influenced by local events, including the attack on the press of James G. Birney during the Cincinnati Riots of 1836, associated himself with the anti-slavery movement. Chase was also a member of the literary Semi-Colon Club, whose members included Harriet Beecher Stowe and Calvin Stowe.[480] Chase became the leader of the political reformers, as opposed to the Garrisonian abolitionist movement.

For his defense of escaped slaves seized in Ohio under the Fugitive Slave Law of 1793, Chase was dubbed the *Attorney General for Fugitive Slaves*. His argument in the case of *Jones v. Van Zandt* on the constitutionality of fugitive slave laws before the U.S. Supreme Court attracted particular attention. In this and similar cases, the court ruled against him, and John Van Zandt's conviction was upheld. Chase contended that slavery was local, not national, and that it could exist only by virtue of positive state law. He argued that the federal government was not empowered by the Constitution to create slavery anywhere and that when a slave leaves the jurisdiction of a state where slavery is legal, he ceases to be a slave; he continues to be a man and leaves behind the law that made him a slave.

Figure 51: *Salmon P. Chase*

Elected as a Whig to the Cincinnati City Council in 1840, Chase left that party the next year. For seven years he was the leader of the Liberty Party in Ohio. He helped balance its idealism with his pragmatic approach and political thought. He was skillful in drafting platforms and addresses, and he prepared the national Liberty platform of 1843 and the Liberty address of 1845. Building the Liberty Party was slow going. By 1848 Chase was leader in the effort to combine the Liberty Party with the Barnburners or Van Buren Democrats of New York to form the Free Soil Party.

The Free Soil movement

Chase drafted the Free-Soil platform, and it was chiefly through his influence that Van Buren was their nominee for President in 1848. In 1849, Chase was elected to the U.S Senate from Ohio on the Free Soil ticket. Chase's goal, however, was not to establish a permanent new party organization, but to bring pressure to bear upon Northern Democrats to force them to oppose the extension of slavery.

During his service in the Senate (1849–1855), Chase was an anti-slavery champion. He spoke ably against the Compromise of 1850 and the Kansas-Nebraska Act of 1854. The passage of the Kansas-Nebraska legislation, and the subsequent violence in Kansas, convinced Chase of the futility of trying to influence the Democrats.

He was a leader in the movement to form a new party opposing the extension of slavery. He tried to unite the liberal Democrats with the dwindling Whig Party, which led to establishment of the Republican Party. "The Appeal of the Independent Democrats in Congress to the People of the United States", written by Chase and Giddings, and published in the *New York Times* on January 24, 1854, may be regarded as the earliest draft of the Republican party creed.

In 1855 he was elected governor of Ohio. Chase was the first Republican governor of Ohio, serving from 1856 to 1860, where he supported women's rights, public education, and prison reform.

Chase sought the Republican nomination for president in 1860. With the exception of William H. Seward, Chase was the most prominent Republican in the country and had done more against slavery than any other Republican. But he opposed a "protective tariff", favored by most other Republicans, and his record of collaboration with Democrats annoyed many Republicans who were former Whigs.

At the 1860 Republican National Convention, he got 49 votes on the first ballot, but he had little support outside Ohio. Abraham Lincoln won the nomination, and Chase supported him.

Chase was elected as a Republican to the U.S. Senate in 1860. However, three days after taking his seat, he resigned to become Secretary of the Treasury under Lincoln. He was a member of the Peace Convention of 1861 held in Washington, D.C., in an effort to prevent the impending war.

Secretary of the Treasury

Chase served as Secretary of the Treasury in President Lincoln's cabinet from 1861 to 1864, during the Civil War. In that period of crisis, there were two great changes in American financial policy, the establishment of a national banking system and the issue of paper currency. The former was Chase's own particular measure. He suggested the idea, worked out the important principles and many of the details, and induced the Congress to approve them. It not only secured an immediate market for government bonds, but also provided a permanent uniform, stable national currency. Chase ensured that the Union could sell debt to pay for the war effort. He worked with Jay Cooke & Company to successfully manage the sale of $500 million in government war bonds (known as 5/20s) in 1862.[482]

Figure 52: *First Reading of the Emancipation Proclamation of President Lincoln by Francis Bicknell Carpenter<ref> Reference[481]. Lincoln met with his cabinet on July 22, 1862 for the first reading of a draft of the Emancipation Proclamation. Sight measurement. Height: 108 inches (274.32 cm) Width: 180 inches (457.2 cm)</ref>Use your cursor to see who is who*

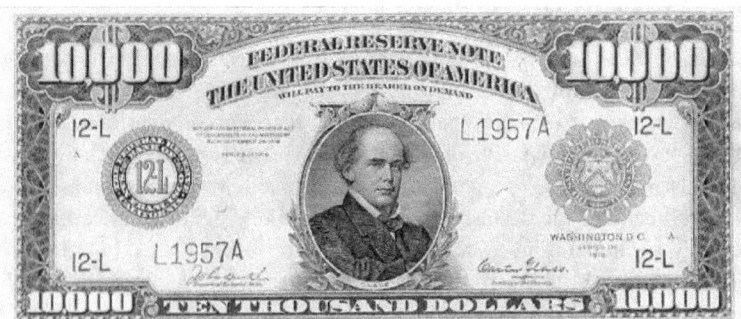

Figure 53: *Obverse of $10,000 bill featuring Salmon P. Chase*

Figure 54: *Salmon P. Chase in his elder years.*

The first U.S. federal currency, the greenback demand note, was printed in 1861-1862, during Chase's tenure as Secretary of the Treasury. These greenbacks formed the basis for today's paper currency. It was Chase's responsibility to design the notes. In an effort to further his political career, his face appeared on a variety of U.S. paper currency, starting with the $1 bill so that the people would recognize him.

Perhaps Chase's chief defect was an insatiable desire for high office.[483] Throughout his term as Treasury Secretary, Chase exploited his position to build up political support for another run at the Presidency in 1864.

He also tried to pressure Lincoln by repeatedly threatening resignation, which he knew would cause Lincoln difficulties with the Radical Republicans.

To honor Chase for introducing the modern system of banknotes, he was depicted on the $10,000 bill printed from 1928 to 1946. Chase was instrumental in placing the phrase "In God We Trust" on United States coins.[484]

Chief Justice of the United States

In June 1864, Lincoln surprised Chase by accepting his fourth offer of resignation; Lincoln had secured renomination and the Federal Treasury was in solid shape, so Lincoln no longer needed Chase.

Figure 55: *The Chase Court, 1866*

But to placate the Radical wing of the party, Lincoln mentioned Chase as a potential Supreme Court nominee. When Chief Justice Roger B. Taney died in October, Lincoln named Chase to replace him. Lincoln issued on the nomination on December 6, 1864. Chase was confirmed by the Senate that very day, and immediately received his commission, holding the office from 1864 until his own death in 1873. Chase was a complete change from the pro-slavery Taney; one of Chase's first acts as Chief Justice was to admit John Rock as the first African-American attorney to argue cases before the Supreme Court.[485]

In his capacity as Chief Justice, Chase presided at the impeachment trial of President Andrew Johnson in 1868. Among his most important decisions while on the court were:

- *Texas v. White* (74 U.S. 700), 1869, in which he asserted that the Constitution provided for a permanent union, composed of indestructible states, while allowing some possibility of divisibility "through revolution, or through consent of the States.";[486,487]
- *Veazie Banks v. Fenno* (75 U.S 533), 1869, on banking legislation of the Civil War that imposed a tax of 10 percent on state banknotes; and
- *Hepburn v. Griswold* (75 U.S. 603), 1870, which declared certain parts of the legal tender acts to be unconstitutional. When the legal tender decision was reversed after the appointment of new Justices, in 1871 and 1872 (Legal Tender Cases, 79 U.S. 457), Chase prepared a very able dissenting opinion.

Toward the end of his life he gradually drifted back toward his old Democratic allegiance, and made an unsuccessful effort to secure the Democratic nomination for the presidency in 1868. He "was passed over because of his stance in favor of voting rights for black men."[485] He helped to found the Liberal Republican Party in 1872, unsuccessfully seeking its presidential nomination. Chase was also a Freemason, active in the lodges of Midwestern society. He collaborated with John Purdue, the founder of Lafayette Bank and Purdue University. Eventually, JP Morgan Chase & Co. would purchase Purdue National Corporation of Lafayette, Indiana in 1984.

As early as 1868 Chase concluded that:

> "Congress was right in not limiting, by its reconstruction acts, the right of suffrage to whites; but wrong in the exclusion from suffrage of certain classes of citizens and all unable to take its prescribed retrospective oath, and wrong also in the establishment of despotic military governments for the States and in authorizing military commissions for the trial of civilians in time of peace. There should have been as little military government as possible; no military commissions; no classes excluded from suffrage; and no oath except one of faithful obedience and support to the Constitution and laws, and of sincere attachment to the constitutional Government of the United States."[488]

Death and legacy

Chase died in New York City in 1873. His remains were interred first in Oak Hill Cemetery in Washington, D.C., and later re-interred in Spring Grove Cemetery, Cincinnati, Ohio.[489,490,491] Chase had been an active member of St. Paul Episcopal Cathedral, Cincinnati.

The Chase National Bank, a predecessor of Chase Manhattan Bank which is now JPMorgan Chase, was named in his honor, though he had no financial affiliation with it.

Chase Hall, the main barracks and dormitory at the United States Coast Guard Academy, is named for Chase in honor of his service as Secretary of the Treasury, and the United States Coast Guard Cutter Chase (WHEC 718) is named for him.

Chase's portrait is on the $10,000 bill, but it is out of circulation.

Chase County, Kansas is named in his honor. As is *Chaseville*, Florida, Massachusetts, North Carolina (which only lasted from 1868–1871), New York, Ohio, and Tennessee.

Figure 56: *Grave of Salmon Chase in Spring Grove Cemetery. Docent is dressed in period clothing.*

Chase Hall at Harvard Business School is also named in his honor.

Also, the Chief Justice of the Connecticut Supreme Court Chase Rodgers is genealogically connected to Salmon P. Chase.

The Salmon P. Chase College of Law at Northern Kentucky University is named in his honor.

References

- Salmon P. Chase[492] at the *Biographical Directory of Federal Judges*, a public domain publication of the Federal Judicial Center.

Secondary sources

- Blue, Frederick J. *Salmon P. Chase: A Life in Politics* (1987)[493]
- Flanders, Henry. *The Lives and Times of the Chief Justices of the United States Supreme Court*[494]. Philadelphia: J. B. Lippincott & Co., 1874 at Google Books.
- Friedman, Leon. "Salmon P. Chase" in *The Justices of the United States Supreme Court: Their Lives and Major Opinions.* Volume 2. (1997)[495] pp 552–67.

- Foner, Eric. *Free Soil, Free Labor, Free Men: The Ideology of the Republican Party before the Civil War* (1970)[496]
- Goodwin, Doris Kearns. Team of Rivals: The Political Genius of Abraham Lincoln (2005) on Lincoln's cabinet.
- Hendrick, Burton J. *Lincoln's War Cabinet* (1946)[497]
- Niven, John. *Salmon P. Chase: A Biography* (1995).
- Randall, James G. "Salmon Portland Chase," Dictionary of American Biography, B, 4: 27-34; Blue, Chase.
- Richardson, Heather Cox. *The Greatest Nation of the Earth: Republican Economic Policies during the Civil War* (1997)[498]
- Salmon P. Chase[499] at the *Biographical Directory of the United States Congress*

This article incorporates text from a publication now in the public domain: Chisholm, Hugh, ed (1911). *Encyclopædia Britannica* (11th ed.). Cambridge University Press.

- J. W. Schuckers, *The Life and Public Services of Salmon Portland Chase*, (1874).
- William M. Evarts. *Eulogy on Chief-Justice Chase* (1874)[500],

Salmon Chase is one of the major figures in the extensively researched historical novel "Lincoln" by Gore Vidal.

Primary sources

- Niven, John, et al. eds. ed. *The Salmon P. Chase Papers* Volume: 2, 1823–57 (1993)[501] vol 1–5 have coverage to 1873
- Niven, John, et al. eds. ed. *The Salmon P. Chase Papers* Volume: 3, 1858–63 (1993)[502]
- Donald, David ed. *Inside Lincoln's Cabinet: The Civil War Diaries of Salmon P. Chase* (1954)[503]

Further reading

- Abraham, Henry J. (1992). *Justices and Presidents: A Political History of Appointments to the Supreme Court. 3d. ed.*. New York: Oxford University Press. ISBN 0-19-506557-3.
- Cushman, Clare (2001). *The Supreme Court Justices: Illustrated Biographies,1789-1995 (2nd ed.)*. (Supreme Court Historical Society, Congressional Quarterly Books). ISBN 1568021267; ISBN 978-1-56802-126-3..

- Frank, John P.; Leon Friedman and Fred L. Israel, editors (1995). *The Justices of the United States Supreme Court: Their Lives and Major Opinions*. Chelsea House Publishers. ISBN 0791013774; ISBN 978-0-7910-1377-9.
- Hall, Kermit L., ed. (1992). *The Oxford Companion to the Supreme Court of the United States*. New York: Oxford University Press. ISBN 0195058356; ISBN 978-0-19-505835-2..
- Martin, Fenton S.; Goehlert, Robert U. (1990). *The U.S. Supreme Court: A Bibliography*. Washington, D.C.: Congressional Quarterly Books. ISBN 0871875543.
- Urofsky, Melvin I. (1994). *The Supreme Court Justices: A Biographical Dictionary*. New York: Garland Publishing. pp. 590. ISBN 0815311761; ISBN 978-0-8153-1176-8..
- Warden, Robert B. (1874). *An account of the private life and public services of Salmon Portland Chase*[504]. Cincinnati: Wilstach, Baldwin and Co.. - Authorized biography.

External links

- *The Life of Salmon P. Chase, Attorney General of Fugitive Slaves*.[505]
- The Salmon P. Chase papers[506], including correspondence and a myriad of biographical materials spanning the years 1820-1884, are available for research use at the Historical Society of Pennsylvania.
- Salmon P. Chase[507] at Tulane University Law School.
- Biography at "Mr. Lincoln's White House"[508]
- Mr. Lincoln and Freedom: Salmon P. Chase[509]
- Eulogy on Chief-Justice Chase[500], delivered by William M. Evarts, 1874
- Bibliography[510], Sixth Circuit U.S. Court of Appeals.
- Biography[511], Sixth Circuit U.S. Court of Appeals.
- Location of Papers[512], Sixth Circuit U.S. Court of Appeals

William P. Fessenden

William Pitt Fessenden	

26th United States Secretary of the Treasury	
In office July 5, 1864 – March 3, 1865	
President	Abraham Lincoln
Preceded by	Salmon P. Chase
Succeeded by	Hugh McCulloch
United States Senator from Maine	
In office February 10, 1854 – July 1, 1864	
Preceded by	James W. Bradbury
Succeeded by	Nathan A. Farwell
In office March 4, 1865 – September 8, 1869	
Preceded by	Nathan A. Farwell
Succeeded by	Lot M. Morrill
Personal details	
Born	October 16, 1806 Boscawen, New Hampshire, U.S.
Died	September 8, 1869 (aged 62) Portland, Maine, U.S.
Political party	Whig, Opposition, Republican
Profession	Politician, Lawyer
Religion	Episcopalian
Signature	*Wm. P. Fessenden*

William Pitt Fessenden (October 16, 1806 – September 8, 1869) was an American politician from the U.S. state of Maine. Fessenden was a Whig (later a Republican) and member of the Fessenden political family. He served in the United States House of Representatives and Senate before becoming Secretary of the Treasury under President Abraham Lincoln during the American Civil War.

A lawyer, he was a leading antislavery Whig in Maine; in Congress, he fought the Slave Power (the plantation owners who controlled southern states). He built an antislavery coalition in the state legislature that elected him to the US Senate; it became Maine's Republican organization. In the Senate, Fessenden played a central role in the debates on Kansas, denouncing the expansion of slavery. He led Radical Republicans in attacking Democrats Stephen Douglas, Franklin Pierce, and James Buchanan. Fessenden's speeches were read widely, influencing Republicans such as Abraham Lincoln and building support for Lincoln's 1860 Republican presidential nomination. During the war, Senator Fessenden helped shape the Union's taxation and financial policies. He moderated his earlier radicalism, and supported Lincoln against the Radicals, becoming Lincoln's Treasury Secretary.[513] After the war, Fessenden was back in the Senate, as chair of the Joint Committee on Reconstruction, which established terms for resuming congressional representation for the southern states, and which drafted the Fourteenth Amendment to the United States Constitution. Later, Fessenden provided critical support that prevented Senate conviction of President Andrew Johnson, who had been impeached by the House.

Youth and early career

Fessenden was born in Boscawen, New Hampshire. He graduated from Bowdoin College in 1823, and then studied law. He was a founding member of the Maine Temperance Society in 1827.[514] That year he was also admitted to the bar. He practiced with his father Samuel Fessenden, who was also a prominent anti-slavery activist. He practised law first in Bridgeton, Maine, a year in Bangor, and afterward in Portland. He was a member of the Maine House of Representatives in 1832, and its leading debater. He refused nominations to congress in 1831 and in 1838, and served in the Maine legislature again in 1840, becoming chairman of the house committee to revise the statutes of the state.

He was elected for one term in the United States House of Representatives as a Whig in 1840. During this term, he moved the repeal of the rule that excluded anti-slavery petitions, and spoke upon the loan and bankrupt bills, and the army. At the end of his term in Congress, he turned his attention wholly to

Figure 57: *The Running Machine*
An 1864 cartoon featuring Fessenden, Edwin Stanton, Abraham Lincoln, William Seward and Gideon Welles takes a swing at the Lincoln administration.

his law business until he was again in the Maine legislature in 1845-46. He acquired a national reputation as a lawyer and an anti-slavery Whig, and in 1849 prosecuted before the United States Supreme Court an appeal from an adverse decision of Judge Joseph Story, and gained a reversal by an argument which Daniel Webster pronounced the best he had heard in twenty years. He was again in the Maine legislature in 1853 and 1854.

Service in U.S. Senate and Cabinet

Fessenden's strong anti-slavery principles caused his election to the U. S. Senate in 1854, with the support of Whigs and Anti-Slavery Democrats. Upon taking office, he immediately began speaking against the Kansas-Nebraska Act. His speech on the Clayton-Bulwer Treaty, in 1856, received the highest praise, and in 1858 his speech on the Lecompton Constitution of Kansas, and his criticisms of the opinion of the supreme court in the Dred Scott Case, were considered the ablest discussion of those topics. He participated in the organization of the Republican Party, being re-elected to the Senate from that group in 1860, this time without the formality of a nomination.

In 1861 he was a member of the Peace congress. By the secession of the Southern senators the Republicans acquired control of the senate, and placed Fessenden at the head of the finance committee. During the Civil War, he was the most conspicuous senator in sustaining the national credit. He opposed the Legal Tender Act as unnecessary and unjust. As chairman of the finance committee, Fessenden prepared and carried through the senate all measures relating to revenue, taxation, and appropriations, and, as declared by Charles Sumner, was "in the financial field all that our best generals were in arms."

President Abraham Lincoln appointed Fessenden United States Secretary of the Treasury upon Salmon P. Chase's resignation. It was the darkest hour of national finances of the United States. Chase had just withdrawn a loan from the market for want of acceptable bids, and the capacity of the country to lend seemed exhausted. The currency had been enormously inflated: the paper dollar was worth only 34 cents; gold was at $280/ounce. Fessenden at first refused the office, but at last accepted in obedience to the universal public pressure. When his acceptance became known, gold fell to $225/ounce. He declared that no more currency should be issued, and, making an appeal to the people, he prepared and put upon the market the seven-thirty loan, which proved a triumphant success. This loan was in the form of bonds bearing interest at the rate of 7.30%, which were issued in denominations as low as $50, so that people of moderate means could take them. He also framed and recommended the measures, adopted by congress, which permitted the subsequent consolidation and funding of the government loans into the 4% and 4.5% bonds.

Fessenden began his service as Secretary of the Treasury on July 5, 1864. The financial situation becoming favorable, in accordance with his expressed intention, he resigned the secretaryship, leaving on March 3, 1865, to return to the Senate, to which he had now for the third time been elected.

From 1865 to 1867, he headed the Joint Committee on Reconstruction, which was responsible for overseeing the readmission of states from the former Confederacy into the Union. He wrote its report, which vindicated the power of congress over the rebellious states, showed their relations to the government under the constitution and the law of nations, and recommended the constitutional safeguards made necessary by the rebellion. At this point, Fessenden was the acknowledged leader in the senate of the Republicans. He was considered a moderate, rather than Radical, Republican.

During President Andrew Johnson's impeachment trial in 1868, Fessenden broke party ranks, along with six other Republican senators, and in a courageous act of political suicide, voted for acquittal. These seven Republican senators were disturbed by how the proceedings had been manipulated in order to give a one-sided presentation of the evidence. He, Joseph S. Fowler, James W. Grimes, John B. Henderson, Lyman Trumbull, Peter G. Van Winkle,[515] and

Figure 58: *Frederic Porter Vinton's portrait of William P. Fessenden, posthumous. Circa. 1870*

Edmund G. Ross[516] defied their party and public opinion and voted against conviction. As a result, a 35-19 vote in favor of removing the President from office failed by a single vote of reaching a 2/3 majority.

He served as chairman of the Finance Committee during the 37th through 39th Congresses (from 1861 to 1867), which led to his Cabinet appointment. He also served as a chairman of the Committee on Public Buildings and Grounds during the 40th Congress, the Appropriations Committee during the 41st Congress and the U.S. Senate Committee on the Library, also during the 41st Congress. In 1867, he was one of two senators who voted against the purchase of Alaska from Russia.[517] His last speech in the Senate was upon the bill to strengthen the public credit. He advocated the payment of the principal of the public debt in gold, and opposed the notion that it might lawfully be paid in depreciated greenbacks.

For several years, he was a regent of the Smithsonian Institution. He received the degree of LL.D. from Bowdoin in 1858, and from Harvard University in 1864. He died in 1869, while still serving in the U. S. Senate, and was interred at Evergreen Cemetery in Portland, Maine.

Family

Two of his brothers, Samuel C. Fessenden and T. A. D. Fessenden, were also Congressmen. He had three sons who served in the American Civil War: Samuel Fessenden, killed at the Second Battle of Bull Run, and Brigadier-General James D. Fessenden and Major-General Francis Fessenden, the latter of whom wrote a two-volume biography of his father which was published in 1907.

- William Fessenden (1694–1756) & Martha Brown (1699–1746)
  - William Fessenden (1718–1758)
    - William Fessenden (1747–1805)
      - Samuel Fessenden (1784–1869)
        - William P. Fessenden (1808–1869)
          - James Deering Fessenden (1833–1897)
          - Francis Fessenden (1839–1907)
          - Samuel Fessenden (1841–1862)
        - Samuel C. Fessenden (1815–1881)
        - T. A. D. Fessenden (1826–1868)
  - Thomas Fessenden (1739–1813)
    - Thomas G. Fessenden (1771–1827)
      - Elisha Hunt Allen (1804–1883)
    - William Fessenden (1779–1815)
      - Sarah Elizabeth Fessenden (1808–1845)
        - William Fessenden Allen (1831–1906)

Posthumous honors

He is the only person to have three streets in Portland named for him: William, Pitt and Fessenden streets in the city's Oakdale neighborhood.

References

- Cook, Robert J. *Civil War Senator: William Pitt Fessenden and the Fight to Save the American Republic* (Louisiana State University Press; 2011) 344 pages; a standard scholarly biography

- Landis, Michael Todd. "'A Champion Had Come': William Pitt Fessenden and the Republican Party, 1854-60," *American Nineteenth Century History,* Sept 2008, Vol. 9 Issue 3, pp 269–285
- Charles A. Jellison. *Fessenden of Maine, Civil War Senator* (1962)[518], a standard scholarly biography
- William P. Fessenden[519] at the *Biographical Directory of the United States Congress*
- This article incorporates text from a publication now in the public domain: Chisholm, Hugh, ed (1911). *Encyclopædia Britannica* (11th ed.). Cambridge University Press.
- "Fessenden, Samuel". *Appletons' Cyclopædia of American Biography.* 1900.
- "Fessenden, William Pitt". *New International Encyclopedia.* 1905.

External links

- William P. Fessenden[519] at the *Biographical Directory of the United States Congress*. Includes *Guide to Research Collections*[520] where his papers are located.
- Biography at Lincoln's White House[521]

Hugh McCulloch

	Hugh McCulloch
	36th United States Secretary of the Treasury
	In office October 31, 1884 – March 7, 1885
President	Chester A. Arthur
Preceded by	Walter Q. Gresham
Succeeded by	Daniel Manning
	27th United States Secretary of the Treasury
	In office March 9, 1865 – March 3, 1869
President	Abraham Lincoln (1865) Andrew Johnson (1865-1869)
Preceded by	William P. Fessenden
Succeeded by	George S. Boutwell
	Personal details
Born	December 7, 1808 Kennebunk, Maine, U.S.
Died	May 24, 1895 (aged 86) Prince George's County, Maryland, U.S.
Political party	Republican
Alma mater	Bowdoin College
Profession	Politician, Lawyer

Hugh McCulloch (December 7, 1808 – May 24, 1895) was an American statesman who served two non-consecutive terms as U.S. Treasury Secretary, serving under three presidents.

Biography

Born at Kennebunk, Maine, he was educated at Bowdoin College, studied law in Boston, and in 1833 began practicing law at Fort Wayne, Indiana. He was cashier and manager of the Fort Wayne branch of the state chartered Bank of Indiana and President of the larger organization from 1835 to 1857, and president of its successor, the private owned Bank of Indiana from 1857 to 1863. Notwithstanding his early opposition to the "National Banking Act of 1862", he was selected by Salmon P. Chase to be the first Comptroller of the Currency in 1863. During McCulloch's 22 months in office, 868 national banks were chartered and no failures occurred. As the first Comptroller, McCulloch recommended major changes in the banking law and the resulting National Banking Act of 1864 remains the foundation of the national banking system.

On March 9, 1865, McCulloch was appointed as the 27th Secretary of the Treasury by President Abraham Lincoln. His appointment was largely due to his influence with existing state banks. On the morning of Lincoln's assassination, newly appointed McCulloch remarked "I never saw Mr. Lincoln so cheerful and happy." He continued to serve in the Presidential Cabinet of Andrew Johnson until the close of his administration in 1869.

Immediately confronted with inflation caused by the government's wartime issue of greenbacks, he recommended their retirement and a return to the gold standard. In McCulloch's first annual report, issued on December 4, 1865, he strongly urged the retirement of the legal tenders or greenbacks as a preliminary to the resumption of specie payments. However this would have reduced the supply of currency and was unpopular during the period of postwar reconstruction and westward expansion.

In accordance with this suggestion an act was passed, on March 12, 1866, authorizing the retirement of not more than $10,000,000 in six months and not more than $4,000,000 per month thereafter. This act met with strong opposition and was repealed on the February 4, 1868, after only $48,000,000 had been retired. The battle over its revival raged for the next fifty years. McCulloch was also disappointed by the decision of the United States Supreme Court upholding the constitutionality of the legal tenders.

During his tenure, McCulloch maintained a policy of reducing the federal war debt and the careful reintroduction of federal taxation in the South.

Soon after the close of his term of office McCulloch went to England, and spent six years (1870–1876) as a member of the banking firm of Jay Cooke, McCulloch & Co.

From October 1884 until the close of President Chester A. Arthur's term of office in March 1885 he was again secretary of the treasury, the 36th in the

Figure 59: *Hugh McCulloch*

line. During his six months in office at that time, he continued his fight for currency backed by gold, warning that the coinage of silver, used by then as backing for currency, should be halted.

He died at his home, Holly Hill in Prince George's County, Maryland, near Washington, D.C. in 1895 and is buried in Rock Creek Cemetery in D.C. McCulloch Hall, a residence hall at Harvard Business School, was named in his honor.

The U.S. Revenue Cutter Service and its successor, the U.S. Coast Guard, each named cutters after McCulloch. Revenue Cutter McCulloch served under George Dewey in the Battle of Manila during the Spanish-American War, and Coast Guard Cutter McCulloch served in World War II and the Vietnam War.

The chief authority for the life of McCulloch is his own book, *Men and Measures of Half a Century* (New York, 1888). McCulloch was the last surviving member of the Lincoln cabinet.

Bank of Indiana

McCulloch began his banking career as the President of the Bank of Indiana. In 1833 the bank was established in response the closure of the Second Bank of the United States. Indiana was still a wilderness and no eastern bank was willing take charge of the fledgling state bank. McCulloch was one of the few prominent businessmen in the young state, and although he had no banking experience, he was appointed because he was the most qualified person willing to take the position.

He ran the bank with great efficiency making it one of the most stable in the nation. He remained president until the bank was closed in 1859 and the bank's notes were exchanged for federal notes from the new national bank. He then went on to become president of the Second Bank of Indiana, where he remained until 1865.

References

- This article incorporates text from a publication now in the public domain: Chisholm, Hugh, ed (1911). *Encyclopædia Britannica* (11th ed.). Cambridge University Press.

External links

- Hugh McCulloch Biography[522]

Attorney General

Edward Bates

Edward Bates	

26th United States Attorney General	
In office March 5, 1861 – November 24, 1864	
President	Abraham Lincoln
Preceded by	Edwin M. Stanton
Succeeded by	James Speed
Personal details	
Born	September 4, 1793 Goochland County, Virginia, U.S.
Died	March 25, 1869 (aged 75) St. Louis, Missouri, U.S.
Political party	Democratic-Republican, Whig, Republican
Profession	Lawyer, Politician
Military service	

Service/branch	Volunteer
Rank	sergeant
Battles/wars	War of 1812

Edward Bates (September 4, 1793 – March 25, 1869) was a U.S. lawyer and statesman. He served as United States Attorney General under Abraham Lincoln from 1861 to 1864. He was the younger brother of Frederick Bates, second governor of Missouri, and James Woodson Bates, who was an attorney and politician in Arkansas.

Biography

Born in Goochland County, Virginia on his family's Belmont plantation, Bates was tutored at home as a boy. When older, he attended Charlotte Hall Military Academy in Maryland.

Career

Edward Bates served in the War of 1812 before moving to St. Louis, Missouri Territory in 1814 with his older brother James, who started working as an attorney. Frederick Bates was already in St. Louis by that time, where he had served as Secretary of the Louisiana Territory and Secretary of the Missouri Territory.

Edward Bates studied the law with Rufus Easton and boarded with his family. Easton was Judge of the Louisiana Territory, the largest jurisdiction in U.S. history after the Louisiana Purchase. After being admitted to the bar, Bates worked as a partner with Easton.[523]

In 1817 the two organized the James Ferry, which ran from St. Charles, Missouri to Alton, Illinois. Easton had founded the latter town, naming it after his first son Alton.[523]

Bates's private practice partner was Joshua Barton, who would be the first Missouri Secretary of State. Barton became infamous for fighting duels on Bloody Island (Mississippi River). In 1816 Bates was the second to Barton in a duel with Thomas Hempstead, brother of Edward Hempstead, the Missouri Territory's first Congressional representative. The fight ended without bloodshed. Barton would be killed in a duel on the island in 1823.

Bates' first foray into politics came in 1820, when he was elected as a member of the state's constitutional convention. He wrote the preamble to the state

Figure 60: *Lincoln met with his Cabinet for the first reading of the "Emancipation Proclamation" draft on July 22, 1862. L-R: Edwin M. Stanton, Salmon P. Chase, Abraham Lincoln, Gideon Welles, Caleb B. Smith, William H. Seward, Montgomery Blair and Edward Bates.*

constitution–an honor that later influenced his fight against the radical Missouri Constitution of 1865. He next was appointed as the new state's attorney general.

In 1822, Bates was elected to the Missouri House of Representatives. He moved up to the United States House of Representatives for a single term (1827–1829). He was elected to the State Senate from 1831 to 1835, then to the Missouri House from 1835. He ran for the U.S. Senate, but lost to Democrat Thomas Hart Benton.

Bates became a prominent member of the Whig Party during the 1840s, where his political philosophy closely resembled that of Henry Clay. During this time, he became interested in the case of the slave Polly Berry, who in 1843 gained her freedom decades after having been held illegally in the free state of Illinois for several months. Bates argued as her attorney in the separate freedom suit which she filed for her daughter Lucy Berry, then about age 14. According to the principle of *partus sequitur ventrum*, since the mother had been proved a free woman at the time of her daughter's birth, Lucy also gained her freedom.[524] During this time, Orion Clemens, brother of Mark Twain, studied law under Bates.

In 1850 President Millard Fillmore asked Bates to serve as U.S. Secretary of War, but he declined. Charles Magill Conrad accepted the position. At the Whig National Convention in 1852, Bates was considered for the vice-presidential slot on the ticket, and he led on the first ballot before losing on the second ballot to William Alexander Graham.

After the breakup of the Whig Party in the 1850s, Bates became a Republican, and was one of the four main candidates for the party's 1860 presidential nomination. He received support from Horace Greeley, who later switched to supporting Abraham Lincoln.[525] The next year, after winning the election, Lincoln appointed Bates as his Attorney General, an office Bates held from 1861 until 1864. Bates was the first Cabinet member to hail from the region west of the Mississippi River.

Attorney General

Bates's tenure as Attorney General generally met with mixed reviews. On the one hand, he was important in carrying out some of Lincoln's earlier war policies, including the arbitrary arrest of southern sympathizers and seditious northerners. On the other hand, as Lincoln's policies became more radical, Bates became increasingly irrelevant. Bates disagreed with Lincoln on emancipation and the recruitment of blacks into the Union Army. In 1864, Lincoln nominated Salmon P. Chase to be Chief Justice, an office which Bates had wanted, and he decided to resign his office.

Later activities

Bates returned to Missouri after leaving the cabinet. He participated in the conservative struggle against the adoption of the Missouri constitution of 1865. He authored seven essays arguing against the constitution. He particularly objected to the "ironclad oath" required as a proof of loyalty, and the disfranchisement of rebel sympathizers. But his efforts proved unsuccessful.

After the new constitution was ratified in the summer of 1865, Bates retired from politics altogether. He provided commentary on political events in the local newspapers, but never again played a prominent role in public policy. He died in St. Louis in 1869.

Marriage and family

Bates married Miss Julia Coalter from South Carolina. They had 17 children together.[525] Her brother David Coalter lived in St. Louis, and her sister Caroline J. Coalter married Hamilton R. Gamble, another attorney of the city, who became the chief justice of the State Supreme Court.[526]

Bates was, for the most part, happy with his large family. During the Civil War, his son Fleming Bates served with the Confederates, under the command of General Sterling Price. This was a cause of tension between the father and the son, and Bates rarely mentioned Fleming in his war-time diary. Another son, John C. Bates, served in the Union Army. The youngest son, Charles, was still at West Point during the war.[525]

References

- Biographical Directory of the United States Congress: BATES, Edward[527]
- Bates, Edward. *The Diary of Edward Bates, 1859-1866,* ed. Howard K. Beale. New York: Da Capo Press, 1971.
- Cain, Marvin R. *Lincoln's Attorney General: Edward Bates of Missouri.* Columbia : University of Missouri Press, 1965.
- Goodwin, Doris Kearns. *Team of Rivals: The Political Genius of Abraham Lincoln.* New York : Simon & Schuster, 2005.
- Judah, Charles and George Winston Smith. *The Unchosen.* New York : Coward-McCann, 1962.

External links

- Biography of Edward Bates[528], Lincoln Institute

James Speed

James Speed	
27th United States Attorney General	
In office December 2, 1864 – July 22, 1866	
Preceded by	Edward Bates
Succeeded by	Henry Stanberry
Personal details	
Born	March 11, 1812 Jefferson County, Kentucky, U.S.
Died	June 25, 1887 (aged 75) Louisville, Kentucky, U.S.
Political party	Whig, Republican
Spouse(s)	Jane Cochran Speed
Alma mater	St. Joseph's College Transylvania University
Profession	Lawyer, Professor, Politician
Military service	
Service/branch	Louisville Home Guard
Battles/wars	American Civil War

James Speed (March 11, 1812 – June 25, 1887) was an American lawyer, politician and professor. In 1864, he was appointed by Abraham Lincoln to be the United States' Attorney General. He previously served in the Kentucky Legislature, and in local political office.

Speed was born in Jefferson County, Kentucky, to Judge John Speed and his second wife Lucy Gilmer Fry. He graduated from St. Joseph's College in

Bardstown, Kentucky, studied law at Transylvania University and was admitted to the bar at Louisville, in 1833. He joined the Whig Party and became a strong opponent of slavery.

Representative

In 1847 Speed was elected to the Kentucky House of Representatives. At this early point in his career, Speed was already agitating for the emancipation of American slaves. Because of these views, his candidacy for becoming a delegate to the 1849 Kentucky Constitutional Convention was rejected. From 1851 to 1854, Speed served on the Louisville Board of Aldermen, including two years as its president. He taught as a professor in the Law Department of the University of Louisville from 1856 to 1858, and would later return to teach from 1872 to 1879. He was one of the founders of the law firm of Stites & Harbison.

Civil War era

As the coming Civil War was increasing in likelihood, Speed worked to keep Kentucky in the Union. He also became a commander of the Louisville Home Guard. Elected to the Kentucky Senate in 1861 he became the leader of the pro-Union forces. In 1862 he controversially introduced a bill to "confiscate the property" of those supporting the Confederacy in Kentucky.

In December 1864, President Abraham Lincoln appointed Speed Attorney General of the United States. After the assassination of Lincoln he became associated with the Radical Republicans and advocated the vote for male African Americans. Disillusioned with the increasingly conservative policies of President Andrew Johnson, Speed resigned from the Cabinet in July 1866 and resumed the practice of law.

After representation

Speed's radical views were unpopular in Kentucky and his attempt to be elected to the Senate in 1867 ended in failure. In 1868, Speed was a candidate for the Republican nomination for Vice President of the United States but lost it to Schuyler Colfax.

Speed was a delegate to the National Union Convention in Philadelphia in 1866 and served as president of the Convention. He was a candidate for U.S. Representative from Kentucky's 5th District in 1870, and was a delegate to Republican National Convention from Kentucky in 1872. He died in Louisville in 1887, and is interred at Cave Hill Cemetery in that city.

He was the brother of Joshua Fry Speed, as well as a distant descendant of the English cartographer John Speed.

Figure 61: *James Speed interment in Cave Hill Cemetery in Louisville, Kentucky*

References

1. "Speed, James" (1 ed.). 2001.

Further reading

- Bush, Bryan S. (2008). *Lincoln and the Speeds: The Untold Story of a Devoted and Enduring Friendship.* Morley, Missouri: Acclaim Press. ISBN 978-0-9798802-6-1.

External links

- Mr. Lincoln's White House: James Speed Biography[529]
- "Joshua and James Speed"[530] — Article by Civil War historian/author Bryan S. Bush
- James Speed[531] at Find a Grave

Postmaster General

Montgomery Blair

Montgomery Blair	

20th United States Postmaster General	
In office March 5, 1861 – September 24, 1864	
Preceded by	Horatio King
Succeeded by	William Dennison, Jr.
Personal details	
Born	May 10, 1813 Franklin County, Kentucky
Died	July 27, 1883 (aged 70) Silver Spring, Maryland, U.S.
Political party	Republican, Democratic
Spouse(s)	Mary Elizabeth Woodbury Blair
Alma mater	United States Military Academy

Profession	Lawyer, Politician
Military service	
Service/branch	United States Army
Battles/wars	Seminole War

Montgomery Blair (May 10, 1813 – July 27, 1883), the son of Francis Preston Blair, elder brother of Francis Preston Blair, Jr. and cousin of B. Gratz Brown, was a politician and lawyer from Maryland. Despite belonging to a prominent slaveholding family, Blair was an abolitionist and a loyal member of the Cabinet of Abraham Lincoln during the American Civil War. Blair was hot-tempered, and in 1864 he launched an all-out attack against Republican liberals.

Life

Blair was born in Franklin County, Kentucky. His father, Francis P. Blair, Sr., was, as editor of the *Washington Globe*, a prominent figure in the Democratic Party during the Jacksonian era, and as a boy Montgomery "often listened to the talk of his father and Andrew Jackson."[532] Blair graduated from the United States Military Academy in 1835, but after a year's service in the Seminole War, he left the Army, studied law, and began practice at St Louis, Missouri. After serving as United States district attorney (1839–43) and as judge of the court of common pleas (1834–1849), he moved to Maryland in 1852 and devoted himself to law practice principally in the United States Supreme Court. He was United States Solicitor in the Court of Claims (1855–58) and was associated with George T. Curtis as counsel for the plaintiff in the *Dred Scott v. Sandford* case of 1857.

The Blairs, like many other nationalist Democrats, but unusually for politicians from the border states, had abandoned the Democratic Party in the wake of the Kansas-Nebraska Act and had been among the founding leaders of the new Republican Party. In 1860 Montgomery Blair took an active part in the presidential campaign on behalf of Abraham Lincoln. After his election, Lincoln invited Blair to be part of his cabinet as Postmaster-General. Lincoln expected Blair, who advocated taking a firm stance with the southern states, to help balance more conciliatory members of his cabinet.[534] Blair served as Postmaster-General from 1861 until September 1864, when Lincoln accepted an earlier offer by Blair to resign. Lincoln's action may have been a response to the hostility of the Radical Republican faction, who stipulated that Blair's retirement should follow the withdrawal of John C. Frémont's name as a candidate for the presidential nomination in that year. Regarding Lincoln's action, Blair told his wife that the president had acted "from the best motives" and that

Figure 62: *First Reading of the Emancipation Proclamation of President Lincoln by Francis Bicknell Carpenter<ref> Reference[533]. Lincoln met with his cabinet on July 22, 1862 for the first reading of a draft of the Emancipation Proclamation. Sight measurement. Height: 108 inches (274.32 cm) Width: 180 inches (457.2 cm)</ref>Use your cursor to see who is who*

"it is for the best all around." After he left the cabinet, Blair still campaigned for Lincoln's re-election and Lincoln and the Blair family retained close ties.[535]

Under Blair's administration, such reforms and improvements as the establishment of free city delivery, the adoption of a money order system, and the use of railway mail cars were instituted — the last having been suggested by George B. Armstrong (d. 1871), of Chicago, who from 1869 until his death was general superintendent of the United States railway mail service.

Differing from the Republican Party on the Reconstruction policy, Blair gave his adherence to the Democratic Party after the Civil War, along with his brother, who was the Democratic vice presidential candidate in 1868.

His manor in present-day Silver Spring, Maryland was named Falkland. It was burned by Confederate troops during their thrust towards Washington, D.C. He died at Silver Spring. Montgomery Blair's wife was Mary Woodbury, a daughter of Levi Woodbury. Together, they were the great-grandparents of actor Montgomery Clift.

Works

- *Speech on the Causes of the Rebellion* (1864)

Honors

Montgomery Blair High School in Silver Spring, Maryland.

Gallery

Figure 63: *Montgomery Blair in his postbellum.*

Figure 64: *Lincoln met with his Cabinet for the first reading of the Emancipation Proclamation draft on July 22, 1862.*

Publications

- Croly, *Seymour and Blair: Their Lives and Services* (1868)

References

- This article incorporates text from a publication now in the public domain: Chisholm, Hugh, ed (1911). *Encyclopædia Britannica* (11th ed.). Cambridge University Press.
- *This article incorporates text from an edition of the* New International Encyclopedia *that is in the public domain.*
- Goodwin, D. K. *Team of Rivals: The Political Genius of Abraham Lincoln*. New York: Simon & Schuster, 2005. ISBN 1-4165-4983-8 (electronic edition).

External links

- Biography[536]
- Mr. Lincoln and Friends: Montgomery Blair[537]
- Mr. Lincoln and Freedom: Montgomery Blair[538]
- Mr. Lincoln's White House: Montgomery Blair[536]
- Montgomery Blair[539] at Find a Grave

William Dennison, Jr.

William Dennison, Jr.

24th Governor of Ohio

In office
January 9, 1860 – January 13, 1862

Lieutenant	Robert C. Kirk
Preceded by	Salmon P. Chase
Succeeded by	David Tod

21st United States Postmaster General

In office
September 24, 1864 – July 25, 1866

President	Abraham Lincoln
Preceded by	Montgomery Blair
Succeeded by	Alexander Randall

Personal details

Born	November 23, 1815 Cincinnati, Ohio
Died	June 15, 1882 (aged 66) Columbus, Ohio
Political party	Whig Republican
Spouse(s)	Anne Neil Dennison
Alma mater	Miami University
Profession	Lawyer

William Dennison, Jr. (November 23, 1815 – June 15, 1882) was a Whig and Republican politician from Ohio. He served as the 24th Governor of Ohio and as U.S. Postmaster General in the Cabinet of President Abraham Lincoln during the American Civil War.

Early life and career

Born in Cincinnati, Dennison graduated from Miami University, studied law, and was admitted to the Ohio bar in 1840. A canny businessman, he led the Exchange Bank and the Columbus and Xenia Railroad, and organized the Columbus and Hocking Valley Railroad, while becoming active in politics.

In 1840, he married to Anne Eliza Neil, the daughter of the wealthy, Columbus, businessman William Neil, whose farm later became the campus of Ohio State University. Together, William and Anne Dennison had seven children. The eldest of them was a son, William Neil Dennison, who later won distinction in the Civil War while serving in the U.S. Horse Artillery Brigade.

William Dennison, Jr., was one of the first major Ohio politicians to leave the dying Whig Party for the new Republican Party. He rose quickly through the party ranks due to his anti-slavery and anti-discrimination efforts in the Ohio State Senate. Dennison was elected to the governorship in 1859, defeating Rufus P. Ranney, and served a single term from 1860 to 1862. Before the outbreak of the American Civil War, he refused the demands of Kentucky and Virginia state authorities for the extradition of fugitive slaves or the punishment of those who helped them.

Civil War

He organized Ohio's mobilization in the opening days of the war, and was generally effective, despite having a small staff and no prior military experience. His efforts led to the creation of several large training camps for newly raised troops, one of which would be named for him (Camp Dennison). Dennison tried but failed to be elected to the United States Senate in 1861, when he was defeated by John Sherman.

Without being asked by the War Department, he sent Ohio troops under George McClellan into western Virginia, where they guarded the Wheeling Convention, which eventually led to the admission of West Virginia as a free state. He also took the initiative to seize control of Ohio's railroads and telegraph lines early in the war to allow military usage, angering Peace Democrats in the Ohio Legislature. He denounced secession and Ohio's "Copperheads", established a consistent supply of arms and equipment for the new troops, and was a vocal supporter of Lincoln's policies. During his term, he raised over 100,000 troops and organized 82 three-years regiments for the Union army.

However, errors by the Governor and his subordinates led to the state's alliance of Republicans and War Democrats to drop Dennison as a candidate in 1862. The parties turned instead to David Tod, a War Democrat. Historian Richard H. Abbott wrote, "No Ohio chief executive [before Dennison] had ever exercised such powers and fulfilled such duties with a greater sense of public responsibility and determination. Nevertheless...politics dictated his demise."

Dennison accepted this turn of events with good grace, capably advised his successor, and provided valuable services in helping recruit black troops for Ohio units. He served as Chairman of the Republican National Convention in 1864. He was appointed U.S. Postmaster General by President Abraham Lincoln, and served from 1864 to 1866, leaving the Cabinet after he decided he could no longer support the policies of President Andrew Johnson.

Postbellum career and memorialization

After the war, Dennison served on the Columbus City Council and organized the Franklin County Agricultural Society. President Ulysses S. Grant appointed him the first President of the Board of Commissioners for the District of Columbia, the highest governing office of Washington, D.C., in which Dennison served from 1874 to 1878. He sought the Republican nomination for the U.S. Senate in 1880, but was defeated by James Garfield. Dennison remained active in state and national politics until his death. He left behind a widow and seven children, and was buried in Green Lawn Cemetery, Columbus, Ohio.

Of Dennison's single term in the opening stages of the Civil War, historian John S. Stilt wrote, "His wisdom and foresight were appreciated by few and condemned by many.... It is doubtful whether any of his predecessors could have met the issues any more successfully."

Camp #1 of the Department of Ohio of the Sons of Union Veterans of the Civil War is named for Governor William Dennison. It was chartered August 1, 1882, shortly after Dennison's death at age 66.

References

- Harper, Robert S., *Ohio Handbook of the Civil War*. Columbus, Ohio: The Ohio Historical Society, 1961.
- Reid, Whitelaw, *Ohio in the War: Her Statesmen, Her Generals, and Soldiers*. 2 vol. Cincinnati: Moore, Wilstach, & Baldwin, 1868.
- Dennison Camp of the SUCV[540]

External links

- William Dennison, Jr.[541] at Find a Grave

Secretary of the Navy

Gideon Welles

Gideon Welles	
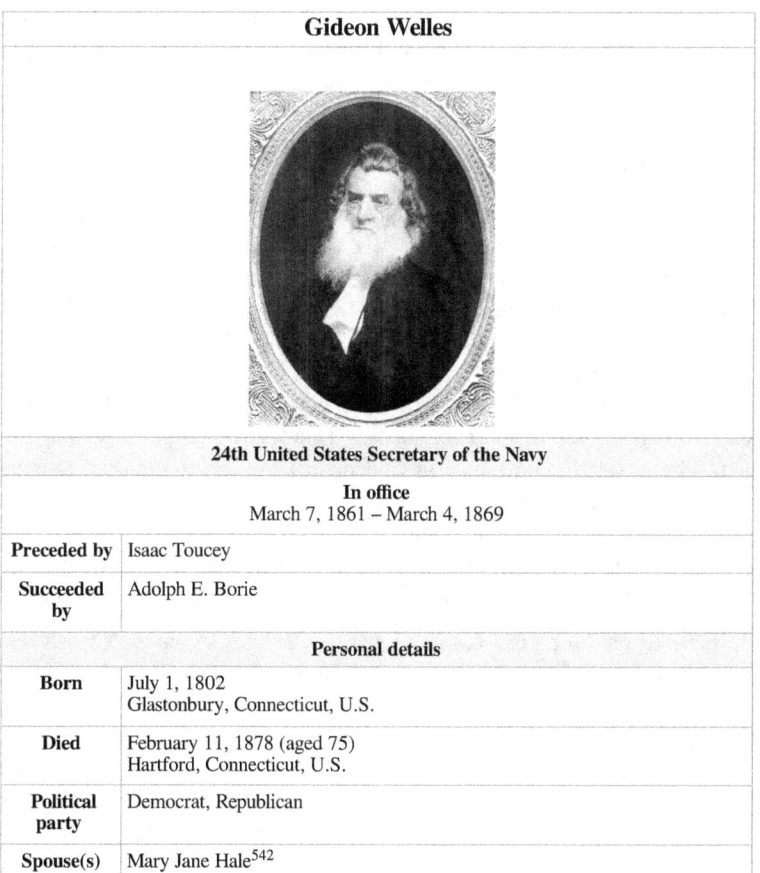	
24th United States Secretary of the Navy	
In office March 7, 1861 – March 4, 1869	
Preceded by	Isaac Toucey
Succeeded by	Adolph E. Borie
Personal details	
Born	July 1, 1802 Glastonbury, Connecticut, U.S.
Died	February 11, 1878 (aged 75) Hartford, Connecticut, U.S.
Political party	Democrat, Republican
Spouse(s)	Mary Jane Hale[542]

Children	Edgar Thaddeus Welles[543] Thomas Glastonbury Welles John Arthur Welles Herbert Welles Samuel Welles Edward Gideon Welles Anna Jane Welles Mary Juanita Welles
Alma mater	Military Academy at Norwich, Vermont
Profession	Politician, Lawyer, Writer, Journalist
Signature	*Gideon Welles*

Gideon Welles (July 1, 1802 – February 11, 1878) was the United States Secretary of the Navy from 1861 to 1869. His buildup of the Navy to successfully execute blockades of Southern ports was a key component of Northern victory of the Civil War. Welles was also instrumental in the Navy's creation of the Medal of Honor.[544]

Biography

Gideon Welles, the son of Samuel Welles and Ann Hale,[545] was born on July 1, 1802 in Glastonbury, Connecticut.[546] His father was a shipping merchant and fervent Jeffersonian;[547] he was a member of the Convention which formed the first state Connecticut Constitution in 1818 that abolished the colonial charter and officially severed the political ties to England. This constitution is also notable for having reversed the earlier Orders and provided for freedom of religion. He was a member of the seventh generation of his family in America. His original immigrant ancestor was Thomas Welles,[548,549] who arrived in 1635 and was the only man in Connecticut's history to hold all four top offices: governor, deputy governor, treasurer, and secretary. He was also the transcriber of the Fundamental Orders. Welles was the second great grandson of Capt. Samuel Welles and Ruth (Rice) Welles, the daughter of Edmund Rice, a 1638 immigrant to Sudbury and founder of Marlborough, Massachusetts.[550]

He married on June 16, 1835, at Lewiston, Mifflin County, Pennsylvania, Mary Jane Hale,[542] who was born on June 18, 1817 in Glastonbury, Connecticut the daughter of Elias White Hale and Jane Mullhallan. Her father, Elias, graduated from Yale College in 1794, and practiced law in Mifflin and Centre Counties, Pennsylvania.[551] She died on February 28, 1886 in Hartford, Connecticut and was buried next to her husband in Cedar Hill Cemetery in Hartford, Connecticut. Gideon and Mary Jane were the parents of six children.

Figure 65: *Gideon Welles*

He was educated at the Episcopal Academy at Cheshire, Connecticut, and earned a degree at the American Literary, Scientific, and Military Academy at Norwich, Vt. (later Norwich University).[546] He became a lawyer through the then-common practice of reading the law, but soon shifted to journalism and became the founder and editor of the *Hartford Times* in 1826. After successfully gaining admission, from 1827–1835, he participated in the Connecticut House of Representatives as a Democrat. Following his service in the Connecticut General Assembly, he served in various posts, including State Controller of Public Accounts in 1835, Postmaster of Hartford (1836–41), and Chief of the Bureau of Provisions and Clothing for the Navy (1846–49).[552]

Welles was a Jacksonian Democrat, who worked very closely with Martin Van Buren and John Milton Niles. His chief rival in the Connecticut Democratic Party was Isaac Toucey, whom Welles would later replace at the Navy Department. While Welles dutifully supported James K. Polk in the 1844 election, he would abandon the Democrats in 1848 to support Van Buren's Freesoil campaign.

Mainly because of his strong anti-slavery views, Welles shifted allegiance in 1854 to the newly-established Republican Party, and founded a newspaper in 1856 (the *Hartford Evening Press*) that would espouse Republican ideals for decades thereafter. Welles' strong support of Abraham Lincoln in 1860

Figure 66: *The Running Machine*
An 1864 cartoon featuring Welles, William P. Fessenden, Edwin M. Stanton, Abraham Lincoln and William H. Seward takes a swing at the Lincoln administration.

made him the logical candidate from New England for Lincoln's cabinet, and in March 1861 Lincoln named Welles his Secretary of the Navy.

Tenure in Lincoln's Cabinet

Welles found the Naval Department in disarray, with Southern officers resigning en masse. His first major action was to dispatch the Navy's most powerful warship, the USS *Powhatan*, to relieve Fort Sumter. Unfortunately, Lincoln had simultaneously ordered the Powhatan to both Fort Sumter and Pensacola, Florida, ruining whatever chance Major Robert Anderson had of withstanding the assault. Several weeks later, when Secretary of State William H. Seward argued for a blockade of Southern ports, Welles argued vociferously against the action but was eventually overruled by Lincoln. Despite his misgivings, Welles' efforts to rebuild the Navy and implement the blockade proved extraordinarily effective. From 76 ships and 7600 sailors in 1861, by 1865 the Navy expanded almost tenfold. His implementation of the Naval portion of the Anaconda Plan strongly weakened the Confederacy's ability to finance the war through limiting the cotton trade, and while never completely effective in

Figure 67: *First Reading of the Emancipation Proclamation of President Lincoln by Francis Bicknell Carpenter<ref> Reference*[553]. *Lincoln met with his cabinet on July 22, 1862 for the first reading of a draft of the Emancipation Proclamation. Sight measurement. Height: 108 inches (274.32 cm) Width: 180 inches (457.2 cm)</ref>Use your cursor to see who is who*

sealing off all 3,500 miles of Southern coastline it was a major contribution towards Northern victory. Lincoln nicknamed Welles his "Neptune".

At the start of the war, David Dixon Porter wrote Wells that "the present allowance of crews . . . if for peace establishment and is not suited at all to times of war."On another occasion, Porter told Wells that his own vessel lacked coal and that small steamers of shallow draft were required to make the blockade effective. From Mobile to the Mississippi River there were numerous inlets through which small Confederate craft could slip through the Federal blockade.[554]

Despite his successes, Welles was never at ease in the Cabinet. His anti-English sentiments caused him to clash with Seward, and Welles's conservative stances led to arguments with Treasury Secretary Salmon P. Chase and War Secretary Edwin M. Stanton.

Tenure in Johnson's Cabinet

After Lincoln's assassination Welles was retained by President Andrew Johnson as Secretary of the Navy. In 1866, Welles, along with Seward, was instrumental in launching the National Union Party as a third party alternative supportive of Johnson's reconciliation policies. Welles also played a prominent part in Johnson's ill-fated "Swing Around the Circle" campaign that fall. Although Welles admitted in his diary that he was dismayed by Johnson's behavior on the trip, particularly the president's penchant for invective and engaging directly with hecklers, Welles remained loyal to Johnson to the end, even congratulating him in 1875 when Johnson, now an ex-president, was launching a comeback political bid with his election to the U.S. Senate from Tennessee.

Welles ultimately left the Cabinet on March 3, 1869, having returned to the Democratic Party after disagreeing with Andrew Johnson's reconstruction policies but supporting him during his impeachment trial.

Later Life and Death

After leaving politics, Welles returned to Connecticut and to writing, editing his journals and authoring several books before his death, including a biography, *Lincoln and Seward*, published in 1874.[546] Towards the end of 1877, his health began to wane. A streptococcal infection of the throat killed Gideon Welles at the age of seventy-five on February 12, 1878.[546] His body was interred at Cedar Hill Cemetery in Hartford, Connecticut.[555]

The Diary of Gideon Welles

Welles' three-volume diary, documenting his Cabinet service from 1861–1869, is an invaluable archive for Civil War scholars and students of Lincoln alike, allowing readers rare insight into the complex struggles, machinations and inter-relational strife within the President's War Cabinet. Although offering a unique and quite non pareil portrayal of the immense personalities and problems facing the men who led the Union to ultimate victory, the first edition (published in 1911) suffers from rewrites by Welles himself and after his death, by his son; the 1960 edition is drawn directly from his original manuscript. The 1911 version of his diary may be found on Google Books: Vol. I (1861-March 30, 1864)[556], Vol. II (April 1, 1864-December 31, 1866)[557], Vol. III (January 1, 1866-June 6, 1869)[558].

Posthumous Dedications

Two ships have been named USS *Welles* in his honor. The Dining Commons at Cheshire Academy and the Gideon Welles School in Glastonbury, Connecticut are also named after him.

References

- Boulard, Garry "The Swing Around the Circle–Andrew Johnson and the Train Ride that Destroyed a Presidency" (iUniverse, 2008)
- Hale, Oscar Fitzalan. *Ancestry and descendants of Josiah Hale: fifth in descent from Samuel Hale of Hartford, Connecticut, 1637* Rutland, Vermont: The Tuttle Company, 1909.
- Niven, John. *Gideon Welles; Lincoln's Secretary of the Navy* Publisher: Oxford University Press US, 1973. ISBN 0195016939
- Norton, Frederick Calvin *The governors of Connecticut: biographies of the chief executives of the commonwealth that gave to the world the first written constitution known to history*, Publisher Connecticut Magazine Co., 1905.
- Siemiatkoski, Donna Holt. *The Descendants of Governor Thomas Welles of Connecticut, 1590–1658, and His Wife, Alice Tomes* Baltimore: Publisher, Gateway Press, 1990.
- John D. Winters, *The Civil War in Louisiana*, Baton Rouge: Louisiana State University Press, 1963, ISBN 0807117250.

External links

- Lincoln and Seward[559]: by Gideon Welles, New York: Publisher, Sheldon and Company, 1874.
- Mr. Lincoln's White House: Gideon Welles[560]
- Gideon Welles[561] at the Naval Historical Center
- Welles Family Association, Inc.[562]
- Biographical sketch of Thomas Welles Connecticut State Library[563]
- Lost Letters of Gideon Welles[564]

Secretary of the Interior

Caleb Blood Smith

Caleb Blood Smith	

6th United States Secretary of the Interior	
In office March 5, 1861 – December 31, 1862	
Preceded by	Jacob Thompson
Succeeded by	John Palmer Usher
Personal details	
Born	April 16, 1808 Boston, Massachusetts, U.S.
Died	January 7, 1864 (aged 55) Indianapolis, Indiana, U.S.
Political party	Whig, Republican
Spouse(s)	Elizabeth B. Watton Smith
Alma mater	Cincinnati College Miami University

Profession	Politician, Lawyer, Journalist
Signature	*Caleb B Smith*

Caleb Blood Smith (April 16, 1808 – January 7, 1864) was an American journalist and politician, serving in the Cabinet of Abraham Lincoln during the American Civil War.

Biography

Born in Boston, Massachusetts, he emigrated with his parents to Ohio in 1814, was educated at Cincinnati College and Miami University, studied law in Cincinnati and in Connersville, Indiana, and was admitted to the bar in 1828. He began practice at the latter place, established and edited the *Sentinel* in 1832, served several terms in the Indiana legislature, and was in the United States Congress in 1843–1849, having been elected as a Whig. During his congressional career, he was one of the Mexican claims commissioners. He returned to the practice of law in 1850, residing in Cincinnati and subsequently in Indianapolis. He was influential in securing the nomination of Abraham Lincoln for the presidency at the Chicago Republican National Convention in 1860.

Lincoln appointed Smith as the United States Secretary of the Interior in 1861 as a reward for his work in the presidential campaign. He was the first citizen of Indiana to hold a Presidential Cabinet position. However, Smith had little interest in the job and, with declining health, delegated most of his responsibilities to Assistant Secretary of the Interior John Palmer Usher. In 1862, he was interested in the empty seat in the United States Supreme Court vacated by John Archibald Campbell's resignation the previous year. However, Lincoln nominated David Davis for the position instead. After Smith resigned in December 1862 as the result of his discord with the Emancipation Proclamation, Usher became Secretary. Smith went home to become the United States circuit judge for Indiana. He died January 7, 1864, from his ill health. President Lincoln ordered that government buildings be draped in black for two weeks in a sign of mourning for Smith's death.

Search for body

It has been said that Caleb B. Smith's body is buried in a Connersville, Indiana cemetery. In 1977, John Walker, a Connersville, Indiana resident, received permission from the Smith family, Norvella Thomas Copes, and Nancy S. Hurley, and the city of Connersville, Indiana, to excavate the body of Caleb

Figure 68: *Caleb Blood Smith*

Figure 69: *First Reading of the Emancipation Proclamation of President Lincoln by Francis Bicknell Carpenter<ref> Reference[565]. Lincoln met with his cabinet on July 22, 1862 for the first reading of a draft of the Emancipation Proclamation. Sight measurement. Height: 108 inches (274.32 cm) Width: 180 inches (457.2 cm)</ref>Use your cursor to see who is who*

Blood Smith. Walker had an interest in President Abraham Lincoln, and discovered in reading about Lincoln that one of his cabinet members was buried in the city he lived in. An excavation was done in November, but Smith's body was not there. It was Smith's son-in-law William Watton Smith. C.B. Smith's wife, Elizabeth B. Watton, had paid $500 for the choice of plots, in *Greenlawn Cemetery*[566] but had to remove the body to Crown Hill Cemetery in Indianapolis for fear of southern dissenters, the Sons of Liberty, desecrating his body and of local teens knocking over the markers. There was also a possibility that his body was in one of the two above ground vaults behind the *Warren Lodge*[567], also known as Elmhurst, but both doors were standing open and had been for years, with nothing inside (also in Connersville, Indiana). A letter inquiring about the whereabouts of Smith's body found in the 1980s arose from a New York public library in the 1930s.

External links

- Caleb Blood Smith[568] at the *Biographical Directory of the United States Congress* Retrieved on 2009-03-26
- "Caleb Blood Smith"[569]. Find a Grave. Retrieved 2009-03-26.
- Mr. Lincoln's White House: Caleb Blood Smith[570]
- Caleb Blood Smith papers at the Indiana Historical Society[571]
- *The Department of Everything Else: Highlights of Interior History*[572] (1989)
- "Smith, Caleb Blood". *Appletons' Cyclopædia of American Biography*. 1900.
- Sanford, Wayne L. "Cemeteries" *The Encyclopedia of Indianapolis*. Bloomington: Indiana University Press, 1994. googlebooks[573] Retrieved May 21, 2009
- Correspondence on excavation and opening of grave-site (See talk page.)

John Palmer Usher

John Palmer Usher	
7th United States Secretary of the Interior	
In office January 1, 1863 – May 15, 1865	
Preceded by	Caleb Blood Smith
Succeeded by	James Harlan
Personal details	
Born	January 9, 1816 Brookfield, New York, U.S.
Died	April 13, 1889 (aged 73) Philadelphia, Pennsylvania, U.S.
Political party	Republican
Profession	Politician, Lawyer

John Palmer Usher (January 9, 1816 – April 13, 1889) was a U.S. administrator who served in the Cabinet of President Abraham Lincoln during the American Civil War.

Born in Brookfield, New York, Usher trekked west in 1839 to locate in Terre Haute in western Indiana where he became a law partner with William D. Griswold in the firm of Griswold & Usher. An outstanding trial lawyer, Usher traveled the circuit in Indiana and Illinois during the 1840s and 1850s, becoming acquainted with Abraham Lincoln of Springfield, Illinois. He also became a mentor to young Joseph Gurney Cannon.

While Usher was serving as the elected Indiana Attorney General in March 1862, Lincoln asked him to serve as Assistant Secretary of the Interior. Then-secretary Caleb Blood Smith had little interest in the job, and, with declining health, soon delegated most of his responsibilities to Usher. When Smith resigned in December 1862, Usher became Secretary effective January 1, 1863.

Usher served as the Secretary of the Interior between 1863 and 1865. He was known as genial, courteous, and unobtrusive secretary. He accompanied Lincoln to Gettysburg, Pennsylvania in November 1863 for the dedication of the Gettysburg National Cemetery and sat on the platform with other dignitaries when Lincoln gave his famous Gettysburg Address.[574] When William P. Fessenden resigned as Secretary of the Treasury in March of 1865, Lincoln nominated Hugh McCulloch from Indiana to replace Fessenden at Treasury. Lincoln did not want two men from Indiana in his cabinet. Usher dated his resignation March 8, 1865 with an effective date of May 15th. His resignation was accepted by Lincoln on March 9th and Usher continued to serve until May 15th, a month after Lincoln's assassination.[575] Lincoln had nominated his close friend James Harlan to replace Usher. Harlan had been confirmed by the Senate and took over as Secretary of Interior under now President Andrew Johnson.

Usher became general solicitor for the Union Pacific Railway, Eastern Division, and was active in promoting the building of the railroad west from Kansas City. Later called the Kansas Pacific, the road was eventually consolidated with the Union Pacific in 1880.

Usher built a house in Lawrence, Kansas, completing it in 1873. Usher served one term as mayor of Lawrence. His house still stands at 1425 Tennessee Street and is on the National Register of Historic Places.[576] It has been the home of the Alpha Nu chapter of Beta Theta Pi Fraternity at the University of Kansas since 1912.

Usher died of cancer at the age of 73. He is buried in Oak Hill Cemetery in Lawrence.[577]

External links

- Mr. Lincoln's White House: John Palmer Usher Biography[578]
- *The Department of Everything Else: Highlights of Interior History*[579] (1989)

Appendix

References

[1] Goodwin, p. 91; Holzer (2004), p. 232.
[2] Tagg,
[3] Randall (1947), pp. 65–87.
[4] Bulla (2010), p. 222.
[5] Donald (1996), pp. 20–22.
[6] Pessen (1984), pp. 24–25.
[7] White, pp. 12–13.
[8] Donald (1996), p. 21.
[9] Donald (1996), pp. 22–24.
[10] Pessen (1984), pp. 24–25.
[11] Lamb, p. 189.
[12] Sandburg (1926), p. 20.
[13] Donald (1996), pp. 30–33.
[14] Donald (1996), p. 20.
[15] Donald (1996), pp. 26–27.
[16] White, pp. 25, 31, 47.
[17] Donald (1996), p. 33.
[18] Donald (1996), p. 41.
[19] Donald (1996), pp. 30–33.
[20] Donald (1996), pp. 28, 152.
[21] Donald (1996), pp. 38–43; Prokopowicz, pp. 18–19.
[22] Donald (1996), p. 36.
[23] Thomas (2008), pp. 23–53; Carwardine (2003), pp. 3–5.
[24] Sandburg (1926), pp. 22–23.
[25] Donald (1996), pp. 55–58.
[26] Donald (1996), pp. 67–69; Thomas (2008), pp. 56–57, 69–70.
[27] Lamb, p. 43.
[28] Sandburg (1926), pp. 46–48.
[29] Donald (1996), p. 86.
[30] Donald (1996), p. 87.
[31] Sandburg (1926), pp. 50–51.
[32] Donald (1996), p. 93.
[33] White, p. 125.
[34] Donald (1996), pp. 95–96.
[35] White, p. 126.
[36] Baker, p. 120.
[37] White, pp. 179–181, 476.
[38] Steers, p. 341.
[39] Shenk, Joshua Wolf (October 2005). "Lincoln's Great Depression" http://www.webcitation.org/62a4fProj. *The Atlantic*. The Atlantic Monthly Group. Archived from the original http://www.theatlantic.com/doc/200510/lincolns-clinical-depression on October 20, 2011.
[40] Foner (1995), pp. 440–447.
[41] Winkle ch 7–8.
[42] Winkle, pp. 86–95.
[43] laughtergenealogy.com – Presidents Personal Information http://www.laughtergenealogy.com/bin/histprof/misc/olio/personal.html
[44] Donald (1996), p. 46.
[45] Winkle, pp. 114–116.
[46] Donald (1996), pp. 53–55.
[47] White, p. 59.

[48] Donald (1996), p. 64.
[49] White, pp. 71, 79, 108.
[50] Donald (1948), p. 17.
[51] Simon, p. 283.
[52] Simon, p. 130.
[53] Donald (1996), p. 134.
[54] Foner (2010), pp. 17–19, 67.
[55] Donald (1996), p. 222.
[56] Boritt (1994), pp. 137–153.
[57] Oates, p. 79.
[58] Harris, p. 54; Foner (2010), p. 57.
[59] Heidler (2006), pp. 181–183.
[60] Holzer (2004), p. 63.
[61] Oates, pp. 79–80.
[62] Basler (1946), pp. 199–202.
[63] McGovern, p. 33.
[64] Basler (1946), p. 202.
[65] "Lincoln's Spot Resolutions" http://www.webcitation.org/62a5gtE9P. National Archives. Archived from the original http://www.archives.gov/education/lessons/lincoln-resolutions/ on October 20, 2011.
[66] Donald (1996), p. 128.
[67] Donald (1996), pp. 124–126.
[68] Donald (1996), p. 140.
[69] Harris, pp. 55–57.
[70] Donald (1996), p. 96.
[71] Donald (1996), pp. 105–106, 158.
[72] Donald (1996), pp. 142–143.
[73] Donald (1996), pp. 156–157.
[74] White, p. 163.
[75] "Abraham Lincoln's Patent Model: Improvement for Buoying Vessels Over Shoals" http://www.webcitation.org/62a7AMeAa. Smithsonian Institution. Archived from the original http://americanhistory.si.edu/collections/object.cfm?key=35&objkey=19 on October 20, 2011.
[76] Donald (1996), p. 155.
[77] Dirck (2007), p. 92.
[78] Handy, p. 440.
[79] Donald (1996), pp. 155–156, 196–197.
[80] Donald (1996), pp. 150–151.
[81] Harrison (1935), p. 270.
[82] "The Peculiar Instution" http://www.webcitation.org/62dB0ccYV. Newberry Library and Chicago History Museum. Archived from the original http://lincolnat200.org/exhibits/show/alwayshatedslavery/peculiarinstitution on October 22, 2011.
[83] "Lincoln Speaks Out" http://www.webcitation.org/62dBlWFGi. Newberry Library and Chicago History Museum. Archived from the original http://lincolnat200.org/exhibits/show/alwayshatedslavery/speaksout on October 22, 2011.
[84] McGovern, pp. 36–37.
[85] Foner (2010), pp. 84–88.
[86] Thomas (2008), pp. 148–152.
[87] White, p. 199.
[88] Basler (1953), p. 255.
[89] Oates, p. 119.
[90] White, pp. 205–208.
[91] McGovern, pp. 38–39.
[92] Donald (1996), p. 193.
[93] Oates, pp. 138–139.
[94] Zarefsky, pp. 69–110.
[95] Jaffa, pp. 299–300.

[96] White, p. 251.
[97] Harris, p. 98.
[98] Donald (1996), p. 209.
[99] McPherson (1993), p. 182.
[100] Donald (1996), pp. 214–224.
[101] Donald (1996), p. 223.
[102] Carwardine (2003), pp. 89–90.
[103] Donald (1996), pp. 242, 412.
[104] Jaffa, p. 473.
[105] Holzer (2004), pp. 108–111.
[106] Carwardine (2003), p. 97.
[107] Holzer (2004), p. 157.
[108] Donald (1996), p. 240.
[109] Donald (1996), p. 241.
[110] Donald (1996), p. 244.
[111] Oates, pp. 175–176.
[112] Donald (1996), p. 245.
[113] Luthin (1994), pp. 609–629.
[114] Hofstadter, pp. 50–55.
[115] Donald (1996), pp. 247–250.
[116] Boritt (1994), pp. 10, 13, 18.
[117] Donald (1996), p. 253.
[118] Donald (1996), pp. 254–256.
[119] Donald (1996), p. 254.
[120] Mansch, p. 61.
[121] Harris, p. 243.
[122] White, p. 350.
[123] Nevins (1950), p. 312.
[124] Edgar, p. 350.
[125] Donald (1996), p. 267.
[126] Potter, p. 498.
[127] White, p. 362.
[128] Potter, pp. 520, 569–570.
[129] White, p. 369.
[130] White, pp. 360–361.
[131] Donald (1996), p. 268.
[132] Vorenberg, p. 22.
[133] Lupton, p. 34.
[134] Donald (1996), pp. 273–277.
[135] Donald (1996), pp. 277–279.
[136] Sandburg (2002), p. 212.
[137] Donald (1996), pp. 283–284.
[138] Donald (1996), pp. 268, 279.
[139] Donald (1996), pp. 292–293.
[140] Nevins (2000), p. 29.
[141] Sherman, pp. 185–186.
[142] Donald (1996), p. 293.
[143] Oates, p. 226.
[144] Heidler (2000), p. 174.
[145] Donald (1996), p. 304.
[146] Scott (1948), pp. 326–341.
[147] Thomas (2007), p. 180.
[148] Donald (1996), pp. 303–304; Carwardine (2003), pp. 163–164.
[149] Donald (1996), pp. 315, 338–339.
[150] Donald (1996), pp. 331–333, 417.
[151] Donald (1996), p. 314; Carwardine (2003), p. 178.

[152] Donald (1996), pp. 314–317.
[153] Carwardine (2003), p. 181.
[154] Adams, pp. 540–562.
[155] Donald (1996), p. 322.
[156] Prokopowicz, p. 127.
[157] Benjamin P. Thomas and Harold M. Hyman, *Stanton, the Life and Times of Lincoln's Secretary of War* (Knopf, 1962)
[158] Donald (1996), pp. 295–296.
[159] Donald (1996), pp. 391–392.
[160] Ambrose, pp. 7, 66, 159.
[161] Donald (1996), pp. 432–436.
[162] Donald (1996), pp. 318–319.
[163] Donald (1996), pp. 349–352.
[164] Donald (1996), pp. 360–361.
[165] Nevins (1960), pp. 2:159–162.
[166] Donald (1996), pp. 339–340.
[167] Goodwin, pp. 478–479.
[168] Goodwin, pp. 478–480.
[169] Goodwin, p. 481.
[170] Donald (1996), pp. 389–390.
[171] Donald (1996), pp. 429–431.
[172] Nevins (1960), pp. 343–367.
[173] Nevins (1960), pp. 318–322, quote on p. 322.
[174] Donald (1996), pp. 422–423.
[175] Nevins (1960), pp. 2:432–450.
[176] Donald (1996), pp. 444–447.
[177] Donald (1996), p. 446.
[178] Mackubin, Thomas Owens (March 25, 2004). "The Liberator" http://www.webcitation.org/62a7fJ9hj. *National Review*. National Review. Archived from the original http://www.nationalreview.com/books/owens200403251139.asp on October 20, 2011.
[179] Guelzo (1999), pp. 290–291.
[180] Donald (1996), pp. 364–365.
[181] McPherson (1992), p. 124.
[182] Donald (1996), p. 368.
[183] Guelzo (2004), pp. 147–153.
[184] Donald (1996), pp. 364, 379.
[185] Donald (1996), p. 407.
[186] Donald (1996), p. 408.
[187] Nevins (1960), pp. 2:239–240.
[188] Donald (1996), pp. 430–431.
[189] Donald (1996), p. 431.
[190] Douglass, pp. 259–260.
[191] Donald (1996), pp. 453–460.
[192] Donald (1996), pp. 460–466.
[193] Wills, pp. 20, 27, 105, 146.
[194] Thomas (2008), p. 315.
[195] Nevins (2000), (Vol. IV), pp. 6–17.
[196] Donald (1996), pp. 490–492.
[197] McPherson (2009), p. 113.
[198] Donald (1996), p. 501.
[199] "The Peacemakers" http://www.webcitation.org/62a8J9jOa. The White House Historical Association. Archived from the original http://www.whitehousehistory.org/whha_about/whitehouse_collection/whitehouse_collection-art-06.html on October 20, 2011.
[200] Thomas (2008), pp. 422–424.
[201] Neely (2004), pp. 434–458.
[202] Thomas (2008), p. 434.

[203] Donald (1996), pp. 516–518.
[204] Donald (1996), p. 565.
[205] Donald (1996), p. 589.
[206] Fish, pp. 53–69.
[207] Tegeder, pp. 77–90.
[208] Donald (1996), pp. 494–507.
[209] Grimsley, p. 80.
[210] Basler (1953), p. 514.
[211] Donald (1996), p. 531.
[212] Randall & Current (1955), p. 307.
[213] Paludan, pp. 274–293.
[214] Noll, p. 426.
[215] Basler (1953), p. 333.
[216] Thomas (2008), pp. 509–512.
[217] Donald (1996), pp. 471–472.
[218] Donald (1996), pp. 485–486.
[219] Nevins (2000), Vol IV., p. 206.
[220] Donald (1996), p. 561.
[221] Donald (1996), pp. 562–563.
[222] "Primary Documents in American History: 13th Amendment to the U.S. Constitution" http://www.webcitation.org/62a9BIwNw. Library of Congress. Archived from the original http://www.loc.gov/rr/program/bib/ourdocs/13thamendment.html on October 20, 2011.
[223] Carwardine (2003), pp. 242–243.
[224] "Presidential Proclamation-Civil War Sesquicentennial" http://www.webcitation.org/62aAPoA6B. The White House. April 12, 2011. Archived from the original http://www.whitehouse.gov/the-press-office/2011/04/12/presidential-proclamation-civil-war-sesquicentennial on October 20, 2011. "...a new meaning was conferred on our country's name..."
[225] Jaffa, p. 399.
[226] Diggins, p. 307.
[227] Foner (2010), p. 215.
[228] Jaffa, p. 263.
[229] Belz (1998), p. 86.
[230] Donald (2001), p. 137.
[231] Paludan, p. 116.
[232] McPherson (1993), pp. 450–452.
[233] Summers, Robert. "Abraham Lincoln" http://www.webcitation.org/62dM1T7zn. *Internet Public Library 2 (IPL2)*. U. Michigan and Drexel U.. Archived from the original http://www.ipl.org/div/potus/alincoln.html on October 22, 2011.
[234] Donald (1996), p. 424.
[235] Paludan, p. 111.
[236] Donald (2001), p. 424.
[237] Cox, p. 182.
[238] Nichols, pp. 210–232.
[239] Donald (1996), pp. 501–502.
[240] Donald (1996), p. 471.
[241] Schaffer, p. 48.
[242] Blue, p. 245.
[243] Donald (1996), pp. 300, 539.
[244] Donald (1996), pp. 586–587.
[245] Donald (1996), p. 587.
[246] Harrison (2000), pp. 3–4.
[247] Donald (1996), pp. 594–597.
[248] Donald (1996), p. 597.
[249] Martin, Paul (April 8, 2010). "Lincoln's Missing Bodyguard" http://www.webcitation.org/62aAqLOzq. *Smithsonian Magazine*. Smithsonian Institution. Archived from the original http:

//www.smithsonianmag.com/history-archaeology/Lincolns-Missing-Bodyguard.html on October 20, 2011.

[250] Donald (1996), p. 599.
[251] Donald (1996), pp. 598–599, 686. Witnesses have provided other versions of the quote, i.e. "He now belongs to the ages." and "He is a man for the ages."
[252] Trostel, pp. 31–58.
[253] Goodrich, pp. 231–238.
[254] Carwardine (1997), pp. 27–55.
[255] Donald (1996), pp. 48–49, 514–515.
[256] Donald (1996), pp. 48–49.
[257] Parrillo, pp. 227–253.
[258] Wilson, pp. 251–254.
[259] Wilson, p. 254.
[260] Donald (1996), p. 514.
[261] Taranto, p. 264.
[262] Chesebrough, pp. 76, 79, 106, 110.
[263] Schwartz (2000), p. 109.
[264] Schwartz (2009), pp. 23, 91–98.
[265] Belz (2006), pp. 514–518.
[266] Graebner, pp. 67–94.
[267] Smith, pp. 43–45.
[268] Boritt (1994), pp. 196, 198, 228, 301.
[269] Harris, p. 2.
[270] Randall (1947), p. 175.
[271] Zilversmit, pp. 22–24.
[272] Smith, p. 42.
[273] Bennett, pp. 35–42.
[274] Dirck (2008), p. 31.
[275] Striner, pp. 2–4.
[276] Cashin, p. 61.
[277] Kelley & Lewis, p. 228.
[278] Schwartz (2009), p. 146.
[279] Donald (1996), p. 15.
[280] Dennis (2002), p. 194.
[281] "Renovation and Expansion of the Historic DC Courthouse" http://www.webcitation.org/62dfFdX74 (PDF). DC Court of Appeals. Archived from the original http://www.dcappeals.gov/dccourts/appeals/pdf/appeals_renovation_expansion.pdf on October 23, 2011.
[282] "Mount Rushmore National Memorial" http://www.webcitation.org/62dfUtolh. U.S. National Park Service. Archived from the original http://www.nps.gov/moru/historyculture/index.htm on October 23, 2011.
[283] "Abraham Lincoln Birthplace National Historic Site" http://www.webcitation.org/62dfhlRLE. U.S. National Park Service. Archived from the original http://www.nps.gov/abli/index.htm on October 23, 2011.
[284] "Lincoln Boyhood National Memorial" http://www.webcitation.org/62fLOWRqX. U.S. National Park Service. Archived from the original http://www.nps.gov/libo/index.htm on October 24, 2011.
[285] "Lincoln's New Salem" http://www.webcitation.org/62fLY6Gyu. Illinois Historic Preservation Agency. Archived from the original http://www.illinoishistory.gov/hs/new_salem.htm on October 24, 2011.
[286] "Lincoln Home National Historic Site" http://www.webcitation.org/62fLhitWd. U.S. National Park Service. Archived from the original http://www.nps.gov/liho/planyourvisit/index.htm on October 24, 2011.
[287] Peterson, pp. 312, 368.
[288] "The Abraham Lincoln Presidential Library and Museum" http://www.webcitation.org/62i1pRLLD. Abraham Lincoln Presidential Library and Museum. Archived from the original http://www.alplm.com/ on October 25, 2011.

[289] "About Ford's" http://www.webcitation.org/62i1ux7Sk. Ford's Theatre. Archived from the original http://www.fordstheatre.org/home/about-fords on October 25, 2011.
[290] "Lincoln Tomb" http://www.webcitation.org/62i23WFGo. Illinois Historic Preservation Agency. Archived from the original http://www.illinoishistory.gov/hs/lincoln_tomb.htm on October 25, 2011. .
[291] Healey, Matthew. "Lincoln Stamps Bring Neary $2 Million at a New York Auction" http://www.nytimes.com/2009/04/20/arts/design/20lincoln.html?adxnnl=1&adxnnlx=1309323210-SHbsvaNW+FeQ/LsMHYd2HA. *New York Times*. Retrieved June 29, 2011.
[292] Cummings, p. 284.
[293] Vinciguerra, Thomas (February 7, 2009). "Now if Only We Could Mint Lincoln Himself" http://www.nytimes.com/2009/02/08/weekinreview/08vinciguerra.html. *The New York Times*: p. WK4. Retrieved October 11, 2011.
[294] Schwartz (2009), pp. 196–199.
[295] Peterson pp. 147, 263.
[296] Carroll, James R. (January 12, 2009). "Let the Lincoln Bicentennial Celebrations Begin" http://www.courier-journal.com/article/20090112/NEWS01/901120364. *The Courier-Journal*. Retrieved October 11, 2011.
[297] Schwartz (2009), pp. 153–155.
[298] http://books.google.com/books?id=H84DAAAAMBAJ&pg=PA35&source=gbs_toc_r&cad=2#v=onepage&q&f=false
[299] http://www.historycooperative.org/journals/jala/18.1/carwardine.html
[300] http://www.lib.niu.edu/2006/ih060934.html
[301] http://muse.jhu.edu/login?uri=/journals/civil_war_history/v050/50.4neely.html
[302] http://www.historycooperative.org/journals/jala/2/zilversmit.html
[303] http://quod.lib.umich.edu/l/lincoln/
[304] http://worldcat.org/identities/lccn-n79-6779
[305] http://memory.loc.gov/ammem/alhtml/alhome.html
[306] http://www.loc.gov/rr/program/bib/prespoetry/al.html
[307] http://www.alplm.org/home.html
[308] http://www.papersofabrahamlincoln.org
[309] http://www.google.com/patents?vid=6469
[310] http://edsitement.neh.gov/spotlight.asp?id=138
[311] http://www.abrahamlincoln200.org/
[312] http://lincoln.lib.niu.edu/
[313] http://www.loc.gov/rr/program/bib/presidents/lincoln/
[314] http://library.umaine.edu/speccoll/FindingAids/Hamlinfamilyinventory.htm
[315] http://www.mrlincolnswhitehouse.org/inside.asp?ID=89&subjectID=2
[316] Augustus C. Smith, *Bangor, Brewer, and Penobscot Co. Directory, 1859–60* (Bangor, 1859)
[317] "The late Hon. Elijah L. Hamlin" http://query.nytimes.com/mem/archive-free/pdf?res=9407EEDC1E38EF34BC4B51DFB1668389669FDE (PDF). *New York Times*. July 23, 1872. Retrieved 2010-12-20.
[318] Warren King Moorhead, *A Report on the Archeology of Maine*, p. 34
[319] Augustus Choate Hamlin (1896). *The Battle of Chancellorsville* http://books.google.com/books?id=sF8fAAAAMAAJ. Bangor, Maine.
[320] http://books.google.com/books?id=uBFCAAAAIAAJ
[321] http://bioguide.congress.gov/scripts/biodisplay.pl?index=H000121
[322] http://www.mlwh.com/inside.asp?ID=89&subjectID=2
[323] http://www.archive.org/details/hannibalhamlin00hamlrich
[324] http://bangorinfo.com/Focus/focus_hannibal_hamlin.html
[325] http://opinionator.blogs.nytimes.com/2010/11/22/lincoln-speaks/
[326] "American President: Andrew Johnson: Family Life" http://millercenter.org/academic/americanpresident/johnson/essays/biography/7. Miller Center of Public Affairs at the University of Virginia. Retrieved May 26, 2009.
[327] Milton, George Fort (1930). *The Age of Hate: Andrew Johnson And The Radicals* http://www.questia.com/PM.qst?a=o&d=14804076. New York: Coward-McCann. p. 80.

ISBN 1417916583. OCLC 739916. "As for my religion, it is the doctrine of the Bible, as taught and practiced by Jesus Christ."

[328] Hall, Kermit; Paul Finkelman, James W. Ely (2005). *American Legal History* (3rd ed.). Oxford: Oxford University Press. pp. 259–260. ISBN 0-19-516225-0.

[329] Trefousse, Hans Louis. *Andrew Johnson: A Biography* (1997), p. 338–339.

[330] National Park Service Questionnaire http://www.nps.gov/anjo/forteachers/curriculummaterials.htm

[331] Hans L. Trefousse, *Andrew Johnson: A Biography* (W. W. Norton, 1989) p, 23.

[332] Karin L Zipf. *Labor Of Innocents: Forced Apprenticeship in North Carolina, 1715–1919* (2005) pp 8–9

[333] Trefousse, *Andrew Johnson: A Biography* pp 27-29

[334] Biography of Andrew Johnson http://www.whitehouse.gov/history/presidents/aj17.html – www.whitehouse.gov

[335] Trefousse, *Andrew Johnson: A Biography* ch 3

[336] Andrew Johnson http://bioguide.congress.gov/scripts/biodisplay.pl?index=J000116 at the *Biographical Directory of the United States Congress*

[337] Trefousse, *Andrew Johnson: A Biography* ch 6

[338] Trefousse, *Andrew Johnson: A Biography* p 126

[339] Trefousse, *Andrew Johnson: A Biography* p 65

[340] Tresouse, p 153

[341] Sledge pg. 1071–1072

[342] *A Review of the Political Conflict in America*, pg. 430 http//books.google.com

[343] Patton p 126

[344] Trefousse, *Andrew Johnson: A Biography* p 150

[345] http://www.senate.gov/artandhistory/history/resources/pdf/andrew_johnson.pdf

[346] Trefousse p. 198

[347] Complete list of U.S. presidents http://australianpolitics.com/usa/president/presidents-list.shtml

[348] Milton 183

[349] Trefousse, Hans L. Andrew Johnson: A Biography (1989)

[350] "Memoirs of W.W. Holden: Electronic Edition". http://docsouth.unc.edu/fpn/holden/holden.html

[351] Rhodes, *History* 6:68

[352] Trefousse pg. 236. Online reference to the quote available at http://www.pbs.org/wgbh/amex/grant/peopleevents/e_impeach.html

[353] Trefousse 1999

[354] Andrew Johnson Cleveland Speech (September 3, 1866) http://www.usa-presidents.info/speeches/cleveland-speech.html

[355] Rhodes, James Ford (1904). *History of the United States from the compromise of 1850 to the final restoration of home rule at the South in 1877* http//books.google.com. Macmillan Co.. p. 589.

[356] Trefousse, 1989 pages 302–3

[357] Tenure of office act – Britannica Online Encyclopedia http://www.britannica.com/eb/article-9071723/Tenure-of-Office-Act

[358] Tenure of office act – Britannica Concise http://concise.britannica.com/ebc/article-9380467/Tenure-of-Office-Act

[359] "The Trial of Andrew Johnson, 1868". http://www.eyewitnesstohistory.com/john.htm

[360] "Andrew Johnson Trial: The Consciences of Seven Republicans Save Johnson". http://law.jrank.org/pages/13490/Andrew-Johnson-Trial.html

[361] The other three presidents are William Henry Harrison, Zachary Taylor and Jimmy Carter.

[362] Consumer Price Index (estimate) 1800–2008 http://www.minneapolisfed.org/community_education/teacher/calc/hist1800.cfm. Federal Reserve Bank of Minneapolis. Retrieved December 7, 2010.

[363] Hereward Senior, *The last invasion of Canada: the Fenian raids, 1866-1870* (1991)

[364] Furs and fish were important but gold was not discovered in Alaska until 1880, 13 years after the purchase and oil was not discovered until 1968.

[365] United States Senate: Death of Andrew Johnson http://www.senate.gov/artandhistory/history/minute/Death_of_Andrew_Johnson.htm

[366] Andrew Johnson http://www.american-presidents.com/andrew-johnson. American-Presidents.com. Accessed November 1, 2009.

[367] Highly favorable were Winston (1928), Stryker (1929), Milton (1930), and Claude Bowers, *The Tragic Era* (1929).

[368] Foner, Eric (December 3, 2006). "He's The Worst Ever" http://www.washingtonpost.com/wp-dyn/content/article/2006/12/01/AR2006120101509.html. *The Washington Post*. Retrieved December 15, 2008.

[369] The 10 Worst Presidents: No. 3 Andrew Johnson (1865-1869) http://www.usnews.com/usnews/news/articles/070216/16president.johnson.htm, Jay Tolson, *U.S. News & World Report*, February 16, 2007; accessed December 15, 2008.

[370] The Worst President in History? http://www.rollingstone.com/news/story/9961300/the_worst_president_in_history/print, Sean Wilentz, *Rolling Stone*, April 21, 2006; accessed December 15, 2008.

[371] Lafantasie, Glenn (February 21, 2011) Who's the worst president of them all? http://www.salon.com/books/history/index.html?story=/politics/war_room/2011/02/21/worst_president_buchanan, *Salon.com*

[372] http://www.questia.com/PM.qst?a=o&d=104078634

[373] http//books.google.com

[374] http://www.questia.com/PM.qst?a=o&d=16224153

[375] http://www.booktv.org/Program/12207/Andrew+Johnson.aspx

[376] http://www.questia.com/PM.qst?a=o&d=89815306

[377] http://www.questia.com/PM.qst?a=o&d=14804076

[378] http://www.questia.com/PM.qst?a=o&d=94962448

[379] http://www.questia.com/PM.qst?a=o&d=24644891

[380] http://books.google.com/books?vid=OCLC15799162&id=p4fAuPxMYPIC&printsec=toc&dq=annual+cyclopedia+1867

[381] http://www.questia.com/PM.qst?a=o&d=295401

[382] http://www.questia.com/PM.qst?a=o&d=101075266

[383] http://www.questia.com/PM.qst?a=o&d=3971949

[384] http://www.impeach-andrewjohnson.com/

[385] http://www.andrewjohnson.com/09ImpeachmentAndAcquittal/ImpeachmentAndAcquittal.htm

[386] http://starship.python.net/crew/manus/Presidents/aj2/aj2obit.html

[387] http://edisoneffect.blogspot.com/2009/09/impeachment-trial-of-president-johnson.html

[388] http://www.nytimes.com/learning/general/onthisday/bday/1229.html

[389] http://www.law.umkc.edu/faculty/projects/ftrials/impeach/articles.html

[390] http://www.whitehouse.gov/history/presidents/aj17.html

[391] http://www.senate.gov/artandhistory/history/resources/pdf/andrew_johnson.pdf

[392] http://www.mlwh.org/inside.asp?ID=91&subjectID=2

[393] http://www.usa-presidents.info/speeches/cleveland-speech.html

[394] http://memory.loc.gov/cgi-bin/ampage?collId=llcg&fileName=069/llcg069.db&recNum=629

[395] http://www.archive.org/details/johnsonjohnson00andrrich

[396] http://discovergreeneville.com/andrewjohnson

[397] http://www.loc.gov/rr/program/bib/presidents/ajohnson/

[398] http://www.tennessee.gov/tsla/history/manuscripts/findingaids/131.pdf

[399] http://www.tennessee.gov/tsla/history/govpapers/findingaids/gp18.pdf

[400] http://www.tennessee.gov/tsla/history/govpapers/findingaids/gp20.pdf

[401] http://bioguide.congress.gov/scripts/biodisplay.pl?index=J000116

[402] http://www.millercenter.virginia.edu/index.php/academic/americanpresident/johnson

[403] http://www.uiu.edu/~shafferd/johnsonclinton_paper

[404] Brian Jenkins (1978) "The "Wise Macaw" and the Lion: William Seward and Britain, 1861-1863" University of Rochester Library Bulletin, Vol. 31 No. 1 http://www.lib.rochester.edu/index.cfm?page=1017

[405] Doris Kearns Goodwin (2005) *Team of Rivals: The Political Genius of Abraham Lincoln*, New York: Simon & Schuster, ISBN 0-684-82490-6, p. 14
[406] Glyndon G. Van Deusen, "The Life and Career of William Henry Seward 1801-1872" http://www.lib.rochester.edu/index.cfm?page=3452
[407] http://www.floridaufsd.org/flufsd/site/default.asp
[408] Julia Lawlor, "If You're Thinking of Living In/Warwick; Wide Open Spaces and 'Funky Flair' (2003)" http://query.nytimes.com/gst/fullpage.html?res=990DE4D7133BF937A2575AC0A9659C8B63&sec=&spon=&pagewanted=2
[409] Union Notable: William H. Seward http://www.union.edu/About/notables/profiles/seward.php, "Union.edu", accessed Oct 9, 2009
[410] William H. Seward Biography, Seward House: A National Historic Landmark http://www.sewardhouse.org/biography/
[411] Doris Kearns Goodwin. Team of Rivals: The Political Genius of Abraham Lincoln, p. 70 (2005).
[412] Seward, William H.. *Discourse on Education* http://books.google.com/books?id=vmoCKqi3Cx8C&printsec=frontcover&dq=seward+discourse+on+education. (Albany: Hoffman & White, 1837).
[413] Seward, Frederick. *William H. Seward an Autobiography from 1801–1834 with a memoir of his life and selections from his letters 1831-1846* Derby and Miller, New York 1891 Page 28.
[414] Frances Seward to William Seward Oct. 16 [1851] University of Rochester Rush Rhees Library Special Collections
[415] Frances Seward to William Seward July 1, 1852 University of Rochester Rush Rhees Library Special Collections
[416] Seward, William. *Works of William H. Seward Vol. I*, (New York: Redfield, 1853) 417.
[417] Seward, William. *Works of William H. Seward Vol. I*, (New York: Redfield, 1853) 471.
[418] Doris Kearns Goodwin. *Team of Rivals: The Political Genius of Abraham Lincoln*, p. 191 (2005).
[419] *Ibid.*, p. 192.
[420] *American Agriculturist*, vol. 19 (1860), p. 330.
[421] Bailey, Thomas A. (1980). *A Diplomatic History of the American People* (10th ed.). Prentice Hall. pp. 360.
[422] Farrar, Victor J. (1937). *The Annexation of Russian America to the United States*. Washington: W.F. Roberts Co.. pp. 113.
[423] Raico, Ralph. America's Will to War: The Turning Point http://mises.org/daily/5236/Americas-Will-to-War-The-Turning-Point, Mises Institute
[424] Doris Kearns Goodwin, *Team of Rivals: The Political Genius of Abraham Lincoln*, pp. 736-37 (2005).
[425] "Alaska's History and Value" http://query.nytimes.com/gst/abstract.html?res=F50E11FC355410738DDDA90A94D1405B8684F0D3. *The New York Times*. 20 September 1886.
[426] Garry Wills, *Henry Adams and the Making of America*, 2005; p. 58, citing Adams' letters, vol. 1, p.223
[427] http://www.seward.com
[428] http://books.google.com/books?vid=OCLC04112122&id=FTTmls3FTcMC&printsec=titlepage
[429] http://hdl.loc.gov/loc.gdc/mtfgc.1000
[430] http://hdl.loc.gov/loc.gdc/mtfgc.1001
[431] http://hdl.loc.gov/loc.gdc/mtfgc.1002
[432] http://hdl.loc.gov/loc.ndlpcoop/mtfxtx.u11846
[433] http://hdl.loc.gov/loc.gdc/mtfgc.1003
[434] http://books.google.com/books?vid=LCCN09004608&id=L0K4-q61Pi4C&printsec=titlepage
[435] http://books.google.com/books?vid=LCCN09004608&id=7Ov7OvmgxaAC&printsec=titlepage
[436] http://books.google.com/books?vid=OCLC13901267&id=Tr4Or7DDI-sC&printsec=toc&dq=intitle:works+intitle:seward
[437] http://bioguide.congress.gov/scripts/biodisplay.pl?index=S000261

[438] http://www.sewardhouse.org
[439] http://www.tulane.edu/~latner/Seward.html
[440] http://www.mrlincolnandfriends.org/inside.asp?pageID=85&subjectID=7
[441] http://www.mrlincolnandnewyork.org/inside.asp?ID=64&subjectID=3
[442] http://www.mrlincolnswhitehouse.org/inside.asp?ID=93&subjectID=2
[443] http://www.gutenberg.org/author/Seward+William+Henry
[444] http://www.frbsf.org/currency/metal/treasury/index2.html
[445] http://www.highbeam.com/doc/1G1-158529009.html?refid=hbw_rd
[446] Allen Johnson (1918). *Chronicles of America Series*. Yale University Press.
[447] Funny Science Quotes - Funny Quotes about Science http://www.basicjokes.com/dquotes.php?cid=16
[448] http://www.history.army.mil/books/sw-sa/CameronS.htm
[449] http://www.spartacus.schoolnet.co.uk/USACWcameron.htm
[450] http://www.npg.si.edu/exh/brady/gallery/71gal.html
[451] http://bioguide.congress.gov/scripts/biodisplay.pl?index=C000068
[452] http://www.mlwh.org/inside.asp?ID=85&subjectID=2
[453] http://www.mrlincolnandfriends.org/inside.asp?pageID=84&subjectID=7
[454] http://www.findagrave.com/cgi-bin/fg.cgi?page=gr&GRid=2876
[455] http://www.dauphincountyhistory.org/mansion/mansionhistory
[456] "Edwin M. Stanton (1814-1869)" http://www.mrlincolnswhitehouse.org/inside.asp?ID=96&subjectID=2. The Lincoln Institute.. Retrieved 18 December 2010.
[457] "Edwin M. Stanton2" http://www.ohiohistorycentral.org/entry.php?rec=356. Ohio History Central. Retrieved 18 December 2010.
[458] Robert C. Kennedy, Harper's Weekly. "The Impeachment of Andrew Johnson" http://www.andrewjohnson.com/11biographieskeyindividuals/EdwinMStanton.htm. Harper's Weekly. Retrieved 20 December 2010.
[459] "Edwin Stanton2" http://www.spartacus.schoolnet.co.uk/USASstanton.htm. Spartacus Educational UK. Retrieved 18 December 2010.
[460] Women of the Civil War, Wife of Secretary of War Edwin Stanton http://www.civilwarwomenblog.com/2010/09/mary-lamson-stanton.html
[461] http://www.senate.gov/artandhistory/art/artifact/Painting_33_00005.htm
[462] Swanson, James L. *Manhunt: The 12-Day Chase for Lincoln's Killer*. 6th ed. New York: Harper Collins, 2006. pp. 426–427. ISBN 978-0060518493
[463] Kunhardt, *Twenty Days*, pg. 186
[464] http://www.supremecourt.gov/about/members.pdf
[465] "Edwin M. Stanton issue of 1871" http://arago.si.edu/index.asp?con=1&cmd=1&tid=2029282. Smithsonian National Postal Nuseum. Retrieved 18 December 2010.
[466] Scotts US Stamp Catalogue
[467] Jeanne Jakle (2011-07-30). "Jeanne Jakle: McGill's profile going higher and higher" http://www.mysanantonio.com/entertainment/entertainment_columnists/jeanne_jakle/article/Jeanne-Jakle-McGill-s-profile-going-higher-and-1643484.php. *mysanantonio.com*. Retrieved 2011-07-30.
[468] http://www.anb.org/articles/04/04-00942.html;
[469] http://www.questia.com/PM.qst?a=o&d=7830940
[470] http://www.impeach-andrewjohnson.com/11BiographiesKeyIndividuals/EdwinMStanton.htm
[471] http://www.mrlincolnandfriends.org/inside.asp?pageID=86&subjectID=7
[472] http://www.mlwh.org/inside.asp?ID=96&subjectID=2
[473] http://www.frbsf.org/currency/civilwar/fractional/s132.html
[474] http://www.frbsf.org/currency/metal/treasury/index2.html
[475] http://www.spartacus.schoolnet.co.uk/USASstanton.htm
[476] http://www.infoplease.com/ce6/people/A0846515.html
[477] "Federal Judicial Center: Salmon Chase" http://www.fjc.gov/servlet/tGetInfo?jid=414. 2009-12-12. Retrieved 2009-12-12.
[478] Niven, John (1995). *Salmon P. Chase*. Oxford University Press. pp. 96. ISBN 9780195046533.
[479] Lydia Rapoza, "The Life of Salmon P. Chase, Attorney General of Fugitive Slaves 1808-1873" http://members.tripod.com/~abernassy/

[480] Gates, Henry Louis, Jr; and Hollis Robbins. "The Annotated Uncle Tom's Cabin" WW. Norton, p. xxxii
[481] http://www.senate.gov/artandhistory/art/artifact/Painting_33_00005.htm
[482] Geisst, Charles R. (1999). *Wall Street*. Oxford University Press. pp. 54. ISBN 9780195115123.
[483] Salmon Portland Chase http://encyclopedia.jrank.org/CHA_CHR/CHASE_SALMON_PORTLAND_1808_1873.html Encyclopedia Britannica, 1911 Edition, Originally appearing in Volume V05, Page 956
[484] http://www.treasury.gov/about/education/Pages/in-god-we-trust.aspx
[485] Chase's biography at HarpWeek http://www.impeach-andrewjohnson.com/11BiographiesKeyIndividuals/SalmonPChase.htm
[486] Aleksandar Pavković, Peter Radan, Creating New States: Theory and Practice of Secession http://books.google.com/books?id=-IjHbPvp1W0C, p. 222, Ashgate Publishing, Ltd., 2007.
[487] *Texas v. White* http://www.law.cornell.edu/supct/html/historics/USSC_CR_0074_0700_ZO.html, 74 U.S. 700 (1868) at Cornell University Law School Supreme Court collection.
[488] J. W. Schuckers, *The Life and Public Services of Salmon Portland Chase,* (1874). p. 585; letter of May 30, 1993, to August Belmont
[489] Salmon P. Chase memorial at http://www.findagrave.com/cgi-bin/fg.cgi?page=gr&GRid=192 Find a Grave.
[490] Christensen, George A. (1983) *Here Lies the Supreme Court: Gravesites of the Justices*, Yearbook http://web.archive.org/web/20050903032026/http://www.supremecourthistory.org/04_library/subs_volumes/04_c20_e.html Supreme Court Historical Society at Internet Archive.
[491] *See also*, Christensen, George A., *Here Lies the Supreme Court: Revisited*, *Journal of Supreme Court History*, Volume 33 Issue 1, Pages 17 - 41 (19 Feb 2008), University of Alabama.
[492] http://www.fjc.gov/servlet/nGetInfo?jid=414&cid=999&ctype=na&instate=na
[493] http://www.questia.com/PM.qst?a=o&d=22807164
[494] http://books.google.com/books?id=ozPVAAAAMAAJ&printsec=frontcover&dq=inauthor:%22Henry+Flanders%22&cd=7#v=onepage&q=&f=false
[495] http://www.questia.com/PM.qst?a=o&d=98855862
[496] http://www.questia.com/PM.qst?a=o&d=90104191
[497] http://www.questia.com/PM.qst?a=o&d=790159
[498] http://www.questia.com/PM.qst?a=o&d=101573920
[499] http://bioguide.congress.gov/scripts/biodisplay.pl?index=C000332
[500] http://www.gutenberg.org/etext/19165
[501] http://www.questia.com/PM.qst?a=o&d=23043578
[502] http://www.questia.com/PM.qst?a=o&d=10424543
[503] http://www.questia.com/PM.qst?a=o&d=10261520
[504] http://books.google.com/books?id=HOopAAAAYAAJ
[505] http://www.webcitation.org/query?url=http://www.geocities.com/CapitolHill/Lobby/6109/salmon1.htm&date=2009-10-25+06:50:12
[506] http://www2.hsp.org/collections/manuscripts/c/Chase0121.html
[507] http://www.tulane.edu/~latner/Chase.html
[508] http://www.mlwh.org/inside.asp?ID=86&subjectID=2
[509] http://www.mrlincolnandfreedom.org/inside.asp?ID=68&subjectID=4
[510] http://www.ca6.uscourts.gov/lib_hist/Courts/supreme/judges/chase/spc-bib.html
[511] http://www.ca6.uscourts.gov/lib_hist/Courts/supreme/judges/chase/spc-bio.html
[512] http://www.ca6.uscourts.gov/lib_hist/Courts/supreme/judges/chase/spc-lop.html
[513] Landis (2008)
[514] Rolde, Neal (1990). *Maine: A Narrative History*. Gardiner, ME: Harpswell Press. pp. 175. ISBN 0-88448-069-0.
[515] "Andrew Johnson Trial: The Consciences of Seven Republicans Save Johnson". http://law.jrank.org/pages/13490/Andrew-Johnson-Trial.html
[516] "The Trial of Andrew Johnson, 1868". http://www.eyewitnesstohistory.com/john.htm
[517] http://memory.loc.gov/cgi-bin/ampage?collId=llej&fileName=017/llej017.db&recNum=249
[518] http://www.questia.com/PM.qst?a=o&d=11883524
[519] http://bioguide.congress.gov/scripts/biodisplay.pl?index=F000099
[520] http://bioguide.congress.gov/scripts/guidedisplay.pl?index=F000099

[521] http://www.mlwh.org/inside.asp?ID=88&subjectID=2
[522] http://www.mlwh.org/inside.asp?ID=92&subjectID=2
[523] Bruce Adamson, *For Which We Stand; the Life of Rufus Easton*
[524] Lucy A. Delaney, *From the Darkness Cometh the Light: or Struggles for Freedom* http://docsouth.unc.edu/neh/delaney/delaney.html, St. Louis: J. T. Smith, 1891, Electronic edition, University of North Carolina, accessed 22 Apr 2009
[525] "Cabinet and Vice President: Edward Bates" http://www.mrlincolnswhitehouse.org/inside.asp?ID=83&subjectID=2, *Mr. Lincoln's White House*, The Lincoln Institute, 1999-2011, accessed 4 January 2011
[526] Dennis K. Boman, *Lincoln's Resolute Unionist: Hamilton Gamble, Dred Scott Dissenter and Missouri's Civil War Governor* http//books.google.com, Louisiana State University Press, 2006, pp. 1-7, accessed 26 February 2011
[527] http://bioguide.congress.gov/scripts/biodisplay.pl?index=B000231
[528] http://www.mlwh.org/inside.asp?ID=9&subjectID=2
[529] http://www.mrlincolnswhitehouse.org/inside.asp?ID=95&subjectID=2
[530] http://www.bryansbush.com/hub.php?page=articles&layer=a0710
[531] http://www.findagrave.com/cgi-bin/fg.cgi?page=gr&GRid=6984109
[532] Allan Nevins, *The War for the Union*, vol. 1: *The Improvised War, 1861-1862* (New York: Charles Scribner's Sons, 1959), p. 43.
[533] http://www.senate.gov/artandhistory/art/artifact/Painting_33_00005.htm
[534] Goodwin, 2005, Chapter 11.
[535] Goodwin, 2005, Chapter 24.
[536] http://www.mlwh.org/inside.asp?ID=84&subjectID=2
[537] http://www.mrlincolnandfriends.org/inside.asp?pageID=83&subjectID=7
[538] http://www.mrlincolnandfreedom.org/inside.asp?ID=67&subjectID=4
[539] http://www.findagrave.com/cgi-bin/fg.cgi?page=gr&GRid=2937
[540] http://members.tripod.com/mcvicker16/GovenorWilliiamDennison.htm
[541] http://www.findagrave.com/cgi-bin/fg.cgi?page=gr&GRid=10423
[542] "Obituary: Mrs. Gideon Welles" http://query.nytimes.com/mem/archive-free/pdf?_r=1&res=9B04E1DE1E38E033A25757C0A9659C94679FD7CF. New York Times. March 4, 1886. Retrieved 2010-08-21.
[543] Obituary: "Edgar T. Welles" http://query.nytimes.com/mem/archive-free/pdf?res=9C05EEDA153FE233A25750C2A96E9C946596D6CF *New York Times*. August 23, 1914.
[544] "The Navy's Medal of Honor" http://www.history.navy.mil/faqs/faq38-1.htm. Department of the Navy – Naval Historical Center. 30 October 2007. Retrieved 2010-08-21.
[545] Hale, p.113
[546] "Obituary: Gideon Welles" http://query.nytimes.com/mem/archive-free/pdf?res=9F01E3DA113FE63BBC4A52DFB4668383669FDE. New York Times. February 12, 1878. Retrieved 2010-08-21.
[547] Niven, p.6
[548] Norton, pp. 19-21
[549] Niven, p.7
[550] "Gideon Welles in ERA database" http://www.edmund-rice.org/era5gens/p37.htm#i350937. Edmund Rice (1638) Association, Inc.. Retrieved 15 March 2011.
[551] Niven, p.16
[552] "Gideon Welles papers, 1777-1911" http://hdl.loc.gov/loc.mss/eadmss.ms003053. Manuscript Division, Library of Congress. 1997, revised April 2010. Retrieved 2010-10-27.
[553] http://www.senate.gov/artandhistory/art/artifact/Painting_33_00005.htm
[554] Winters, p. 47
[555] Gideon Welles http://www.findagrave.com/cgi-bin/fg.cgi?page=gr&GRid=5993736 at Find A Grave
[556] http://books.google.com/books?id=jsdFt7XOr9QC&pg=PR26&dq=welles+diary&lr=#PPR3,M1
[557] http://books.google.com/books?id=Zaqe6XCgJsUC&pg=PA1&dq=welles+diary+%22volume+II%22

[558] http://books.google.com/books?id=4RGDUlZ-SREC&pg=PA1&dq=welles+diary+volume+III
[559] http//books.google.com
[560] http://www.mlwh.org/inside.asp?ID=200&subjectID=2
[561] http://www.history.navy.mil/danfs/w5/welles-i.htm
[562] http://www.wellesfamily.com/
[563] http://www.cslib.org/gov/wellest.htm
[564] http://www.forbes.com/2009/04/24/collecting-lincoln-valuable-lifestyle-collecting-lincoln.html
[565] http://www.senate.gov/artandhistory/art/artifact/Painting_33_00005.htm
[566] Sanford, pp. 392-93. In 1890 the Greenlawn Cemetery was closed.
[567] http://www.warrenlodge.org/elmhurst.html
[568] http://bioguide.congress.gov/scripts/biodisplay.pl?index=S000519
[569] http://www.findagrave.com/cgi-bin/fg.cgi?page=gr&GRid=7666329
[570] http://www.mlwh.org/inside.asp?ID=94&subjectID=2
[571] http://www.indianahistory.org/library/manuscripts/collection_guides/sc1359.html
[572] http://www.cr.nps.gov/history/online_books/utley-mackintosh/index.htm
[573] http//books.google.com
[574] This Consecrated Ground http://www.nps.gov/history/history/online_books/civil_war_series/16/sec20.htm
[575] Collected Works of Abraham Lincoln. Volume 8 http://quod.lib.umich.edu/l/lincoln/lincoln8/1:743?rgn=div1;sort=occur;subview=detail;type=simple;view=fulltext;q1=usher
[576] National Register Application http://pdfhost.focus.nps.gov/docs/NRHP/Text/75000710.pdf
[577] Burial Site http://www.findagrave.com/cgi-bin/fg.cgi?page=gr&GRid=10535
[578] http://www.mlwh.org/inside.asp?ID=98&subjectID=2
[579] http://www.cr.nps.gov/history/online_books/utley-mackintosh/index.htm

Article Sources and Contributors

The sources listed for each article provide more detailed licensing information including the copyright status, the copyright owner, and the license conditions.

Abraham Lincoln *Source:* http://en.wikipedia.org/w/index.php?oldid=457400332 *License:* Creative Commons Attribution-Share Alike 3.0 Unported *Contributors:* !melquiades, $1LENCE D00600D, (aeropagitica), (jarbarf), 07matmoo, 08brung, 123asd, 172, 1fingerwillie, 1up, 208.60.196.xxx, 23-03-33, 24.114.93.xxx, 36hourblock, 3ICE, 3in1, 842U, 8r13n, 95j, @pple, A bit iffy, AGC5445, AJseagull1, AKGhetto, ALargeElk, AP1787, Aaftabj, Aaron, Aaron Schulz, AaronY, Abe Lincoln, Abelincoln98, Abqsteve, Academic Challenger, Acdx, AceTeaser, Aclamicela, Acorrection, Acroterion, Adam Carr, Adam sk, Adashiel, Addshore, AdjustShift, Admikkelsen, AdrianoA, AdventureCaverns, Aeshir Aurion, Aetas-nex, Afterwriting, Agateller, Agathman, Agm1243, AgnosticPreachersKid, Agoodall, Ahoerstemeier, Ajstov, Akamad, Akerans, Alai, Alanscottwalker, Alansohn, Alanthwaits, Alethiophile, Alex Kinloch, Alex Middleton, Alex2706, AlexPlank, Alexle1992, Alexwilson101, Algernon Moncrieff, Alight, Alison, All Hallow's Wraith, Allen3, AlleywayRover, Allixpeeke, AllyUnion, Alpha Quadrant (alt), Alphachimp, Amakuru, American Eagle, AmericanCentury21, Americanadian, AmiDaniel, Amigo737, Amorrow, AnOddName, Anam Gumnam, Andkore, Andonic, Andreac, Andreas Kaganov, Andrevan, Andrew Kelly, Andrewlp1991, Andrewpmk, Android79, Andropod, Andy M. Wang, Andy Marchbanks, Andy120290, Andycjp, Andylinn, Andypandy.UK, Andyparkerson, Angela, Angelic Wraith, Angelofdeath275, Angusmclellan, Animum, Anna512, Anniika, AnonMoos, Anonymous Dissident, Anonymous editor, Antandrus, Antidote, Anton198, Antonrojo, Antranik, Anythingyouwant, Apeloverage, Apeman33, Apollomelos, Applebirthday, AquaTeen191, Aragupta, Arathjp, Arcadie, Arcdemonic, ArchStanton69, Archiver, Arfan, Ari Publican, Aris Katsaris, Arisa, Arknascar44, Arman88, Art LaPella, ArticleImprover, Artoasis, Ashimar, Asklepiades, AstroPig7, Astronautics, Astynax, AtStart, Atavi, Atilla5, Atlant, Atlpedia, AtticusX, Attucks, Aude, Auntof6, Ausir, Avicennasis, Avram Fawcett, Awesomeman7788, Awesomeman8822, Azslande, AzureSyaoran, B34ny, BBrad31, BD2412, BHS Sux, BRPXQZME, BWMSDogs, BWRatliff94, Babjie, BabyStabber, Badbilltucker, Badseed, Banes, Banjop, BanyanTree, Bardnet, Barneyboo, Baron von Chickenpants, Barrettmagic, Bart Versieck, BartBenjamin, Basketballlver22, Bastique, Batvette, Bayerischermann, Bbatsell, Bbsrock, Bcrowell, Bdesham, Beao, Bearcat, Beaster77, Beastmix, Beatle mop, Becker122, Becksguy, Before My Ken, Beidlerp, Bellczar, Belovedfreak, Ben Ben, Ben-Zin, Ben76266, Benandorsqueaks, BenjaminTsai, Benjimonkeyface, Bennettsnider, Bentley4, Berean Hunter, Berkut, Betacommand, Betos01, Betsyk, Bettymnz4, Bevelw, Bevo, Bevo873, Bhadani, Bhuck, Bidabadi, Bigjake, Bigmama123, Bigtimepeace, Bigturtle, Bill Trantham, Bill37212, BillTunell, Billare, Billy Hathorn, Binabik80, Biogcontrib109, BirdKr, Biruitorul, BismarckTheIronChancellor, Bkonrad, Bla Bla Boy, Blackhawk003, Blackthunder326, Blahaccountblah, Blake222, BlankVerse, Blasphemous, BlastOButter42, Blayrp, Blightsoot, Blood sliver, BloodGrapefruit2, Blowski, BlueAg09, BlueMoonlet, Bluezy, Blulull, BobTheTomato, Bobamnertiopsis, Bobblewik, Bobet, Boblikepie, Bobo192, Bodenner, Bogdangiusca, Bongwarrior, Boo100, Boo1210, Bored portal, Borisblue, Bosox24, Bostbart, Bostonian Mike, Boudiccat, BovineBeast, Brad101, Bratsche, Brett2829, Briaboru, Brian Kendig, Brian0918, Brian1979, BrianGV, BrianHansen, BrokenSegue, BrownHairedGirl, Brozhnik, Bryan Derksen, Btbrickner, BubbleGumGrrl86, BuddyJesus, BuffaloBob, BugeyeMcGee, Bull Market, BullRangifer, Bulldog73, Bumslaw, Bunkermikaela, Burroughsks88, BusterD, Bytwerk, C45207, CAPS LOCK, CBDunkerson, CGSwimmer101, CIreland, CJ, CJLL Wright, CLW, CPMcE, CSWarren, CTSWyneken, Cactus Wren, Cactus.man, CalicoCatLover, Calicore, Califa22651, Calm Seas101, Calmypal, CambridgeBayWeather, Camden123, Camillus McElhinney, Can't sleep, clown will eat me, CanadianCaesar, Canihaveacookie, CantStandYa, CapitalR, Capnned, Caponer, CaptainChurch, Carabinieri, Caracaskid, Carajou, CardinalDan, Carl.bunderson, Carlw4514, CarpeCerevisium, Carptrash, Carstodm, Catbar, Cathytreks, Causesobad, Cb6, Cbrodersen, Cburnett, Cdc, Cdml1975, Cdoesche81, Cenarium, Centereagle, Centrx, Ceranthor, Certaindeath127, Cgingold, Ch'marr, ChEsKake, Chamberlain63, Chanting Fox, Chaostails, Charleenmerced, Charles Edward, CharlesGillingham, ChazBeckett, CheckeredFlag200, Cheesehead Fan, CheetahEBI, Chensiyuan, ChessPlayer, Chica995, Chiefmartinez, Chikinpotato11, Childzy, Chitt66, Chocolatethunda69, Choster, Chowbok, Chowells, Chris Capoccia, Chris is me, Chrisn4255, Christofurio, Christopher Parham, ChristopherWillis, Chuck Carroll, Cilibinarii, Cindamuse, Citicat, Civil Engineer III, Ckatz, Cladeal832, ClamDip, Clarityfiend, Claude girardin, Cleared as filed, Closedmouth, Cloud109, Cmb0219, Cmdrjameson, Cmguy777, Cnairne, Coelacan, Coemgenus, Coldness, Collin0320, Comemitmier, CommonsDelinker, Complex (de), Computerjoe, Connelly, Connormah, Conny, Contaldo80, Conversion script, Cookie8191, Coolfrood, Corax, Cori.schlegel, Corlen, Cornince, Courcelles, Cowboyfromhell6054, Cowmanlightsaber, Crash Underride, Crazycomputers, Crazymonkey1123, Crazytales, Crocmike24, Crotchety Old Man, CrucifiedChrist, Cryptic, Cryptic C62, CryptoDerk, Csari, Cubs Fan, Cuchullain, Curiouscdngeorge, Curps, Cwcarlson, Cwilson336, Cyberevil, Cyclone231, CylonCAG, Cymsdale, D6, DESiegel, DEmerson3, DGJM, DINNERS4SUCKERSS, DIREKTOR, DJ Clayworth, DL79OL, DLJessup, DLMahnken, DOSGuy, DRosenbach, DVD R W, DaAnHo, Dabomb87, Dadsawq3, Dadthelawyer, Dale Arnett, DaltinWentsworth, Dan100, Dana boomer, Daniel, Daniel J. Leivick, Daniel Olsen, Daniel Quinlan, Daniel Simanek, Daniel,levine, DanielCD, Danielfolsom, Dank, Danny, Dantheman2007, Dar-Ape, Darcrist, DarkFalls, Darkmega42, Darkwarz, Darkwind, Darth Kalwejt, Darth Panda, DarthBinky, DaughterofSun, Davemcarlson, Daven200520, David Gerard, David H. Flint, David Justin, David.Mestel, DavidFarmbrough, DavidH, DavidOaks, Davidcannon, Davidhein, Dbtfz, Dcamp314, Dcflyer, Dcoetzee, Dcsohl, De Moriarty, DeAceShooter, DeanHinnen, Deathphoenix, Deb, Debresser, Deckiller, Decumanus, Dedalus, Defyconformity, Dekisugi, DeknMike, Delldot, Delta x, Democraticsystem, Den fjättrade ankan, DennisPNorman, DerHexer, Deskana, Deville, Deweyfamily, Deyyaz, Dgrade69, Dhbr, Dialoguejournal, Dicforeabe, Diegomgarcia, Digitalme, Diligent Terrier, Dimadick, Dino, Dinopup, Dirtyman101, Dirtyvampire, Discobandit98, Discospinster, Dispenser, Ditka, Djma12, Djsunzi, Dm46607, Dmerthe, Doc glasgow, Dococe, Dodiad, Doktorschley, Dondavide, Donkeyballs, Donnie Love, DooGooder, Doprendek, DorkButton, Dotcolin95, DoubleBlue, Dougie monty, Dovid, Downey360, Dpbsmith, Dppowell, Dr who1975, Dr. Dan, Draco249, DragonflySixtyseven, Dralwik, Dreamrabbit, Drexlerlk, Drgonzo321, Drilnoth, Drmies, Droob, Drpickem, DrunkenSmurf, Dryke, Drz1627, Dsmdgold, Dual Freq, DubaiTerminator, Dudegoogle, Dudeman5685, Dudesleeper, Dugwiki, Duke of Kent, Duke904311, DuncanHill, Dungodung, Durga rulz, Durin, Durova, Dwcsite, Dwheeler, Dycedarg, Dyingdreams, DÅ‚ugosz, EDM, EDUCA33E, EKMichigan, ESkog, EagleEye1303, EagleFalconn, Easter Monkey, Eastfrisian, Eatchomp, Eco-Mono, Ecopirate, Ecorwin, Ed Poor, Ed g2s, EdHalstram, Edeans, Edgar181, Edgester, Editor182, Editor911, Edivorce, Edward, Edwy, Eegorr, Effsee, Egk14@juno.com, Ehardman80, Ehistory, Ejile, Ejstarchuk, El C, ElKevbo, Eldredo, Electrified mocha chinchilla, Electron9, Eleos, Eliteowner, Elkman, Ellmist, Elmmapleoakpine, Emijrp, Emoabe, Enbob89, Engineer Bob, Englatar8888, Engleham, Enosfam, Entirelybs, Enviroboy, Environnement2100, Eoghanacht, Epicadam, Eppmur divad, EpsilonJSTC, Equinox137, Er-vet-en, Eric119, Ericamick, Esanchez7587, Esteele, Estiv, Ettenro, Eubulides, Euchiasmus, Eutychus, Evercat, EveryDayJoe45, Everyking, Evil Monkey, Evil mcnuggets, Evil saltine, EvocativeIntrigue, Excirial, Exoir, Extermino, Exvicious, Ezeu, FCYTravis, FF2010, Fact check, Fahrgo, Faithlessthewonderboy, Falcon8765, FallOutBoyLuvur, Fang Aili, Fanman904, Farmer22, Fastily, Fat pig73, Faustus37, Favonian, FeanorStar7, Feezo, Ferdinand Pienaar, Fergy122, Ferix, Fetchcomms, Feydey, Fhavenvt, FiggyBee, Fightfightfight, FigmentJedi, FinFangFoom, Finetooth, Finlay McWalter, Finngall, Fireplace, Firespread3, FisherQueen, Fizbin, Fkr, Flcelloguy, Flockmeal, Florentino floro, Floria L, Flubbit, Foofighter20x, Footballexpert, Fotoguzzi, Fram, Francs2000, Freakofnurture, Fred J, Freddieandthedreamers, Freedomlinux, Freepablo, FreplySpang, Friday, Frietjes, Frymaster, Funandtrvl, Func, Funnybunny, Funnyhat, Fuzheado, Fuzzyblob, Fvw, Fys, G Clark, GB fan, GCarty, GDonato, GHe, GIR, GK, GOD ACRONYM, GXSilver, Gabbe, Gael, Gaff, Gagamela, Gaius Cornelius, Gamaliel, Gammaknight, Gammistparty, Garion96, Garret Beaumain, Garrett54540, Gary King, Gaviidae, Gaytan, Gazpacho, Gbraing, GenQuest, General Veers, Geni, Georgette2, Gerchak3, Geriand, Getaway, Gettingtoit, Ghollingsworth, GhostofSuperslum, Gidonshaviv, Gilliam, Gillis, Gimboid13, Gimmetrow, Gizmonicgamer, Globalearth, Glory311, Gmags2003, Gmaxwell, Go54321, GoLeafsGo2626, Godvideogamer, Goetter, Gogo Dodo, GoingBatty, Golbez, GoldRingChip, Goldface, Good Intentions, Good Olfactory, GoodDay, Goodoldpolonius2, Googie man, Goosesg, Gorgoth0, Gorilla Jones, Gorrister, Gracenotes, GraemeL, Graham87, Grammarspellchecker, Grant 93, Grantmidnight, Grapplequip, Grazon, Greatal386, Greatestrowerever, Green caterpillar, Gregory j, Gremio, Grenavitar, Greswik, GringoInChile, Griot, GrouchyDan, Ground, Groundsquirrel13, Grover cleveland, Grr, Grsz11, Grunge6910, Grunt, Gtbob12, Gtrmp, Guanaco, Guersk, Gugilymugily, Gumbini, Gurch, GusF, Guy546, Guy91, GuyDoe, Guyom, Gwen Gale, Gwillhickers, H.J., HJ32, Hadal, Hajor, HalJor, HalfShadow, Hall Monitor, Hamburgler69, Hamiltondaniel, HandGrenadePins, Hanse, Happy138, HappyJake, Happyme22, Harayda, Harej, Harris43, Harris7, Harro5, Harryboyles, Harrynyc, Hartfelt, Haru24, Has164, Hats1$, Haukurth, Hawkestone, Hazard-SJ, Headbomb, Heaven12345, Heavyrunner, Hectard, HeeroYuiX, Heimstern, HeinzzzderMannn, Hekerui, Henry Flower, HenryLi, Hephaestos, Herschel, Herschelkrustofsky, Hertz1888, Hgrenbor, Higherededitor2, Hilltoppers, Hinze, Hlj, Hmains, Homagetocatalonia, Homes83189, Honette, Honker, Hoponpop69, Hoppyh, Hoshie, House Boy, HowardDean, HowardJWilk, Hqb, Hstrybff, Hu12, Hudsoncasiple, HughGRex, Humanman42, HunterDx777, Hushpuckena, Hut 8.5, HutchWilco, Hydriotaphia, Hégésippe Cormier, I like to change stuff..., ILuvTea, IU2002, IXella007, Iamunknown, Icairns, Icehomie417, Idols of Mud, Ikh, Improved, InShaneee, Indexme, IndieJones, Indochinese man, Indon, Infamous30, Infrogmation, Ingolfson, Inner Earth, Intangible, Into The Fray, Invader Chason 123456, Inwind, Ipatrol, Iridescent, Irishguy, Irishtatterz, IronDuke, Irregulargalaxies, Isababe, Ish ishwar, Isis, Isokrates, Italiandevil0505, Italianman, Italus, IvoShandor, Ixfd64, J Di, J M Rice, JCGentry, JCO312, JEDCJT, JEHCubsrule, JForget, JFreeman, JGHowes, JHMM13, JHP, JHunterJ, JJstroker, JNeal, JONJONAUG, JRM, JSmith9579, JTBX, JW1805, JYolkowski, Jaanussilla, Jacek Kendysz, Jack O'Lantern, Jack turnip, Jack248, JackofOz, Jacoplane, Jaganath, Jajhill, Jak86, Jakeandtd, Jakeboritt, James Arboghast, Janeky, Janus Shadowsong, Jao, Jaranda, Jaredwt13, Jason Gastrich, Jason M, Jason Potter, Jauhienij, Java13690, Java7837, Javaweb, Jaxl, Jay, JayJasper, Jayenes, Jayjg, Jaysweet, Jbarfield, Jc713, Jcrocker15, Jdaw4210, Jdlyahiko23, Jdoniach, Jeepday, Jeff G., Jeff810, Jeffd187, Jeffrey O. Gustafson, Jengod, Jenlight, Jenniferlong, Jeremy Bentham, JeremyA, Jeremymahoney, Jersey Devil, Jess567, Jessblp, Jesse.kelly, JesseHogan, Jesster79, Jesusfreekao, Jezar, Jfknrh, Jguk, Jh51681, Jhendin, Jhutchluva, Jiang, Jiddisch, Jim Michael, JimGar, JimWae, Jimerb, Jimmuldrow, Jimmy historian, Jimwal54, Jinian, Jinxed, JjJjJjC, Jjb, Jjjccc, Jjmillerhistorian, Jjpepper, Jjron, Jklin, Jliberty, Jmcbean69, JoanneB, Joao.caprivi, Joe512, JoeBlogsDord, JoeSmack, Joedeshon, Joelr31, John 61912, John ISEM, John K, John Paul Parks, JohnC, JohnClay, JohnJHenderson, JohnSawyer, JohnWinterMadisonSouthDakota, JohnWittle, Johndoe316, Johnhardcastl, Johnissoevil, Johnleemk, Johnny carson, Johnnybriggs, Johnnyhoward, Jojhutton, Jon Awbrey, Jonathunder, Jopa00, Jorvik, Joseph Solis in Australia, Joshbuddy, Joshdboz, Joshmaul, Joshthek,

Josias Bunsen, Jossi, Joyous!, Jpepper, Jpers36, Jpgordon, Jprg1966, Jradke, Jrcrin001, Jreferee, Jrkarp, Jrtayloriv, Jtdirl, Jtkiefer, Juggleandhope, Juliancolton, Jupiter Fire, JustPhil, Jwissick, K61824, KHirsch, Kafziel, Kaiser matias, Kaldari, Kalmia, Kane5187, Kaptincapo, Karanacs, Katalaveno, Katya0133, Katydidit, Kauffner, Kazvorpal, Kbdank71, Kbh3rd, Kbi911, Kchishol1970, Kcurtin, Ke4roh, Kelapstick, Kenatipo, Kendrick7, Kenny-r-r, Kerttie, Ketchup krew, Kevin B12, Kevin Myers, Kfont, Kfreeland, Kgrad, Khmoro99, Khukri, Kiba67, Kida6000, Killa Kitty, Killerflowers, Kimon, King 00007, King 0007, King DeaN, King of Hearts, Kingdon, Kingturtle, Kinneyboy90, Kisch, Kittykat2010, Kjzenn, Kkm010, KnowledgeOfSelf, Knucmo2, Knulpd, Koavf, Kolyavmk, Korath, Kornfan12100, Kossack4Truth, Kotniski, Kotra, Krakatoa, Kranar drogin, Kratos3895, Krich, Kross, Krs5603, Ksargent, Kstingily, Kukini, Kumioko, Kungfuadam, Kuru, Kurykh, Kusma, Kwamikagami, Kyros, LOL, La goutte de pluie, LaDanza, LaggedOnUser, Lairor, Lalalala7789, Lampman, Larast, LarryGilbert, Latics, Lcarscad, LeContexte, Lectonar, Ledzeppelin321295, Leebo, Leemfrank, LegCircus, Legoboy2000, Lenoxus, Leolaursen, Leon7, Leujohn, Levelistchampion, Levineps, Lewis246, Lexicon, Lhb1239, Liamdaly620, LifeStar, LightSpectra, Lightdarkness, Lightmouse, Lights, Lightstarsleaderdarkstar, Ligulem, Lilosi, Lincher, Lindsay658, Ling.Nut, Liptonicetea, Lir, Lisam1, Little Mountain 5, Living large, Lnh27, Localmopeder24, Lockeheed, Lockesdonkey, Logoskakou, LonelyMarble, LonelyPilgrim, LonesomeDrifter, Longhair, Loodog, Looper5920, Looxix, Lord Valanx, LordCodeman, LordHarris, Lordthees, Lotusduck, Loveshoes, Lowellian, Luigifan, Luna Santin, Lupin, Lupo, M dorothy, M.O.X, M.nelson, MBK004, MC MasterChef, MC10, MD87, MDolson22, MECU, MELWOOD, MER-C, MK, MONGO, MSGJ, MZMcBride, MacTire02, Macgregorc, Mad2rox, MadMax, Madchester, Maddenplayer, Magicpiano, Magioladitis, Magister Mathematicae, Magnus Manske, Mailer diablo, Makemi, Malarious, Malber, Malcolm Farmer, Malo, Maltmomma, Malvolio80, Mangoe, Manning Bartlett, Manticore126, Manuel Trujillo Berges, Manushand, Marc9510000, Marcika, Marcus2, MarcusGraly, Mareino, Mario and Zelda Nut, Mark Sublette, Markmor57277, Marktreut, Markvo, Markwiki, MarmadukePercy, Marnik, Martin451, MartinDK, Martious, Master Jay, Matijap, Matt Yeager, Matt smoke, Mattabat, Mattis, Mattsenate, Mattweng, Mauratanner, Mav, Max Powers, Max conformist, MaxEnt, Maxamegalon2000, Maximus Rex, Maybellyne, Mayorcheese, Mayumashu, Mboverload, McNeight, Mcarling, Mdd, Me9292, MeNext, MearsMan, Mebden, Meelar, MegaSloth, Meggy-Eggy-Head, Memotype, Mendaliv, Merotoker1, Merovingian, Messenger boi, Metalhead94, Meteorit, Methnor, Mets501, Miamilake, Michael Devore, Michael L. Kaufman, Michael Snow, MichaelJE2, Michaelmross, Michaeltmccorkle, Midnight12, Miguellarios, Mike 7, Mike Garcia, Mike Rosoft, Mike-Kerkhoven, Mikestone8, Miliberty, MillerRotary, Minesweeper, Minnecologies, Minnesotatwins15, Mipsi75, MisfitToys, Misortie, Mistercow, Mjmarcus, Mkbk91, Mkpumphrey, Mlet, Mmortal03, Mmxx, Mocko13, Mogden, Mogden92, Mohsinwaheed, Moncubus, Monegasque, Moni3, Monkeyjb1988, Monkeyman, MookieZ, Mooman820, Moondyne, Moormand, Moreschi, Morevisit, Morhange, Morwen, Motorneuron, Moverton, Mpolick, Mr Adequate, MrBudDude, MrFish, MrWhich, MrZeebo, Mrwilly123, Mrwojo, Mschlindwein, Msclguru, Msm2007, Mssgill, Mstahl, MuZemike, Muboshgu, Muchness, Muddb, Muhandis, Mulad, Mulder416, Mullibok, Mumpsy, Musical Linguist, Mutableye, Mvincec, Mwanner, Mysdaao, Mystalic, Mythbound, NB-NB, NSLE, Nach0king, Najoj, Nakon, Nambladude, NameIsRon, Namekal, Naraht, Nat Krause, Natalie Erin, Nateinbliss, NativeForeigner, NawlinWiki, Naysie, Nbaxley, Negasable, Nehrams2020, NeilCoughlin, Neilc, Nemmons, Nessim99, Netoholic, Neutrality, Newmanbe, Newportm, Newyorkbrad, Nfgii, Nfleming, Nformoso, NicholasSThompson, Nick81, Nickel Lad, Nickvaughn49, Nicolas Begley, Nietzsche 2, NightCrawler, Nightscream, Nikkimaria, Nilli, Nima1024, Nirvana77, Nishkid64, Nivix, Nizamarain, Nkayesmith, Nlu, Nmg20, No Guru, NoSeptember, Noah Peters, Noclador, Noelle343, Noitall, Nomadre, Nommonomanac, Norm mit, NormaPierce, Noroton, North Shoreman, Northmeister, NovaTabula, Nsigniacorp, Nterage, Nubsnubbed, NuclearWarfare, Nufy8, Nunh-huh, Nut-meg, Nuttish, Nv8200p, Nymf, O p e t h, ONEder Boy, Octavian history, Odin 85th gen, Odoyle5150, Offtheheezy, Ohconfucius, Ohiowa, Ohnoitsjamie, OldEmpire, Olir, Olleicua, Olorin28, Omegaespeon, Omegatron, Omicronpersei8, Onekopaka, Onenex1000, Oneoffedit, Onexblackgoodbye, Oni Ookami Alfador, Onorem, Opaldragon1, Opelio, OpenToppedBus, Optim, Orangemike, OrbitOne, Orpheus, OuroborosCobra, OutRIAAge, Owen, OwenX, P-TownLegit, PAL1809, PFHLai, PJM, Packerfansam, Palantini, Pammysue, Pandaman829, Pandaslayer69, Pandawatch321, Panserbjorn, Panther502002, Paradox4600, Parallel or Together?, Parkwells, Pascal.Tesson, Patcambias, Pathoschild, Paul Arnott, Paul August, Paul Erik, Pegasus1138, PenComputingPerson, Pennylover, Pepsidrinka, Peregrine Fisher, Perey, Peripitus, Permethius, Persian Poet Gal, Peruvianllama, Peter, Peterklevy, Pfalstad, Pg2114, Pgk, Phaedriel, Phantomsteve, Phatcat68, Phenz, Phil Boswell, PhilKnight, Philip Stevens, Philip Trueman, Philippe, PhotoBox, Photohistorian, Phuzion, Physchim62, Picaroon, Pigsonthewing, Pilcrow, Pilotguy, Pioneer-12, Pitt, Pizzaghost, Pjbflynn, Plasticspork, Plasticup, Plastikspork, PlatinumX, Please Don't Block, Pmmenneg, Pmsyyz, Pointlessforest, Poitypoity, Poiuyhjk, Pokemon1989, Politepunk, Pollinator, Polynova, PonileExpress, Porqin, Postdlf, Poulsen, Preetkamal metla, PresN, President Rhapsody, Preslethe, Prez2016, Pridian, Private Butcher, Priyanath, Prolog, Propaniac, Protostan, Psantora, Pscott22, PseudoRichard, PseudoSudo, Psy guy, Ptfreak, Puchiko, Purplebackpack89, Qaddosh, Qqqqqq, Qrc2006, Qtoktok, Quadell, Quagga, Quarl, Que-Can, Quebec99, Qutezuce, Qwe, RFerreira, RG2, RJASE1, RJII, RMc, RTFlemingWhit, RaCha'ar, Raazman, RadclyffeHall, RadioFan, RadioKirk, Radman219, Radzinski, Rainbowkage, Rajah, Rake, Ral315, Rambone, Ramneek, Rande M Sefowt, Randy Johnston, Randy Kryn, RandySavageFTW, Randyc, Rangerdude, Rangilo Gujarati, Rasheed3036, Ratchet213, Raul654, Ravenhull, Rayven the Crook, Rbuicki, Rdsmith4, Realm of Shadows, RebirthThom, Redd Baron1, RedneckCSA15, Redthoreau, Redwarz, Redwasp889, Reedy, Republicofjosh01, Resavednineteen, Ret3, Rethgryn, Retiono Virginian, Retired username, Rettetast, Review california64, Revolución, RexNL, Reywas92, Rfernand, Rfl, Rhatsa26X, Rhion, Rhobite, Rhythm, Rich Farmbrough, Richard Arthur Norton (1958-), Richard L. Peterson, Richard75, RichardF, Richdoss, RickK, Ridan, Riganomic, Rito Revolto, Riurik, Riverstepstonegirl, Rj, Rjd0060, Rjensen, Rjwilmsi, Rklawton, Rmerik, Rmhainlen, Rmhermen, Rmky87, Rnedbal, Rob Hooft, RobLa, Robby, RobertG, Robertgreer, Robertsteadman, Robocon, Roc2120, Rocastelo, Rocknrollanoah, Rodhullandemu, Rodney Boyd, Rogerd, Rogered, Rogsheng, Rollinsk, RonaldMcDonald, Rontrigger, Rorschach, Rory096, Rosemaryamey, Rosspz, Rougher07, RoyBoy, RoyV, Royalguard11, Royboycrashfan, Rreagan007, Rshane, Rugbyhelp, RugerMK1, RussBlau, Rutherfordjigsaw, RxS, RyanCross, Ryanislegend, Ryoji.kun, S davis, S. Ditry, SDJ, SFrank85, SJL III, SMasters, SNIyer1, SNIyer12, ST47, SVera1NY, SWTR, SabineCretella, Sahasrahla, Sailboatd2, Saintjimmy777, Saladbar, SallyForth123, Saltwynd110, SaltyPig, Sam, Sam Korn, Sammy Houston, Samside101, Samsonite07, SamuraiClinton, Sandhillcrane, SandyGeorgia, Sango123, Saphiralite, Sarazip1, Sardanaphalus, Saruwine, Saviorof scottland, Scaife, Scarian, Sceptre, Scewing, Schadigung, Scharb, SchuminWeb, Schzmo, Scientizzle, Scifiintel, Sciurinæ, Scm83x, Scmods, Scohoust, Scotia Scotia, Scott Mingus, Scott Sanchez, Scottperry, Scottydude, Screamorox, Scrubby, Scubadiver99, Sdornan, Seaalm, Sean William, Search4Lancer, Searchme, Seckelberry, SecretAgentMan00, Seicer, Selket, Selmo, Semperfid, Seraphimblade, Sesu Prime, Seth Ilys, Sethsetsfire, Settler, Sfahey, Shabbirraju, Shadow2700, Shadowjams, Shaizakopf, Shanel, Shanes, ShaunES, ShelfSkewed, Sherlock1016, Shiakazee.1, Shicoco, Shimmera, Shizhao, Shoaler, Shoeofdeath, Shsilver, Siber79, SickWilly, Sietse Snel, Signinstranger, Silander, Silarnon, Silverhorse, Silversink, Simon Beavis, SimonATL, SimonD, SimonP, SineWave, Sinead ate your baby, Sinisterscrawl, Sinn, Sintonak.X, Sir Richardson, Sir Samuel, Siroxo, Sjakkalle, Skizzik, Slambo, Sligocki, SlimVirgin, Slippery Mudhills, Slowking Man, Smart Fox, Smedley Hirkum, Smee, Smeggles, Smelialichu, Smoothpenatratingwind, Smurrayinchester, SnappingTurtle, Snarklesnappleblast, Snowdog, Soccermay26, Sogospelman, Solipsist, Solitude, Some thing, SomeGuy11112, Someguy1221, Someoneinmyheadbutit'snotme, Sonjaaa, Sonnenberg99, Sortior, Soxwon, Spacestar8765, Spangineer, Spartan55, Spartaprince, Sperm123, Spittips101, Splash, Splat, Spliffy, Splintermonkey2, Spoocky, SpookyMulder, Spotty11222, SpuriousQ, Sputnikcccp, Squidd, Srcrowl, Srich32977, Srikeit, Srushe, Ssiruuk25, Staceyerdman, Stakelover, Stanleyfisher, Starbane, Starnestommy, Steel, Stefanomione, SteinbDJ, Stephanolmedo, Stephen Deken, Stephenb, Stephoswalk, Steve03Mills, Steve112, Steve2011, Steve64, Stevertigo, Stevewk, Steviedanger2, Stevietheman, Stewie814, Stickee, Sticky Parkin, Stilgar135, Sting au, Stix9693, Storm Rider, StradivariusTV, Stubblyhead, Student7, Studerby, Stupidjuice, Sundog61, Sunnyboi14, Sunray, SuperNova, Superdude99, Superneoking, Supersima, Supertask, Suruena, SusanLesch, Susurrus, Suvablee0506, Svenares, Sverdrup, Swedenman, SweetcocaJ, Swimmeringer, Symane, Syrthiss, Syvanen, T-bonham, TEO-emo12, TGC55, TOttenville8, Tabletop, Tabortiger, Tad Lincoln, Takethemud, Talfethag7, Tangotango, Tannin, Tapir Terrific, Taras, Tatarize, Tawheatley, Tawker, Taxman, Taylor3150, Tbhotch, Tcvanp3570, TechPurism, Ted Wilkes, Tedder, Tellyaddict, TenPoundHammer, Texas David, TexasAndroid, Texture, Tghe-retford, The Commuter, The Cunctator, The Duke of Waltham, The Epopt, The Letter J, The Little Blue Frog, The Man72, The Mystery Man, The Rogue Penguin, The Twenty Thousand Tonne Bomb, The Utahraptor, The Wordsmith, The masterpedia, The stuart, The tooth, The undertow, The wub, TheBlazikenMaster, TheDJ, TheEemingTree, TheKMan, TheRanger, Theblueaquabat, Thebss, Thecurran, Theda, Theodork, Thepignut, Therealsquee, Therequiembellishere, Theshibboleth, Thewellman, Thinduck, Thingg, Thinking of England, This user has left wikipedia, Thiseye, Thivierr, Thizz1011, Thmcmahon, Thomas Gilling, Thomas Paine1776, ThomasK, Thorn in Side, Thorsmitersaw, Threeafterthree, Thue, Thylacine lover, Tide rolls, TigerShark, Tim010987, Timberlax, Timothy Muggli, Timrem, Timwi, TiroDeAethra, Tiroth, Tito4000, Titoxd, Tjr4, Tmangray, Tmoney2677, Tmopkisn, Toliet347, Tom, Tom harrison, Tomas417, Tomlillis, Tommy2010, TommyBoy, Tomseb, Tony Sidaway, TonySt, TonyTheTiger, Toocool6814, Toonmon2005, TorynHill, Toussaint, Toya, Tpbradbury, Tpetross, Tradnor, Trainmanlars, Trampton, Traumerei, Tree Biting Conspiracy, Trevor GH5, Trevor MacInnis, Treybien, Trfasulo, Tricky Victoria, Trin23, Tripssouth, Trödel, Tstockma, Tsusurfanami, Tuneman42, Tupac 2, Tyrano, Tyrol5, UBeR, Ucanlookitup, Uga Man, Ugur Basak, Ujm90, UkPaolo, Ukabia, Ukgreg, Ultraexactzz, Ulysse2000, Uncle Dick, Unimaginative Username, Unitanode, UnitedStatesIndia, UnitedStatesian, Unschool, Useight, User F203, User2004, Uskerdoo, Utmandafodio, VMS Mosaic, Vampirehunter45, Vanais, Vanished user, Vary, VegaDark, Vegaswikian, Veniceslug1, Ventur, Vera Cruz, Verde Flash, Vfp15, Vgy7ujm, Vicki Rosenzweig, Victuallers, Vidor, Vilerage, Viridae, Viriditas, ViriiK, VolatileChemical, Voldemort, Volumerocks, Von Tamm, Voyagerfan5761, Vrenator, Vsan94, Vsmith, Vzbs34, Vzlj, W377!M, WCityMike, WJBscribe, WTF23434, Wachholder0, Wafflepjs, Wahabijaz, Walidatwell, Wandering Ghost, Warfvinge, Wars, Wavelength, Wayne, Waynem, Wayward, Wcquidditch, Webnet, Websterkntz7, Well, girl, look at you!, Weniswenis, Wereon, Werideatdusk33, Wetman, Weyes, Where, WhisperToMe, Whoop whoop pull up, Why Not A Duck, Wifione, Wik, WikHead, Wikasmart, Wiki Girl 234, Wiki alf, Wiki-art-name, WikiLaurent, Wikiacc, Wikibob, Wikidea, Wikifier, Wikiklrsc, Wikilibrarian, Wikisux, Wikster72, Wildhartlivie, Will Beback, Will Beback Auto, Will2k, WillC, WillMak050389, Willarthur32, William Beckett, William Loeb, William S. Saturn, William Saturn, Williamevoss, Williebaz, Williebone, Wilt, Wimt, Windyjarhead, Winhunter, Wisco, Wjhonson, Wkerney, Wknight94, Wmahan, Wmannin4, Wonkothesane42, Woodykass, Woohookitty, Word to Mother, World, Writtenright, Wshs315, Wtmgeo, Wtmitchell, Wutizevrybudylookingat?, X1a4muse, X3210, Xaosflux, Xenophon777, Xezbeth, Xgmx, Xiahou, Xiner, Xogns, Xoloz, Xyzzyplugh, Y1234567890, Y2kcrazyjoker4, Yaf, Yakle, Yamamoto Ichiro, YankeeDoodle14, Yannickbrant, Yappers, Yeaforme, Yellow Rain, YellowMonkey, Yelyos, Yepmatt@hotmail.com, Yllosubmarine, Yojimbo312, YolanCh, Yoteshio, Youandme, Youdontsmellbad, Yougo1000, Yuliya1887, Yump12345, Zachary Klaas, Zakkuro, Zanimum, Zanshin, Zaui, Zaurus, Zeimusu, ZekeMacNeil, ZenCopian, ZeroOne, Zetterberg40, ZincOrbie, Zoe, Zoso, Zsinj, Zzuuzz, Zzyzx11, Zzzelch, ריינהארט, לערי 3144 anonymous edits 3

Hannibal Hamlin *Source:* http://en.wikipedia.org/w/index.php?oldid=456594713 *License:* Creative Commons Attribution-Share Alike 3.0 Unported *Contributors:* A.C. Norman, AKGhetto, Adavidb, AdjustShift, Aitias, AlanK, Alex2706, Allen3, Altenmann, Annalise, Annie May, Anomalocaris, Ashley Pomeroy, Astynax, BMRR, Badbilltucker, Bbsrock, Blakecarlile, Blowedupt, Bob frasier, Bobblehead, Bobblewik, Bobo192, Burzmali, Buskahegian, BusterD, Canuckian89, CardinalDan, Charles Matthews, Choster, Chris the speller, Chrisn4255, Clasqm, Coachb68, Connormah, ContiAWB, Conversion script, Crazydjman, D6, DLJessup, DanMS, Danny, Davidcannon, Dimitris, Discospinster, Dk1965, Dodiad, Dominus, Donner60, Doulos Christos, Dralwik,

Dudeman5685, Durova, Dysepsion, East718, Edton, Eggy49er, Elipongo, Emops, Emperorbma, Escape Orbit, Everyking, Floydspinky71, Foofighter20x, Fram, FrankMJohnson, Freakmighty, Funnyhat, GateKeeper, Gbr3, GcSwRhIc, Generalkookypants, Gilliam, Gmcd, Golbez, GoldRingChip, Good Olfactory, GoodDay, Gtstricky, Gurch, HHamlin, Harland1, Hmains, Iamwisesun, Ithacagorges, J.delanoy, JCGentry, JClark4626, JForget, Jack Cox, Jajhill, Javaweb, JayJasper, Jengod, Jetman, Jim2710, Joal Beal, John K, Jojhutton, Josejuan.Blanco10, Jtdirl, Kas1234, KathodeRay, Ken Gallager, Koavf, Krazykenny, KuatofKDY, Kumioko, Kungfuadam, Lee Daniel Crocker, Lightmouse, LonelyBeacon, Lst27, Luna Santin, MAINEiac4434, MK, Madeline K, Madelmutter, Mark Heiden, MarkSweep, Mary-Christ, Massimo Macconi, Maximillion Pegasus, Mendaliv, Mentifisto, MiFeinberg, Mighty Lord And King, Mikebar, Million Moments, Minesweeper, Monegasque, NL-Ninane, Namiba, NathanoNL, NatureA16, Neutrality, Newyorkbrad, NlynchN, Olivier, Oregonrains, Paleorthid, Pitchka, Pomf26651, Possum, Postdlf, Pres-scholar, R'n'B, RadioKirk, Rajah, RandySavageFTW, Rasheed3036, Rich Farmbrough, Richard75, Roadrunner, Robertgreer, Rodkovel, Rrburke, Ryan Roos, Sardanaphalus, SarekOfVulcan, Schmerguls, Schmiteye, SchreyP, Scott Mingus, Semperf, Shelllbyl, SidP, Stephennarmstrong, Stephensuleeman, Stepp-Wulf, Stormyhawn, Tahu199397, Tedickey, Template namespace initialisation script, The Mystery Man, TheMaestro, Tide rolls, Tihanyi Joci, Tom, TonyTheTiger, Treybien, TutterMouse, UnitedStatesIndia, Valadius, Versus22, Waytogoro, Wildhartlivie, Willking1979, Wjddbsals, Wknight94, XKL, Xinoph, Xnatedawgx, Youngamerican, Zeno Gantner, Zsero, 204 anonymous edits
53

Andrew Johnson *Source:* http://en.wikipedia.org/w/index.php?oldid=457195596 *License:* Creative Commons Attribution-Share Alike 3.0 Unported *Contributors:* .mau., 123Hedgehog456, 123qwertasdfg, 172, 1q2w12, 288icegator288, 2D, 5GemTroll, A p3rson, A. B., A. Parrot, A8UDI, AJseagull1, AKGhetto, Aachiang, Ace ETP, Adamtrevillian, Adashiel, Adavidb, Adherent of the Enlightenment 10.0, AdjustShift, Ahc, Ahkond, Ahoerstemeier, Aitias, Alansohn, Ale jrb, Alectess1, Alex.muller, Alex2486, Alison22, All Hallow's Wraith, Allstarecho, Allynfolksjr, Amcaja, AmiDaniel, Anastrophe, AndreNatas, Andreas Kaganov, Andrew wilson, Andy120290, Anglius, Animum, AnnaFrance, Antandrus, Anthony, Appalachianangler, Apparition11, Aremith, Ari Publican, Aris Katsaris, Arjun01, Arthena, Asb14, Ash773, Asteriks, Astynax, AuburnPiIot, AuburnPilot, Audacity, AudiomanJS, Auntof6, Autumn Hawk, Avoided, B00P, BCV, BD2412, BGOATDoughnut, Babbage, Bachrach44, Badgernet, Barliman Butterbur, Bastique, Belugaperson, Ben76266, Bender235, Benjaburns, Bento00, Bidabadi, BigDunc, BigFatBuddha, BigHairRef, BigJimDawsonSaysHi, Bigturtle, Billyfutile, Bkonrad, Blackthunder326, BlastOButter42, Blue520, BlueDevil, BlueMoonlet, Bluerasberry, Bob9doy, BobTheTomato, Bobblehead, Bobo192, Boing! said Zebedee, Bolt Vanderhuge, Bongwarrior, Bossmancalling, Brambleclawx, Breed Zona, Brholden, Briaboru, Brighterorange, Brittadudette, Bsegina16, Bubbacow21, Burtont1, BusterD, Byakuren, Byrial, CIreland, CJCurrie, CJLL Wright, Cadsuane Melaidhrin, Calanus, CalicoCatLover, Calmypal, Caltas, Calvin 1998, Can't sleep, clown will eat me, Canadian-Bacon, CanadianLinuxUser, Canthusus, Canuckian89, CapSexton40, Captain panda, Caracaskid, CardinalDan, Catapult, Catgut, Cenarium, Centralperk6, Centrx, Chick Bowen, Chill doubt, Chipuni, Chramchram, Chris 73, Chrisn4255, Cicillioron, Citroënist, Civil Engineer III, Cjewell, Clarince63, Clio'sdaughter, Cmguy777, Coburnpharr04, Coemgenus, Colonel Bask, CommonsDelinker, Con587, Confeds, Connormah, Conversion script, Courcelles, CraigRNielsen, Csigabi, Cube lurker, Cylon, CylonCAG, Cyrus Andiron, D, DCEdwards1966, DESiegel, DLJessup, DMCer, DNewhall, Dadofsam, Dadude3320, Dale Arnett, Daniel 1992, Danny, Darrenhusted, Darth Kalwejt, Darwinek, Das Nerd, Dat11, Davewild, David Shankbone, Dcljr, Dcn8943, Deckiller, Declare, Deed89, Delirium, Delldot, DerHexer, Diligent Terrier, Dimadick, Diotti, DiprotiumOxide, Discospinster, Djus, Dlohcierekim, Dmn, Dodo bird, Don4of4, Doublew, Doulos Christos, Download, Dp462090, Draeco, DreamHaze, Drexlerlk, Drsowell, Dryazan, Dudeman5685, Durova, Eddieandnick, Edeans, Edivorce, Edward Z. Yang, Ekspiulo, El C, Ellinoisisme, Ellsworth, Emperorbma, Emperyan, Endjinn8, Epbr123, Ericamick, Ericl, Erik Kennedy, Erik9, Ernest, The Importance of Being, Etineskid, Euryalus, Evercat, Everyking, Evrik, Excirial, Falcon8765, Falconclaw5000, Fanman904, Fat pig73, Fatalbert, Favonian, Fdewaele, FeanorStar7, Ferdiaob, FinFangFoom, FisherQueen, Fisherking38, Fishyfred, Flawiki, Flockmeal, Fluri, Foetusized, Foofighter20x, Foxdog5410, FrankCostanza, Frankenpuppy, French Onion, Frosted14, Funandtrvl, Funky1234, Funnyhat, Fvw, Fæ, GB fan, GRSUS, Gail, Garion96, Gary King, Gazpacho, Geneb1955, Genes123, Geographer, Gerrish, Giants27, Gilliam, Gjd001, Glassworks35, Gogo Dodo, Golbez, GoldRingChip, Good Olfactory, GoodDay, Goodvac, Grafen, Graham87, Graydoncarter, Great Scott, Grenavitar, Greycap, Ground, Gtrmp, Guersk, Gurch, Gwernol, Gwillhickers, Hager jeff, Hahaurscrewed, Hajhouse, HalfShadow, Halmstad, HamburgerRadio, Happylobster, Harvestdancer, Haukurth, Hazuki, Hdt83, Heimstern, Helldjinn, Hephaestos, Herbm1, HexaChord, Hgilbert, HiLo48, Hmains, Hoj263, Hornlitz, Htfiddler, Hulek, Hullaballoo Wolfowitz, Hult041956, Husond, Hvnlynigma, Hydriotaphia, Hydrogen Iodide, Hysteria18, ILuvTea, IW.HG, Iamdalto, Iamwisesun, Ian Pitchford, Ianlopez12, Icairns, Icarus' Dream, IceJew, Idols of Mud, Iknowyourider, Illnab1024, Immunize, Imperial Monarch, Incka, Indon, Infoliteracy, Infrogmation, Iridescent, Irishguy, Itai, Ixfd64, J.delanoy, JForget, JHunterJ, JW1805, Jaakobou, Jackfork, Jacoblala7, Jajhill, Jake Wartenberg, JamesAM, JamesBWatson, JamesReyes, Janus Shadowsong, Jauhienij, Javierito92, JayJasper, Jbw1291, Jeepday, Jeff G., Jengod, Jer443932, JesseHogan, Jhartz, Jiang, Jiddisch, JimWae, Jlord534, Jmalatino93, Jmolinx, John, John K, John Paul Parks, John254, JohnInDC, JohnnyB256, Johnor, Jojhutton, Jon Harald Søby, Jonathan.s.kt, Joseph Solis in Australia, Joyous!, Jpgordon, Jptdrake, Jsc83, Jsd7190, Jtkiefer, Juliancolton, Junnyb14, Jusdafax, Just Another Dan, K1Bond007, KGasso, KPH2293, Kaisershatner, Karlhahn, KathodeRay, Katieh5584, Kauffner, Kdshaw2, Keilana, Kevin j, Khanartist, Kingturtle, Kingwhick, KirinX, KnowledgeOfSelf, Koavf, Kpjas, Kresock, Kross, Ksnow, KuatofKDY, Kukini, Kumioko, Kurochunda, Kuru, La goutte de pluie, LarryJeff, LarryQ, Laurinavicius, Lefairh, Levineps, Libraryteacher, Libs23, LightSpectra, Lightmouse, Lights, Lincolnite, LittleOldMe, Lockesdonkey, Lolz idiot, LonelyPilgrim, Loostick, Lord Pistachio, Lpstubbs, Lst27, Ludicolo, Luk, Lupinsmyman, Lwaltzman, M.O.X, MBK004, MC10, MK, MLHalls08, MZMcBride, MacTire02, Mackensen, Maddy600, Maelnuneb, Magioladitis, Magnus Manske, Makemi, Maksim L., Mandarax, Mangojuice, Maniac323074, Manuel Trujillo Berges, Mareino, Marek69, Marie Callendar, Marin274, Martin451, MartinSpacek, Martinlc, Master of Puppets, Mathwizard1232, Mausy5043, Mav, Maximillion Pegasus, Mayumashu, Mayur, Mboverload, McGrupp10799, Me390, Meepster, Meldor, Mendaliv, Mentifisto, Meowmeow52132, Mercury, MetallicaRulez77, Michael Snow, MichaelWheeley, Michaeltmccorkle, Microchip08, Midnight12, Mike Rosoft, MikeDero, Mikehelms, Miller17CU94, MillerCenter, Millionsandbillions, Minesweeper, Minimac's Clone, Mliggett, ModRocker86, Mona, Monegasque, Mooseofshadows, MosheA, Moverton, Mrpink2605, Mrsblink182, Msclguru, Mufka, Mumia-w-18, Myanw, Nakon, Nam, Nascar1996, Natalie Erin, Natl1, NawlinWiki, Nebular110, Neckbelow, Neutrality, Neverquick, NewEnglandYankee, Newyorkbrad, Nikai, Nivix, Nmviw, Noah Salzman, Noctibus, North King, North Shoreman, Nothing.co, Nothing444, Nposs, Nsaa, NuclearWarfare, Numbo3, Nunh-huh, O Fenian, Ohnoitsjamie, Ojigiri, Omicronpersei8, Opelio, Orlady, Oroso, Owen, Owl cakes, Oxymoron83, Packerfansam, Paitsch, Pajfarmor, Parkwells, Parvazbato59, Pascal.Tesson, PastorMatt, Pastorwayne, PaulHanson, Pb30, Pdcook, Peruvianllama, Peter Fleet, Peter.C, PeterSymonds, Phfootball, Philip Stevens, Philip Trueman, Phoephus, Piano non troppo, Pictish Defender, Pillseller32, Pinethicket, Plumber, Poisonink, PoliticalJunkie, Polutlas, Popopopopopopopop, Popuup, Postdlf, Potatoexz, Potatoswatter, Pres-scholar, Presumptive, PrimeHunter, Princess Lirin, PrincessofLlyr, Prodego, Prolog, Psmith, Purplebackpackonthetrail, Quantpole, Quentin X, Qxz, R'n'B, RFD, RG2, ROSSJW1, Raeky, Rafaelthomas, Raider Duck, RainbowOfLight, Rajah, RandySavageFTW, Rathersane, Razorflame, Rbaul, Rcgorman5698, ReignMan27, Reinoutr, RexNL, Rhobite, Riana, Rich Farmbrough, Richard75, RickK, Rjensen, Rjwilmsi, Rlquall, Rmosler2100, RobLa, RobbieFal, Robby, Robert K S, Robertgreer, Robwingfield, Rocastelo, Rockpeasonmyhead, RodC, RoosterBubble82, Rorschach, Rrburke, Rufous-crowned Sparrow, Ruy Pugliesi, Ryan Postlethwaite, SDJ, SGT141, SHIMONSHA, SNIyer1, SNIyer12, Saforrest, Samwisebruce, Sanda427, SandyDancer, Sardanaphalus, Sarenne, Satch7, Savidan, Sceptre, SchfiftyThree, Schwindtd, Sciurinæ, Scott Mingus, ScottyBerg, Seaphoto, Serein (renamed because of SUL), Sesesq, Setanta747 (locked), Settler, Sfiller, Shalom Yechiel, Shanes, Shimmera, Shizane, Shoeofdeath, Showy8, Silver Streak, SkepticMuhs, Skywriter, Slakr, Slambo, Smith03, Soccaplaya, Soliloquial, Southleft, Spangineer, Specs112, Spitfire19, Spongerobme, Squids and Chips, Stacyjj, StaticVision, Steelersfano, Stephennarmstrong, Stmoose, Str1977, Studerby, Stwalkerster, Sumergocognito, Supercoop, Sushiflinger, Swampyank, Swarm, Synchronism, System6669, THEN WHO WAS PHONE?, TJ Spyke, Taties20, Tbabyy43, Tbhotch, Tedickey, Tedius Zanarukando, Teeeim, Template namespace initialisation script, Tempshill, Terranovia1661, Tesseran, Tex, The Duke of Waltham, The Filmaker, The Giant Puffin, The Love Train, The Mystery Man, The Thing That Should Not Be, The Twenty Thousand Tonne Bomb, The masterpedia, The sock that should not be, TheJediCouncil, TheRealFennShysa, TheSilentPhotographer, Thedjatclubrock, Thefinaladvent9, Thehelpfulone, Therequiembellishere, Thewayforward, Thingg, Thivierr, Thomas Gilling, ThomasK, Thue, Tiddly Tom, Tide rolls, Tigga en, Tilden76, Tim Thomason, Timc, Time3000, Timwi, Titoxd, Tktru, Tocino, Tom, TonyTheTiger, Toonerh, TorynHill, Tpbradbury, TransUtopian, Tresiden, Treybien, Triona, Triwbe, Truedancer87, Truthanado, Trxr4kds, Tryptofish, Ttwaring, TurabianNights, UDScott, Uncle Dick, Unitanode, UnitedStatesIndia, Unknown1402, Unschool, UpstateNYer, Uwillnvrgetthis1, Valkyrie Red, ValleyOfMegiddo, Velocicaptor, Ventusa, Verdlanco, Versus22, Vicenarian, Vicki Rosenzweig, Vilcxjo, Vipinhari, Vrenator, Vulturell, WBcoleman, Wahabijaz, WarPigs7890, Warfieldian, Wars, Wayne Slam, Webucation, WereSpielChequers, Wertuose, West.andrew.g, WhiteKMJK, Whouk, WikHead, Wiki alf, Wikidrew1632, Wikilibrarian, Wikipelli, Wilee, WillC, William S. Saturn, Willking1979, Winchelsea, Wjejskenewr, Wjhonson, Wknight94, Wmannin4, Woogee, Wow Scotland !, Wysprgr2005, XRK, Xavexgoem, Xtreme1090, Yamamoto Ichiro, Yellow Hat17, YellowMonkey, Yettie0711, Zach20245, Zafiroblue05, Zanibas, Zaui, Zentuk, Zocky, Zoe, Zscout370, Zsero, Zzedar, Zzyzx11, 1841 anonymous edits 60

William H. Seward *Source:* http://en.wikipedia.org/w/index.php?oldid=457540619 *License:* Creative Commons Attribution-Share Alike 3.0 Unported *Contributors:* ADTS1, AKGhetto, Acidradio, Adambondy, Adambro, Adashiel, Addisonbr, Addshore, Alansohn, Alborghetti, Americus55, Andycjp, Antoine Gautier, Ary29, Avraham, BD2412, Bam127, Bbsrock, Bdefore, Bender235, Bentley4, Bgs022, Big pin, Billy Hathorn, Bkonrad, Bob Burkhardt, Bobblewik, Brewcrewer, Brozozo, Busaccsb, BusterD, Buyo, Bwithh, C45207, CFLeon, CJ Wengler, Calmer Waters, Canuckian89, Capricorn42, Captainktainer, Cb6, CheetahMan1, Chensiyuan, Chickencracker, Chris the speller, Christopher Parham, Citicat, Civil Engineer III, Cjensen, Cladestine, Colonies Chris, CommonsDelinker, Connormah, D C McJonathan, D6, DCNanney, DLJessup, DNewhall, Daniel Case, Darwinek, DerBorg, Dgphilli, Dimadick, Dinabutterfly, Dogru144, Doncram, Dragons225, Drpickem, DwightKingsbury, EJF, Echozdog, Edison, Edward321, Eldredo, Epolk, Eran of Arcadia, Eternal Pink, Everyking, Executor Tassadar, Exeunt, Fanra, FinalRapture, Firsfron, FrisoHoltkamp, Frozenport, Fusionmix, GenQuest, Genehisthome, Ghostalker, Giggy, Gilliam, GonzosTorment, Good Olfactory, GoodDay, HOT L Baltimore, Hanse, HennessyC, Hertz1888, Hinotori, Hipgnostic, HistoryBA, Hmains, Hydrogen Iodide, Ianblair23, Immunize, Inter16, Invisible Flying Mangoes, Isis, Ixfd64, J.delanoy, JForget, JSquish, Jack O'Lantern, Jajhill, Jakebrettell, JayJasper, Jdelombard, Jengod, Jfruh, Jim.henderson, JimWae, Jj137, John, John K, Johngrisham6, Johntinker, Jojhutton, Jpgordon, Jun Nijo, Justin Eiler, KathodeRay, Keilana, Keithtambo, Kimon, KnowledgeOfSelf, Koavf, Kraxler, Kubigula, Kumioko, La Pianista, Lamro, Leslie Mateus, Levineps, Libs23, Lightmouse, Lupinelawyer, MSGJ, MSTCrow, Magnus Manske, Mark K. Jensen, MarkSutton, Michael A. White, Michaelh2001, Michaelsbll, Mikehillman, Minesweeper, Mklobas, ModRocker86, Moodyfloydwhofan, Mouse Nightshirt, MrOllie, MrPrada, Mscottjones, Mstewart47, NY-13021, Nicholejean04, Nik42, Niteowlneils, North Shoreman, Notorious4life, Oceangod8, OldestManOnMySpace, Omicronpersei8, Oswaldojh, PBS-AWB, Packerfansam, Panther502002, Patriarca12, Perfect Tommy, Periphron, Petri Krohn, Pilcrow, Pmanderson, Politicaljunkie23, Polylerus, Popsracer, Postdlf, Pudge MclameO, R'n'B, RMc, RWReagan, RadioKirk, Rande M Sefowt, Ray-Ginsay, Red Harvest, RepublicanJacobite, Reywas92, Riccomario96, Rich Farmbrough, Richard Arthur Norton (1958-), Rigga101, Rjensen, Rkmlai, Robert Skyhawk, RockLeesLilShadow, Roncon, Rrostrom, Ryuhaku, Saga

City, Salamurai, Sam Francis, Samrica, Sardanaphalus, Scartol, ScottyBerg, Settler, SewardHouse, ShakingSpirit, Shearonink, Sixteen Left, Sjbostian, SouthernNights, Spacemanspiff066, Spitfire, SpuriousQ, Stephenb, Stepp-Wulf, Stevieg2123, Sulfiteboy, Superiority, TBGNumber9, THEN WHO WAS PHONE?, Tad Lincoln, Tagishsimon, Taskinen, Tassedethe, Tbhotch, Tempodivalse, ThaddeusB, That Guy, From That Show!, The Mystery Man, The Thing That Should Not Be, The wub, Thismightbezach, Tirerim, Tkleve146, Tom, Tomas417, TonyTheTiger, Trikiwi, Ttwaring, TurabianNights, Unschool, UpstateNYer, VMAAXT, W E Hill, Wames, WillC, Wknight94, Wperdue, Wwoods, Xavier black, Zachlipton, Zdtrlik, Zoe, Zwoom, Æthelwold, 494 anonymous edits 81

Simon Cameron *Source:* http://en.wikipedia.org/w/index.php?oldid=456604078 *License:* Creative Commons Attribution-Share Alike 3.0 Unported *Contributors:* A.bit, AlexPlank, AndreasPraefcke, Appraiser, Bbsrock, BillFlis, Bob Burkhardt, Brian0918, Canuckian89, Carom, Choess, CommonsDelinker, Complex01, Connormah, D6, DMG413, Davepape, David Gerard, Dimadick, Dodiad, Dr who1975, Everyking, Fat&Happy, Floydspinky71, GVP Webmaster, Ganymead, Goobergunch, Good Olfactory, Ground Zero, Hlj, Hmains, Incredibleshrinkingman, J Clear, Jengod, John K, KathodeRay, Kbdank71, Krsont, Kumioko, Looxix, LouI, Mieczkowski, Minesweeper, Morwen, MrDolomite, Neutrality, North Shoreman, Npeters22, Perl, Petri Krohn, PurpleChez, RFD, RWReagan, Robth, Sadads, Schnitzi, Scott Mingus, Sietse Snel, Stefanomione, Stilgar135, The Mystery Man, Thismightbezach, Tlincoln, Tom, TonyTheTiger, Veinor, WikiContributor, Wizardman, Wouterhagens, Wrightchr, Xploita, 28 anonymous edits 99

Edwin M. Stanton *Source:* http://en.wikipedia.org/w/index.php?oldid=454778544 *License:* Creative Commons Attribution-Share Alike 3.0 Unported *Contributors:* 8th Ohio Volunteers, A Werewolf, AKGhetto, Abcdezyxwv, Aesopos, Alchimista, AlexPlank, Americasroof, Angela, Aznshark4, BCV, BD2412, Babbage, Bam63, Beemer69, Bender235, Bentley4, Billy Hathorn, Blakeud, BookWorm, Bped1985, Brian0918, BusterD, CRKingston, Can't sleep, clown will eat me, Canuckian89, Cbustapeck, Chaser, Chrisminter, Chrisn4255, Chrumps, Civil Engineer III, Civil WarAuthor, Coemgenus, Complex01, Connormah, Cvllelaw, D6, DMG413, Dabomb87, Darkwind, Darwinek, Davepape, December21st2012Freak, Dehn Larson, Dimadick, Dodiad, Dr. Dan, DrunkenSmurf, Dukeofomnium, E0steven, Edarrell, Edeans, Eharley, Einbierbitte, Emurphy42, Enosfam, Ericl, Eruption162, Eubulides, Firemanic9, Firsfron, Foofighter20x, Friginator, Gimmetrow, Grazon, Gurch, Gwillhickers, Harland1, HennessyC, Hlj, Hmains, Iamnotachicken, Isomorphic, J.delanoy, JNW, JPMcGrath, Jack Cox, Jajhill, Jareha, Jengod, Jimknut, JoDonHo, John K, John Reaves, John254, Joshmaul, Jpetry, KTC, KathodeRay, Kbdank71, KdWiki, Kevin Myers, Koavf, Konczewski, Kralizec!, Kumaryu, Kumioko, LB-Versender, Levg, Levineps, MD1937, Madcat peter, Magnus Manske, Manushand, Mexaguil, Midnightdreary, Mifter, Miranda, Mkpumphrey, MrDolomite, Msilver727, Neutrality, NotMittRomney, Nunh-huh, Nyttend, Ohconfucius, Packerfansam, Paradoxian, Penthamontar, Poccil, PurpleChez, QuizzicalBee, RWReagan, Reywas92, Rjensen, Rontrigger, Scott Mingus, Silvercobra100, SiobhanHansa, Smallfixer, Snoyes, SoWhy, SockPuppet20742, Srich32977, Stepshep, TarquiniusWikipedius, Tassedethe, Tedder, The Frog, The Mystery Man, TheKMan, TheRanger, Thismightbezach, Tim1965, TonyTheTiger, TopGUN71691, Troobeeleever, Ugen64, Utopies, Vanished 6551232, Victuallers, WOSlinker, WillC, Willking1979, Zeimusu, 202 anonymous edits 104

Salmon P. Chase *Source:* http://en.wikipedia.org/w/index.php?oldid=452168834 *License:* Creative Commons Attribution-Share Alike 3.0 Unported *Contributors:* 7&6=thirteen, 8th Ohio Volunteers, 91Bear, AP1787, Ahoerstemeier, Akcarver, Akferia, Anomalocaris, Anonymous56789, Antonsson, Anythingyouwant, Auntof6, Aymatth2, BD2412, Barticus88, Bbsrock, Ben Manski, Binabik80, Binarybits, Bissinger, Bkonrad, Bob Burkhardt, Bobak, Bobblehead, BorgHunter, Brian A Schmidt, Btphelps, BusterD, CRKingston, Cairel, Canuckian89, Carolmooredc, Cbrown285, Cgingold, Chaser, Choster, Chrisn4255, Clariosophic, Clawson, Coemgenus, CommonsDelinker, Connormah, Conscious, Critic11, D6, DFRussia, DIDouglass, DLJessup, DMG413, Daderot, Darkwind, Darth Kalwejt, Darwinek, Davepape, DavidLevinson, Daysleeper47, Deon, DerHexer, Dimadick, Dinopup, Discospinster, Djmutex, Dlohcierekim, Dr who1975, Duffy2032, Dukeofomnium, EncMstr, Engineer Bob, EoGuy, Epbr123, Epolk, Ericl, Esrever, Evercat, Evets70, Excirial, Fastily, Fishal, Flauto Dolce, Flynzy, Foofighter20x, Foonly, ForgottenManC, Frmorrison, Fry1989, G34j, Gang14, GcSwRhIc, Gdarin, Geni, Geoff Plourde, Gezellig, Good Olfactory, GoodDay, Greensburger, Greg5030, Grunt, Hilltoppers, Hmains, Homagetocatalonia, HughMor, Infrogmation, Isaac Rabinovitch, J'onn J'onzz, JCGentry, JForget, JW1805, Jack Cox, Jasonnaas, JayJasper, Jengod, Jewbacca, Jhobson1, Jmcneill2, John, John K, John Spraggs, Josephabradshaw, Jpbrenna, Jrgilb, Jstosko, Jun Nijo, Karlos the Jackal, KathodeRay, Kelson, Kine, Koavf, Kraxler, Kross, Krscal, Kukini, Kumioko, L1A1 FAL, LaidOff, Levineps, LilHelpa, LinaMishima, MZMcBride, MarcusGraly, Mario 64 Master, Maximus Rex, McGrupp10799, Mhardcastle, Midnightdreary, Mike Dillon, Minesweeper, Mm6119, ModRocker86, Monegasque, MosheA, Moverton, Mxn, Nick Number, Noitall, North Shoreman, Nytimes19992000, OCNative, OfficePuter, Ohio09, Old64mb, Ottawa4ever, PJPerkins, Packerfansam, Papajfd, Parks5541, Parkwells, Passionless, Pauljeffersonks, Philosopher, Philwelch, Phmtbs, Piperh, Pmanderson, Pollinator, Postdlf, Quadell, R. fiend, RFD, RFKFREAK, Raprchju, Reaper Eternal, Reywas92, Rhopkins8, Rich Farmbrough, Richard75, RickK, RickReinckens, Rjensen, Robert K S, Robert Prummel, Rockhopper10r, RogDel, Roseohioresident, Rrostrom, Ruzulo, Sagaciousuk, SalineBrain, Samuel 69105, Sannse, Sardanaphalus, Scott Mingus, SebRovera, Shimmin, Sholom, Simesa, Sirex98, Smith120bh, Son of lucas, SonPraises, SoundGod3, Spc101, StillmanMorison, TGC55, Tagishsimon, Tangledupinblue7, Tassedethe, Template namespace initialisation script, The Mystery Man, The Photon, TheBakerz, Thismightbezach, Tide rolls, Tktru, Tom, Tomas417, TonyTheTiger, TurabianNights, Ulric1313, UnitedStatesIndia, Victuallers, W E Hill, Wavelength, WilliamJE, Wlly n Whlls, Yooden, Zealandman, Zoe, Zoicon5, Zzuuzz, ^demon, Александр Мотин, 178 anonymous edits 115

William P. Fessenden *Source:* http://en.wikipedia.org/w/index.php?oldid=442622517 *License:* Creative Commons Attribution-Share Alike 3.0 Unported *Contributors:* Americus55, AnnaFrance, Anythingyouwant, Ari Publican, Awbeal, Bbsrock, Bearcat, Bob Burkhardt, Breffni Whelan, Brian0918, Canuckian89, Cgascoig, Chris the speller, Closedmouth, Complex01, D6, Davidcannon, Epolk, GRBerry, Goddard123, Good Olfactory, HennessyC, Hmains, Iohannes Animosus, Jengod, John K, Jun Nijo, KathodeRay, Kenatipo, Kumioko, Leonard^Bloom, Mandsford, MarkHB, Monegasque, Namiba, Neutrality, Postdlf, Qmwne235, Rjensen, Scott Mingus, SoundGod3, Tagishsimon, Template namespace initialisation script, The Mystery Man, Thismightbezach, Tomas417, TonyTheTiger, TubularWorld, Twinsrulemlb, W Nowicki, Александр Мотин, 13 anonymous edits 127

Hugh McCulloch *Source:* http://en.wikipedia.org/w/index.php?oldid=447030907 *License:* Creative Commons Attribution-Share Alike 3.0 Unported *Contributors:* Alexf, Algabal, Bbsrock, Bfoaz, Bobet, Brian0918, Burgundavia, Cgascoig, Charles Edward, Complex01, Cuppysfriend, D6, DMG413, Dblandford, Epolk, Epsilon60198, HennessyC, Hmains, Hubbardbk, Jajhill, Jengod, John K, KathodeRay, Kellogg257, Kross, Kumioko, LilHelpa, Lotje, Mandarax, Maximus Rex, Mdnavman, Namiba, NekoDaemon, NoSeptember, Packerfansam, PaulHanson, Scott Mingus, SoundGod3, Spongefrog, Tabletop, Tagishsimon, Template namespace initialisation script, The Mystery Man, Thismightbezach, TonyTheTiger, Twinsrulemlb, WOSlinker, WillC, Александр Мотин, 9 anonymous edits 134

Edward Bates *Source:* http://en.wikipedia.org/w/index.php?oldid=453571631 *License:* Creative Commons Attribution-Share Alike 3.0 Unported *Contributors:* 8th Ohio Volunteers, A Werewolf, AKGhetto, Americasroof, Americus55, Awbeal, Badbilltucker, Boleyn, Brian0918, Canuckian89, Chrisn4255, Complex01, D6, DMG413, Davepape, Dimadick, Finn-Zoltan, Good Olfactory, Hmains, Jengod, KathodeRay, Kumioko, LouI, MarkNeels, Narwhalhistory, Onemoregain, Packerfansam, Parkwells, Pubdog, Rjwilmsi, Rrostrom, Scott Mingus, Serein (renamed because of SUL), Son of lucas, Steve Casburn, Stilgar135, Template namespace initialisation script, The Mystery Man, Themij, Thismightbezach, TonyTheTiger, TysK, Vyselink, William S. Saturn, Woohookitty, Zzuuzz, 24 anonymous edits 139

James Speed *Source:* http://en.wikipedia.org/w/index.php?oldid=428671610 *License:* Creative Commons Attribution-Share Alike 3.0 Unported *Contributors:* AKGhetto, Alanscottwalker, BeckyJDan, Bedford, Brian0918, Cantus, Canuckian89, Chrisn4255, Complex01, D6, DIDouglass, Daboss99, Gaius Cornelius, Gamaliel, Good Olfactory, Grazon, Hmains, Jack Cox, Jackyd101, Jajhill, JamesAM, Jengod, JimWae, KathodeRay, Kbdank71, Kumioko, Neonblak, Neutrality, NoSeptember, Ost316, Packerfansam, Paul A, Popsracer, Quadell, RWReagan, Retired username, Robomanx, Stevietheman, The Mystery Man, Thismightbezach, TonyTheTiger, WillC, Yellowdesk, 8 anonymous edits 144

Montgomery Blair *Source:* http://en.wikipedia.org/w/index.php?oldid=441717077 *License:* Creative Commons Attribution-Share Alike 3.0 Unported *Contributors:* Adavidb, BillFlis, Bluemoose, Bugmuncher, Carl.bunderson, CheckeredFlag200, Complex01, D6, DMG413, Daveisall, Everyking, Gamaliel, Good Olfactory, HennessyC, HenryLi, Hephaestos, Hmains, Isaac Rabinovitch, Jengod, John K, KathodeRay, Kumioko, Llakais, Lyctc, MOhistory, Mark K. Jensen, Monegasque, Neutrality, North Shoreman, Packerfansam, PaulHanson, Scattered0, Scientizzle, Scott Mingus, Ser Amantio di Nicolao, Settler, Stopperettaetta, Taychert, Tedickey, Texture, The Duke of Waltham, The Mystery Man, Thismightbezach, Tom, TonyTheTiger, Victuallers, Wwoods, Zsinj, 14 anonymous edits 147

William Dennison, Jr. *Source:* http://en.wikipedia.org/w/index.php?oldid=424064297 *License:* Creative Commons Attribution-Share Alike 3.0 Unported *Contributors:* 8th Ohio Volunteers, AP1787, B93, Bluemoose, Brian0918, Brianyoumans, Burgundavia, Cantus, Chris the speller, Complex01, D6, DIDouglass, DMG413, Eastfrisian, Elendil's Heir, Flauto Dolce, Fry1989, Good Olfactory, GoodDay, HOT L Baltimore, Hmains, Jack Cox, Jajhill, Jcbarr, Jengod, John K, Joseph Solis in Australia, Jrp, Kumioko, LilHelpa, Llakais, Mlsekeres, Msclguru, NE2, Packerfansam, Parsecboy, Philip Trueman, Postdlf, RogDel, Roseohioresident, Sardanaphalus, Scott Mingus, Tassedethe, The Duke of Waltham, The Mystery Man, Thismightbezach, Tomas417, TonyTheTiger, Welsh, Zundark, 12 anonymous edits 152

Gideon Welles *Source:* http://en.wikipedia.org/w/index.php?oldid=445854624 *License:* Creative Commons Attribution-Share Alike 3.0 Unported *Contributors:* 15lsoucy, Abau50, Abrowneckel, Adam Bishop, Adam sk, AlexPlank, Ari Publican, Auntof6, BME, Bazj, Beginning, Berean Hunter, Bihco, Billy Hathorn, Bob Burkhardt, Bobdobbs1723, Brian0918, Bryan Derksen, Bunnyhop11, CSWarren, Carcharoth, Chrissypan, Civil Engineer III, Complex01, Connormah, Courcelles, D6, DMG413, Danny, Darwinek, Denisarona, Dranster, ERcheck, Ebang, Everyking, Gaius Cornelius, Giovanni-P, Good Olfactory, Grondemar, GusF, Hartfelt, Hmains, Innapoy, Jajhill, Javabeanrush, Jengod, JesseLeiman, Jinian, Jwrosenzweig, KathodeRay, Kbdank71, Kumioko, Kuralyov, Lordoliver, Markvs88, Minesweeper, Neutrality, North Shoreman, Old64mb, One, Packerfansam, Pharaoh of the Wizards, RFD, Rebrane, Rjwilmsi, Stefanomione, Sustructu, The Mystery Man, TheParanoidOne, Thismightbezach, TonyTheTiger, Ulric1313, Vanished 6551232, Victuallers, WOSlinker, Warpozio, Wolfman, Xdamr, Zariane, Æthelwold, 31 anonymous edits 157

Caleb Blood Smith *Source:* http://en.wikipedia.org/w/index.php?oldid=452172655 *License:* Creative Commons Attribution-Share Alike 3.0 Unported *Contributors:* 8th Ohio Volunteers, BD2412, Bearcat, Bhadani, BigrTex, Bkonrad, Bob Burkhardt, Brian0918, Charles Edward, Chevymontecarlo, Cindy L. Clarke, Colonies Chris, Complex01, Connormah, Cynthia Clarke, Cynthia Lynnette Long, D6, DIDouglass, Dananderson, Daytrivia, Dust312, Ground Zero, Hmains, Ian Pitchford, J Di, JHawk88, Jeandré du Toit, Jengod, KathodeRay, Kbdank71, Kumioko, Leujohn, Maplewooddrive, Mentifisto, Nyttend, Packerfansam, Rich Farmbrough, Rjwilmsi, ST47, ScooterDe, Scott Mingus, SoundGod3, The Mystery Man, TheHoosierState89, Thismightbezach, TonyTheTiger, Victuallers, WillC, YUL89YYZ, 13 anonymous edits 165

John Palmer Usher *Source:* http://en.wikipedia.org/w/index.php?oldid=430158332 *License:* Creative Commons Attribution-Share Alike 3.0 Unported *Contributors:* Ari Publican, Bigturtle, Brian0918, Cantus, Canuckian89, Cohesion, Complex01, D6, Dananderson, Fuzzy510, Good Olfactory, Hmains,

Jajhill, Jengod, Jhawksince54, KathodeRay, Kbdank71, Kingka, Michael David, Mike Dillon, OldakQuill, Pauljeffersonks, Postdlf, ScooterDe, Scott Mingus, SoundGod3, The Mystery Man, Thismightbezach, TonyTheTiger, WOSlinker, YUL89YYZ, 11 anonymous edits 169

Image Sources, Licenses and Contributors

The sources listed for each image provide more detailed licensing information including the copyright status, the copyright owner, and the license conditions.

Image *Source:* http://en.wikipedia.org/w/index.php?title=File:Abraham_Lincoln_head_on_shoulders_photo_portrait.jpg *License:* Public Domain *Contributors:* Bkell, Brad101, Closeapple, Cwbm (commons), Daderot, Howcheng, INeverCry, Infrogmation, Jatkins, Mxn, Outriggr, Selket, Shizhao, Tharnton345, Tom, UpstateNYer, Wutsje, Zzyzx11, 8 anonymous edits ... 3

Image *Source:* http://en.wikipedia.org/w/index.php?title=File:Abraham_Lincoln_Signature.svg *License:* Public Domain *Contributors:* Abraham Lincoln ... 4

Image *Source:* http://en.wikipedia.org/w/index.php?title=File:Speakerlink.svg *License:* Creative Commons Attribution 3.0 *Contributors:* Woodstone. Original uploader was Woodstone at en.wikipedia ... 4

Figure 1 *Source:* http://en.wikipedia.org/w/index.php?title=File:Young_Lincoln_By_Charles_Keck.JPG *License:* Creative Commons Zero *Contributors:* Sculpture: Charles Keck (1875-1951) Photograph: Work of uploader: Alanscottwalker (talk) 11:21, 12 October 2010 (UTC) ... 6

Image *Source:* http://en.wikipedia.org/w/index.php?title=File:A&TLincoln.jpg *License:* Public Domain *Contributors:* Anthony Berger, photographer. Brady National Photographic Art Gallery (Washington, D.C.) ... 7

Image *Source:* http://en.wikipedia.org/w/index.php?title=File:Mary_Todd_Lincoln_1846-1847_restored_cropped.png *License:* Public Domain *Contributors:* Mary_Todd_Lincoln_1846-1847_restored.png: *Mary_Todd_Lincoln_1846-1847.jpg: Shepherd, Nicolas H., photographer. derivati ... 8

Figure 2 *Source:* http://en.wikipedia.org/w/index.php?title=File:Abe_Lincoln_young.jpg *License:* Public Domain *Contributors:* Brad101, Conny, Daderot, Elcobbola, Maksim, Mattes, Professorscatman, Ralf Roletschek, Sven Manguard ... 10

Figure 3 *Source:* http://en.wikipedia.org/w/index.php?title=File:Abelincoln1846.jpeg *License:* Public Domain *Contributors:* Nicholas H. Shepherd 12

Figure 4 *Source:* http://en.wikipedia.org/w/index.php?title=File:DredScott.jpg *License:* Public Domain *Contributors:* Alanscottwalker, Conscious, G.dallorto, Infrogmation, Jnn, Martin H., Materialscientist, Sebmol, Wst ... 14

Figure 5 *Source:* http://en.wikipedia.org/w/index.php?title=File:Abraham_Lincoln_by_Alexander_Helser,_1860-crop.jpg *License:* Public Domain *Contributors:* Alexander Hesler (1823–1895) ... 15

Figure 6 *Source:* http://en.wikipedia.org/w/index.php?title=File:The_Rail_Candidate.jpg *License:* Public Domain *Contributors:* Maurer, Louis, 1832-1932 ... 17

Image *Source:* http://en.wikipedia.org/w/index.php?title=File:1860_Electoral_Map.png *License:* Public Domain *Contributors:* EurekaLott, Gauravjuvekar, Koavf, Tallicfan20 ... 19

Image *Source:* http://en.wikipedia.org/w/index.php?title=File:Abraham_lincoln_inauguration_1861.jpg *License:* Public Domain *Contributors:* Clindberg, Evrik, Infrogmation, Jbarta, Jospe, Lotsofissues, Maksim, Man vyi, Mangoman88, Ranveig, 2 anonymous edits ... 19

Figure 7 *Source:* http://en.wikipedia.org/w/index.php?title=File:Major_Robert_Anderson.jpg *License:* Public Domain *Contributors:* Christophe cagé, Frank C. Müller, Gusvel, Homo lupus, Kelson ... 21

Figure 8 *Source:* http://en.wikipedia.org/w/index.php?title=File:RunningtheMachine-LincAdmin.jpg *License:* Public Domain *Contributors:* Cameron, John, b. ca. 1828 , artist ... 23

Figure 9 *Source:* http://en.wikipedia.org/w/index.php?title=File:Lincoln_and_McClellan_1862-10-03.jpg *License:* Public Domain *Contributors:* Beao, Brad101, Daderot, Evrik, Hlj, Infrogmation, Meteor2017, Outriggr, Wolfmann ... 25

Figure 10 *Source:* http://en.wikipedia.org/w/index.php?title=File:Emancipation_proclamation.jpg *License:* Public Domain *Contributors:* 32X, Alensha, Bob Burkhardt, Bogdan, Brad101, Clindberg, Dodiad, Ebcdic, Elcobbola, Evrik, Hohum, Jarekt, Maksim, Mentifisto, Shyam, Sole Soul, Victuallers, Väsk, Ww2censor, 9 anonymous edits ... 27

Figure 11 *Source:* http://en.wikipedia.org/w/index.php?title=File:The_Peacemakers_1868.jpg *License:* Public Domain *Contributors:* Berrucomons, Bob Burkhardt, Brad101, CommonsDelinker, Docu, Infrogmation, Scewing, Singapore1, Thierry Caro, 5 anonymous edits ... 30

Image *Source:* http://en.wikipedia.org/w/index.php?title=File:1864_Electoral_Map.png *License:* Public Domain *Contributors:* Nakor, Tallicfan20, 1 anonymous edits ... 32

Image *Source:* http://en.wikipedia.org/w/index.php?title=File:Lincoln_second.jpg *License:* Public Domain *Contributors:* Brad101, Clindberg, Evrik, Infrogmation, Jospe, Mangoman88, Philip Stevens, Reisio, UpstateNYer, ZZT32, 1 anonymous edits ... 33

Figure 12 *Source:* http://en.wikipedia.org/w/index.php?title=File:Lincoln_and_Johnsond.jpg *License:* Public Domain *Contributors:* Joseph E. Baker 34

Figure 13 *Source:* http://en.wikipedia.org/w/index.php?title=File:Lincoln-Warren-1865-03-06.jpeg *License:* Public Domain *Contributors:* Warren, Henry F., photographer ... 36

Figure 14 *Source:* http://en.wikipedia.org/w/index.php?title=File:The_Assassination_of_President_Lincoln_-_Currier_and_Ives_2.png *License:* Public Domain *Contributors:* Currier & Ives, 1865. ... 40

Figure 15 *Source:* http://en.wikipedia.org/w/index.php?title=File:AbrahamLincolnOilPainting1869Restored.jpg *License:* Public Domain *Contributors:* Brad101, Nehrams2020 ... 41

Figure 16 *Source:* http://en.wikipedia.org/w/index.php?title=File:Lincoln_Museum_Exterior.jpg *License:* GNU Free Documentation License *Contributors:* w:en:User talk:WinonaveUser talk:Winonave ... 43

Figure 17 *Source:* http://en.wikipedia.org/w/index.php?title=File:Aerial_view_of_Lincoln_Memorial_-_east_side_EDIT.jpeg *License:* Public Domain *Contributors:* Aerial_view_of_Lincoln_Memorial_-_east_side.jpg: Carol M. Highsmith derivative work: upstateNYer ... 44

Image *Source:* http://en.wikipedia.org/w/index.php?title=File:Hannibal_Hamlin,_photo_portrait_seated,_c1860-65-retouched-crop.jpg *License:* Public Domain *Contributors:* User:Connormah ... 53

Image *Source:* http://en.wikipedia.org/w/index.php?title=File:Hannibal_Hamlin_Signature.svg *License:* Public Domain *Contributors:* Connormah & Hannibal Hamlin ... 54

Figure 18 *Source:* http://en.wikipedia.org/w/index.php?title=File:Younger_Hannibal_Hamlin.jpg *License:* Public Domain *Contributors:* Kelly 55

Figure 19 *Source:* http://en.wikipedia.org/w/index.php?title=File:Hamlin_button_1860.jpg *License:* Public Domain *Contributors:* Durova, Foroa 56

Figure 20 *Source:* http://en.wikipedia.org/w/index.php?title=File:HHamlin.jpg *License:* Public Domain *Contributors:* . Original uploader was The Mystery Man at en.wikipedia ... 58

Image *Source:* http://en.wikipedia.org/w/index.php?title=File:16_Andrew_Johnson_3x4-Edit1.jpg *License:* Public Domain *Contributors:* Matthew Brady, Retouched by Mmxx ... 60

Image *Source:* http://en.wikipedia.org/w/index.php?title=File:Andrew_Johnson_Signature.svg *License:* Public Domain *Contributors:* Connormah, Andrew Johnson ... 61

Figure 21 *Source:* http://en.wikipedia.org/w/index.php?title=File:Andrew_Johnsons_First_Home_2006.jpg *License:* Creative Commons Attribution 2.5 *Contributors:* Original uploader was Mikehelms at en.wikipedia ... 63

Figure 22 *Source:* http://en.wikipedia.org/w/index.php?title=File:Younger_Andrew_Johnson.jpg *License:* Public Domain *Contributors:* Chick Bowen, Evrik, WTCA ... 64

Figure 23 *Source:* http://en.wikipedia.org/w/index.php?title=File:Republican_presidential_ticket_1864b.jpg *License:* Public Domain *Contributors:* Currier and Ives ... 66

Figure 24 *Source:* http://en.wikipedia.org/w/index.php?title=File:Andrew_Johnson.jpg *License:* Public Domain *Contributors:* Dbenbenn, Grenavitar, Makthorpe, Parpan05, Quadell, Schaengel89, WTCA, 1 anonymous edits ... 67

Figure 25 *Source:* http://en.wikipedia.org/w/index.php?title=File:Lincoln_and_Johnsond.jpg *License:* Public Domain *Contributors:* Joseph E. Baker 68

Figure 26 *Source:* http://en.wikipedia.org/w/index.php?title=File:Andew_Johnson_impeachment_trial.jpg *License:* Public Domain *Contributors:* Theodore R. Davis (1840-1894) ... 70

Figure 27 *Source:* http://en.wikipedia.org/w/index.php?title=File:AJohnsonimpeach.jpg *License:* Public Domain *Contributors:* Original uploader was Great Scott at en.wikipedia ... 71

Figure 28 *Source:* http://en.wikipedia.org/w/index.php?title=File:The_situation.jpg *License:* Public Domain *Contributors:* en:Harper's Weekly 72

Figure 29 *Source:* http://en.wikipedia.org/w/index.php?title=File:Andrew_Johnson_House_Greeneville_year1886_153142pu.png *License:* Public Domain *Contributors:* Hill & Ramkin Studio ... 75

Figure 30 *Source:* http://en.wikipedia.org/w/index.php?title=File:Andrew_Johnson,_1875.jpg *License:* Public Domain *Contributors:* unknown 76

Figure 31 *Source:* http://en.wikipedia.org/w/index.php?title=File:Andrew_Johnson_1938_Issue-17c.jpg *License:* Public Domain *Contributors:* US Post Office ... 77

Image *Source:* http://en.wikipedia.org/w/index.php?title=File:William_Henry_Seward_-_edited.jpg *License:* Public Domain *Contributors:* User:Connormah ... 81

Image *Source:* http://en.wikipedia.org/w/index.php?title=File:William_Henry_Seward_Signature.svg *License:* Public Domain *Contributors:* Connormah, William Henry Seward ... 82
Figure 32 *Source:* http://en.wikipedia.org/w/index.php?title=File:Frances_Adeline_Miller_Seward.jpg *License:* Public Domain *Contributors:* Original uploader was The Mystery Man at en.wikipedia ... 84
Figure 33 *Source:* http://en.wikipedia.org/w/index.php?title=File:WmHSeward.jpg *License:* Public Domain *Contributors:* User:SreeBot ... 86
Figure 34 *Source:* http://en.wikipedia.org/w/index.php?title=File:Emancipation_proclamation.jpg *License:* Public Domain *Contributors:* 32X, Alensha, Bob Burkhardt, Bogdan, Brad101, Clindberg, Dodiad, Ebcdic, Elcobbola, Evrik, Hohum, Jarekt, Maksim, Mentifisto, Shyam, Sole Soul, Victuallers, Väsk, Ww2censor, 9 anonymous edits ... 87
Figure 35 *Source:* http://en.wikipedia.org/w/index.php?title=File:RunningtheMachine-LincAdmin.jpg *License:* Public Domain *Contributors:* Cameron, John, b. ca. 1828 , artist ... 88
Figure 36 *Source:* http://en.wikipedia.org/w/index.php?title=File:FSewardLPaine.jpg *License:* Public Domain *Contributors:* National Police Gazette 89
Figure 37 *Source:* http://en.wikipedia.org/w/index.php?title=File:Alaska_purchase.jpg *License:* Public Domain *Contributors:* Original uploader was The Mystery Man at en.wikipedia ... 91
Figure 38 *Source:* http://en.wikipedia.org/w/index.php?title=File:William_H_Seward_Madison_Sq_jeh.jpg *License:* Creative Commons Zero *Contributors:* User:Jim.henderson ... 92
Figure 39 *Source:* http://en.wikipedia.org/w/index.php?title=File:Seward_House_South.jpg *License:* Creative Commons Attribution-Sharealike 3.0 *Contributors:* User:SewardHouse2 ... 93
Figure 40 *Source:* http://en.wikipedia.org/w/index.php?title=File:Seward_Statue.jpg *License:* Creative Commons Attribution-Sharealike 3.0 *Contributors:* User:JSquish ... 94
Figure 41 *Source:* http://en.wikipedia.org/w/index.php?title=File:Volunteer_Park_Seward.jpg *License:* Public Domain *Contributors:* Oswaldojh 94
Figure 42 *Source:* http://en.wikipedia.org/w/index.php?title=File:WilliamHSewardBust.jpg *License:* Public Domain *Contributors:* en:User:michaelh2001 ... 95
Image *Source:* http://en.wikipedia.org/w/index.php?title=File:Smn_Cameron-SecofWar.jpg *License:* Public Domain *Contributors:* Original uploader was The Mystery Man at en.wikipedia ... 99
Image *Source:* http://en.wikipedia.org/w/index.php?title=File:Simon_Cameron_Signature.svg *License:* Public Domain *Contributors:* Simon Cameron ... 100
Figure 43 *Source:* http://en.wikipedia.org/w/index.php?title=File:Simon_Cameron.jpg *License:* Public Domain *Contributors:* Original uploader was The Mystery Man at en.wikipedia ... 101
Figure 44 *Source:* http://en.wikipedia.org/w/index.php?title=File:Nast_asks_Pardon.jpg *License:* Public Domain *Contributors:* Bob Burkhardt, Jospe, Mutter Erde ... 101
Figure 45 *Source:* http://en.wikipedia.org/w/index.php?title=File:SCameron.jpg *License:* Public Domain *Contributors:* Original uploader was The Mystery Man at en.wikipedia ... 102
Image *Source:* http://en.wikipedia.org/w/index.php?title=File:Edwin_McMasters_Stanton_Secretary_of_War.jpg *License:* Public Domain *Contributors:* Original uploader was The Mystery Man at en.wikipedia. ... 104
Image *Source:* http://en.wikipedia.org/w/index.php?title=File:Edwin_McMasters_Stanton_Signature.svg *License:* Public Domain *Contributors:* Edwin M. Stanton ... 104
Figure 46 *Source:* http://en.wikipedia.org/w/index.php?title=File:Edwin-Stanton-and-son.jpeg *License:* Public Domain *Contributors:* Photographer is unknown. ... 105
Figure 47 *Source:* http://en.wikipedia.org/w/index.php?title=File:Emancipation_proclamation.jpg *License:* Public Domain *Contributors:* 32X, Alensha, Bob Burkhardt, Bogdan, Brad101, Clindberg, Dodiad, Ebcdic, Elcobbola, Evrik, Hohum, Jarekt, Maksim, Mentifisto, Shyam, Sole Soul, Victuallers, Väsk, Ww2censor, 9 anonymous edits ... 107
Figure 48 *Source:* http://en.wikipedia.org/w/index.php?title=File:RunningtheMachine-LincAdmin.jpg *License:* Public Domain *Contributors:* Cameron, John, b. ca. 1828 , artist ... 109
Figure 49 *Source:* http://en.wikipedia.org/w/index.php?title=File:Stanton_1871-7c.jpg *License:* Public Domain *Contributors:* U.S. Post Office 111
Figure 50 *Source:* http://en.wikipedia.org/w/index.php?title=File:The_situation.jpg *License:* Public Domain *Contributors:* en:Harper's Weekly 112
Image *Source:* http//en.wikipedia.org *License:* Public Domain *Contributors:* Connormah, Jacklee, Jbarta ... 115
Image *Source:* http://en.wikipedia.org/w/index.php?title=File:Salmon_P_Chase_Signature.svg *License:* Public Domain *Contributors:* Connormah, Salmon Portland Chase ... 116
Figure 51 *Source:* http://en.wikipedia.org/w/index.php?title=File:SPChase.jpg *License:* Public Domain *Contributors:* Original uploader was The Mystery Man at en.wikipedia ... 118
Figure 52 *Source:* http://en.wikipedia.org/w/index.php?title=File:Emancipation_proclamation.jpg *License:* Public Domain *Contributors:* 32X, Alensha, Bob Burkhardt, Bogdan, Brad101, Clindberg, Dodiad, Ebcdic, Elcobbola, Evrik, Hohum, Jarekt, Maksim, Mentifisto, Shyam, Sole Soul, Victuallers, Väsk, Ww2censor, 9 anonymous edits ... 120
Figure 53 *Source:* http://en.wikipedia.org/w/index.php?title=File:10000-1f.jpg *License:* Public Domain *Contributors:* Infrogmation, Klare Kante, OttomanJackson, Red devil 666, Vizu, 1 anonymous edits ... 120
Figure 54 *Source:* http://en.wikipedia.org/w/index.php?title=File:CJ-SPC.jpg *License:* Public Domain *Contributors:* Original uploader was The Mystery Man at en.wikipedia ... 121
Figure 55 *Source:* http://en.wikipedia.org/w/index.php?title=File:SC-1868.jpg *License:* Public Domain *Contributors:* Bobak, Innotata, Rrius, Tpal3 122
Figure 56 *Source:* http://en.wikipedia.org/w/index.php?title=File:SalmonChaseGrave.jpg *License:* Creative Commons Attribution-Sharealike 2.5 *Contributors:* Photo by Greg Hume (Greg5030) ... 124
Image *Source:* http://en.wikipedia.org/w/index.php?title=File:Hon._Wm._Pitt_Fessenden_of_Maine.png *License:* Public Domain *Contributors:* Original uploader was Brian0918 at en.wikipedia ... 127
Image *Source:* http://en.wikipedia.org/w/index.php?title=File:Appletons'_Fessenden_Samuel_-_William_Pitt_signature.jpg *License:* Public Domain *Contributors:* William P. Fessenden ... 127
Figure 57 *Source:* http://en.wikipedia.org/w/index.php?title=File:RunningtheMachine-LincAdmin.jpg *License:* Public Domain *Contributors:* Cameron, John, b. ca. 1828 , artist ... 129
Figure 58 *Source:* http://en.wikipedia.org/w/index.php?title=File:Portrait_of_William_P._Fessenden.jpg *License:* Public Domain *Contributors:* Aphasic, Bob Burkhardt, Vincent Steenberg ... 131
Image *Source:* http://en.wikipedia.org/w/index.php?title=File:Wikisource-logo.svg *License:* logo *Contributors:* Nicholas Moreau ... 133
Image *Source:* http://en.wikipedia.org/w/index.php?title=File:Hugh_McCulloch.png *License:* Public Domain *Contributors:* Original uploader was Brian0918 at en.wikipedia ... 134
Figure 59 *Source:* http://en.wikipedia.org/w/index.php?title=File:HMcCulloch.jpg *License:* Public Domain *Contributors:* Gardner, Alexander, 1821-1882, photographer. ... 136
Image *Source:* http://en.wikipedia.org/w/index.php?title=File:Edward_Bates_-_Brady-Handy.jpg *License:* Public Domain *Contributors:* Davepape, Ebcdic, Howcheng ... 139
Figure 60 *Source:* http://en.wikipedia.org/w/index.php?title=File:Emancipation_proclamation.jpg *License:* Public Domain *Contributors:* 32X, Alensha, Bob Burkhardt, Bogdan, Brad101, Clindberg, Dodiad, Ebcdic, Elcobbola, Evrik, Hohum, Jarekt, Maksim, Mentifisto, Shyam, Sole Soul, Victuallers, Väsk, Ww2censor, 9 anonymous edits ... 141
Image *Source:* http://en.wikipedia.org/w/index.php?title=File:James_Speed.jpg *License:* Public Domain *Contributors:* Mutter Erde, ברוקולי . 144
Figure 61 *Source:* http://en.wikipedia.org/w/index.php?title=File:JamesSpeedInterment.jpg *License:* GNU Free Documentation License *Contributors:* Original uploader was Stevietheman at en.wikipedia ... 146
Image *Source:* http://en.wikipedia.org/w/index.php?title=File:Montgomery_Blair,_photo_three-quarters_length_seated.jpg *License:* Public Domain *Contributors:* Bob Burkhardt, Davepape, Docu, Scooter, Tom, W Nowicki ... 147
Figure 62 *Source:* http://en.wikipedia.org/w/index.php?title=File:Emancipation_proclamation.jpg *License:* Public Domain *Contributors:* 32X, Alensha, Bob Burkhardt, Bogdan, Brad101, Clindberg, Dodiad, Ebcdic, Elcobbola, Evrik, Hohum, Jarekt, Maksim, Mentifisto, Shyam, Sole Soul, Victuallers, Väsk, Ww2censor, 9 anonymous edits ... 149
Figure 63 *Source:* http://en.wikipedia.org/w/index.php?title=File:PG-MBlair-Postbellum.jpg *License:* Public Domain *Contributors:* Brady-Handy Photograph Collection (Library of Congress) ... 150
Figure 64 *Source:* http://en.wikipedia.org/w/index.php?title=File:Emancipation_proclamation.jpg *License:* Public Domain *Contributors:* 32X, Alensha, Bob Burkhardt, Bogdan, Brad101, Clindberg, Dodiad, Ebcdic, Elcobbola, Evrik, Hohum, Jarekt, Maksim, Mentifisto, Shyam, Sole Soul, Victuallers, Väsk, Ww2censor, 9 anonymous edits ... 150
Image *Source:* http://en.wikipedia.org/w/index.php?title=File:William_Dennison,_Jr.jpg *License:* Public Domain *Contributors:* Davepape, Julius Morton, Roseohioresident, 1 anonymous edits ... 152
Image *Source:* http://en.wikipedia.org/w/index.php?title=File:Gideon_Welles_-_Ambrotype.jpg *License:* Public Domain *Contributors:* probably Mathew Brady ... 157
Image *Source:* http://en.wikipedia.org/w/index.php?title=File:Gideon_Welles_Signature.svg *License:* Public Domain *Contributors:* Connormah, Gideon Welles ... 158

Figure 65 *Source:* http://en.wikipedia.org/w/index.php?title=File:GideonWellesPortrait.jpg *License:* Public Domain *Contributors:* unknown ..159
Figure 66 *Source:* http://en.wikipedia.org/w/index.php?title=File:RunningtheMachine-LincAdmin.jpg *License:* Public Domain *Contributors:* Cameron, John, b. ca. 1828, artist 160
Figure 67 *Source:* http://en.wikipedia.org/w/index.php?title=File:Emancipation_proclamation.jpg *License:* Public Domain *Contributors:* 32X, Alensha, Bob Burkhardt, Bogdan, Brad101, Clindberg, Dodiad, Ebedic, Elcobbola, Evrik, Hohum, Jarekt, Maksim, Mentifisto, Shyam, Sole Soul, Victuallers, Väsk, Ww2censor, 9 anonymous edits 161
Image *Source:* http://en.wikipedia.org/w/index.php?title=File:CBSmith.jpg *License:* Public Domain *Contributors:* en:Mathew Brady 165
Image *Source:* http://en.wikipedia.org/w/index.php?title=File:Caleb_Blood_Smith_Signature.svg *License:* Public Domain *Contributors:* Caleb Blood Smith 166
Figure 68 *Source:* http://en.wikipedia.org/w/index.php?title=File:CalebBloodSmith-seated-left.jpg *License:* Public Domain *Contributors:* Civil War glass negative collection (Library of Congress) 167
Figure 69 *Source:* http://en.wikipedia.org/w/index.php?title=File:Emancipation_proclamation.jpg *License:* Public Domain *Contributors:* 32X, Alensha, Bob Burkhardt, Bogdan, Brad101, Clindberg, Dodiad, Ebedic, Elcobbola, Evrik, Hohum, Jarekt, Maksim, Mentifisto, Shyam, Sole Soul, Victuallers, Väsk, Ww2censor, 9 anonymous edits 167
Image *Source:* http://en.wikipedia.org/w/index.php?title=File:John_Palmer_Usher.jpg *License:* Public Domain *Contributors:* Original uploader was Brian0918 at en.wikipedia 169

License

Creative Commons Attribution-Share Alike 3.0 Unported
//creativecommons.org/licenses/by-sa/3.0/

Index

Abolitionism, 10, 105, 117, 145
Abolitionist, 153
Abraham Lincoln, **3**, 53, 54, 56, 60, 61, 81, 82, 89, 99, 100, 102, 104, 115, 116, 119, 127–130, 134, 135, 139–142, 144, 145, 148, 152–154, 159, 160, 166, 168, 169
Abraham Lincoln (captain), 5
Abraham Lincoln Association, 45
Abraham Lincoln Bicentennial Commission, 45
Abraham Lincoln Birthplace National Historical Park, 44
Abraham Lincoln Peoria speech, 13
Abraham Lincoln Presidential Library and Museum, 43, 45
Abraham Lincoln and religion, 4
Abraham Lincoln assassination, 58, 61, 66, 82, 135
Actor, 91
Adirondack High Peaks, 95
Adjutant general, 100
Admission to the bar in the United States, 9
Adolph E. Borie, 157
African American, 76, 85
Alabama Claims, 74
Alaska, 131
Alaska purchase, 74, 82, 90, 91, 93
Alexander H. Stephens, 31
Alexander II of Russia, 88
Alexander Randall, 73, 152
Alfred Dwight Foster Hamlin, 59
Alfred Marshall (congressman), 53
All men are created equal, 16
Allan Nevins, 20
Allan Pinkerton, 20
Allen C. Guelzo, 47
Alma mater, 82, 104, 116, 134, 144, 147, 152, 158, 165
Alpha Delta Phi, 117
Alternate history (fiction), 112
Alton Railroad, 12
Alton, Illinois, 140
Ambrose Burnside, 25

American Civil War, 4, 54, 58, 61, 62, 64, 82, 100, 105, 119, 128, 130, 132, 144, 145, 148, 150, 153, 158, 166, 169
American Colonization Society, 10, 44
American Missionary Fellowship, 117
Amnesty, 73
Amos Nourse, 54
Anaconda Plan, 160
Anchorage, Alaska, 96
Andersonville Prison, 59
Andrew Jackson, 63, 148
Andrew Johnson, 3, 32, 35, 37, 40, 53, 57, **60**, 81, 82, 104, 109, 112, 122, 128, 130, 134, 135, 145, 154, 161, 162, 170
Andrew Johnson National Cemetery, 75
Andrew Johnson National Historic Site, 75
Anglicanism, 82, 127
Ann Rutledge, 8
Anthology series, 91
Anti-Masonic Party, 83
Anti-Nebraska Party, 86
Anti-slavery, 159
Antoine-Henri Jomini, 24
Appletons Cyclopædia of American Biography, 133, 168
Appomattox Court House, 31
Apprentice, 100
Army of Virginia, 24
Army of the Potomac, 56
Aroostook War, 55
Assassination, 66
Assassination of Abraham Lincoln, 4
Atlantic slave trade, 88
Attorney General of the United States, 145
Attrition warfare, 30
Auburn Doubledays, 96
Auburn, New York, 82, 83, 91–93
Augustus Henry Seward, 83
Automaton, 112
Ayub Beg Tarabulsy, 87

B. Gratz Brown, 148
Baltimore Plot, 20
Baltimore riot of 1861, 21

Bangor Theological Seminary, 59
Bangor, Maine, 54, 57, 59, 128
Bank of Indiana, 135, 137
Banknote, 121
Bar (law), 106
Bar association, 117
Bardstown, Kentucky, 145
Barnburners and Hunkers, 118
Baton Rouge, 163
Battle of Antietam, 25
Battle of Chancellorsville, 26, 59
Battle of Cold Harbor, 30
Battle of Five Forks, 31
Battle of Fort Stevens, 31
Battle of Fort Sumter, 20, 22
Battle of Fredericksburg, 26
Battle of Gettysburg, 29
Battle of Hampton Roads, 25
Battle of Manila, 136
Battle of Shiloh, 29
Battle of the Wilderness, 30
Belmont, 140
Benjamin Wade, 34
Biographical Directory of Federal Judges, 124
Biographical Directory of the United States Congress, 60, 79, 97, 125, 133, 168, 178
Bishop, 117
Black Americans, 56
Black Codes in the USA, 68
Black Hawk War, 4, 9
Black Reconstruction, 76
Bleeding Kansas, 119
Blockade, 158
Bloody Island (Mississippi River), 140
Booktv, 78
Border states (American Civil War), 5
Boscawen, New Hampshire, 127, 128
Boston, 135
Boston, Massachusetts, 165, 166
Bowdoin College, 128, 134, 135
Brigadier general (United States), 65
Brookfield, New York, 169
Brookins Campbell, 61
Bruce McGill, 113
Bureau of Provisions and Clothing, 159
Bureau of Refugees, Freedmen and Abandoned Lands, 68

CSPAN, 78
CSS Texas, 112
Cabinet (government), 153
Cadiz, Ohio, 106
Caleb B. Smith, 37, 141
Caleb Blood Smith, **165**, 169
Cameron County, Pennsylvania, 102
Cameron Estate, 102

Cameron Parish, Louisiana, 102
Camp Dennison, 153
Canada, 74
Canadian Confederation, 74
Cancer, 170
Cardinal Richelieu, 87
Carl Russell Fish, 47
Carl Schurz, 82
Cave Hill Cemetery, 145, 146
Cedar Hill Cemetery (Hartford, Connecticut), 162
Charles Beard, 76
Charles Hamlin (general), 58
Charles Leale, 40
Charles Magill Conrad, 141
Charles Sumner, 23, 130
Charlotte Hall Military Academy, 140
Chase County, Kansas, 123
Chase Hall, 123
Chase Manhattan Bank, 123
Chase National Bank, 123
Cheshire Academy, 159, 162
Chester A. Arthur, 134, 135
Chicago, 149
Chief Justice of the United States, 66, 115, 122
Chief Justice of the United States Supreme Court, 116
Child actor, 58
Cincinnati, 153
Cincinnati College, 116, 117, 165, 166
Cincinnati Riots of 1836, 117
Cincinnati, Ohio, 117, 123, 152, 166
Civil Rights movement, 76
Clayton-Bulwer Treaty, 129
Clive Cussler, 112
Coal, 161
Cold War, 42
Coles County, Illinois, 7
Colonization, 28
Columbia University, 59
Columbus and Hocking Valley Railroad, 153
Columbus and Xenia Railroad, 153
Columbus, Ohio, 152
Commander-in-chief, 22
Commentaries on the Laws of England, 9
Commissioner, 100
Compensated emancipation, 27
Compositor, 54
Compromise Measures of 1850, 55
Compromise of 1850, 85, 118
Compromise of 1877, 76
Comptroller of the Currency, 135
Confederate States of America, 4, 19, 62, 66, 130, 143, 149
Confiscation Act of 1861, 22
Confiscation Acts, 27

196

Connecticut Constitution, 158
Connecticut General Assembly, 159
Connecticut House of Representatives, 159
Connersville, Indiana, 166
Conscription, 26
Conservatism in the United States, 43
Constitution of the United States, 64, 65
Constitutional Union Party (United States), 18
Cooper Union speech, 16
Copperheads, 5, 22
Copperheads (politics), 22, 33, 153
Cornelia Seward, 83
Cornell University Law School, 182
Cornish, New Hampshire, 116, 117
Corwin Amendment, 19
Court-martial of Fitz John Porter, 107
Cravath, Swaine & Moore, 93
Crittenden Compromise, 19
Crown Hill Cemetery, 168
Cummings, 177
Currency, 119
Currier and Ives, 66
Cybernetics, 112
Cyrus Hamlin, 59
Cyrus Hamlin (general), 58

Dakota War of 1862, 38
Daniel Chester French, 96
Daniel E. Sickles, 106
Daniel Manning, 134
Daniel Webster, 129
Danish West Indies, 74, 88
Dartmouth College, 116, 117
David Davis (Supreme Court justice), 39, 166
David Dixon Porter, 161
David Farragut, 33
David Goodman Croly, 151
David Herbert Donald, 46
David Herold, 90, 108
David Hunter, 27
David M. Key, 61
David T. Patterson, 61
David Tod, 152, 154
David Zarefsky, 51
Decatur, Illinois, 17
Demand note, 121
Democratic Party (U.S.), 83
Democratic Party (US), 148
Democratic Party (United States), 55, 61, 100, 104, 116, 141, 157
Democratic-Republican Party (United States), 139
Demosthenes, 87
Denton Offutt, 7
Department of the West, 22
Dictionary of American Biography, 125

Disfranchisement, 142
District of Columbia, 117
District of Columbia City Hall, 44
Don Carlos Buell, 25
Donegal Springs, 102
Doris Kearns Goodwin, 47
Dred Scott, 14
Dred Scott Case, 129
Dred Scott v. Sandford, 15, 148
Duel, 140

East Tennessee, 62
Eastern United States, 137
Editing, 99, 100
Edmund G. Ross, 72, 131
Edmund Rice (1638), 158, 183
Edmund Spangler, 108
Edward Baker Lincoln, 4, 8
Edward Bates, 37, 104, **139**, 144
Edward Hempstead, 140
Edwin M. Stanton, 32, 37, 73, 88, 99, 102, **104**, 129, 139, 141, 160, 161
Edwin Stanton, 24, 71, 72
Electoral College (United States), 19, 32
Electoral fusion, 18
Elihu B. Washburne, 81
Elijah Miller, 83
Elisha Hunt Allen, 132
Eliza McCardle Johnson, 61, 63
Elizabeth B. Watton Smith, 165
Elizabethton, Tennessee, 61, 75
Ellen Vesta Emery, 55
Ellen Vesta Emery Hamlin, 54
Emancipation Proclamation, 4, 56, 87, 141, 142, 150, 166
Emergence of the term "popular sovereignty" and its pejorative connotation, 13
Emma Willard, 83
Emma Willard School, 83
Emory M. Thomas, 50
Encyclopædia Britannica Eleventh Edition, 98, 125, 133, 137, 151
England, 135
Episcopal Church in the United States of America, 116, 117
Eric Foner, 47, 76
Eugene Hale, 54
Evergreen Cemetery (Portland, Maine), 131

Farm, 54
Farmers Almanac, 13
Federal Judicial Center, 124
Federal government of the United States, 116, 117
Fenian Raids, 74
Fessenden, Samuel, 133

Fessenden, William Pitt, 133
File:Abraham Lincoln Airmail 1960 Issue-25c.jpg, 45
File:Lincoln.ogg, 4
Find a Grave, 103, 146, 151, 155, 168, 182, 183
First Transcontinental Railroad, 37
Fitz John Porter, 107
Flatboat, 7
Florida, New York, 92
Florida, Orange County, New York, 82, 83
Fords Theater, 58, 66
Fords Theatre, 5, 39, 45
Fort Hill Cemetery, 91
Fort Sumter, 160
Fort Wayne, Indiana, 135
Founding Fathers of the United States, 27
Fourteenth Amendment to the United States Constitution, 69, 128
France, 74
Frances Adeline Fanny Seward, 83
Frances Adeline Seward, 82–84
Francis Bicknell Carpenter, 27, 107, 120, 149, 161, 167
Francis Fessenden, 132
Francis Preston Blair, 148
Francis Preston Blair, Jr., 148
Francis Scott Key, 106
Franklin County, Kentucky, 147, 148
Franklin County, New York, 95
Franklin Pierce, 55, 128
Frederic Porter Vinton, 131
Frederick Bates, 140
Frederick Douglass, 29, 47
Frederick Steele, 35
Frederick William Seward, 82, 83, 89, 96
Free Soil Party, 116, 118
Freedmans Bureau, 35
Freedmen, 31, 35, 68
Freedom suit, 141
Freeman Thorp, 101
Freemason, 123
Freeport Doctrine, 16
Fugitive Slave Act, 86
Fugitive Slave Law of 1793, 117
Fundamental Orders, 158

Gabor Boritt, 46
Garry Wills, 50, 180
General Land Office, 11
George Atzerodt, 66, 90, 108
George B. Armstrong, 149
George B. McClellan, 24, 153
George Dewey, 136
George E. Pugh, 116
George McGovern, 48

George Meade, 26
George Peter Alexander Healy, 41
George S. Boutwell, 134
George T. Curtis, 148
George William Brown, 21
Gettysburg Address, 5, 170
Gettysburg Campaign, 26
Gettysburg National Cemetery, 29, 170
Gideon Welles, 37, 73, 88, 109, 129, 141, **157**
Glastonbury, Connecticut, 157, 158, 162
Gold standard, 135
Goochland County, Virginia, 139, 140
Google Books, 124
Gore Vidal, 125
Governor of Maine, 54, 56, 58
Governor of New York, 81, 83
Governor of Ohio, 115, 152
Governor of Tennessee, 61, 64
Green Lawn Cemetery, Columbus, Ohio, 154
Greeneville, Tennessee, 62, 63, 75
Guano Islands Act, 93

Hamilton R. Gamble, 142
Hamlin County, South Dakota, 59
Hamlin, New York, 59
Hammondsville, Ohio, 111
Hampden, Maine, 54
Hampton Roads, 31
Hannibal Hamlin, 3, 17, 37, **53**, 60, 65
Hardin County, Kentucky, 5
Harpers Weekly, 72, 112
Harriet Beecher Stowe, 117
Harrisburg Cemetery, 102
Harrisburg, Pennsylvania, 100, 102
Hartford Evening Press, 159
Hartford Times, 159
Hartford, Connecticut, 157, 159, 162
Harvard Business School, 136
Harvard University, 131
Hawaiian Islands, 88
Hebron Academy, 54
Henry Brooks Adams, 93
Henry Clay, 10, 141
Henry Halleck, 23
Henry Rathbone, 40
Henry Stanberry, 144
Henry Stanbery, 73, 74
Henry Wager Halleck, 24
Hepburn v. Griswold, 122
Herschel Vespasian Johnson, 18
Historical Society of Pennsylvania, 126
Historical rankings of United States Presidents, 42, 62
History of the Democratic Party (United States), 62

History of the Republican Party (United States), 64, 128
History of the United States Republican Party, 56, 62
Hodgenville, Kentucky, 4
Holland Land Company, 83
Homestead Act, 37, 64
Horace Greeley, 28, 87, 142
Horatio King, 147
Horatio Seymour, 151
Houghton Mifflin Harcourt, 49
Housing cooperative, 96
Howard K. Beale, 76
Hugh McCulloch, 37, 73, 127, **134**, 170

Illinois, 3, 169
Illinois 7th congressional district, 3
Illinois Central Railroad, 13
Illinois General Assembly, 9
Illinois House of Representatives, 4, 10
Impeachment, 71
Impeachment in the United States, 62
Impeachment of Andrew Johnson, 62, 130
In God We Trust, 121
Independent agencies of the United States government, 169
Indiana, 67, 166, 169
Indiana Attorney General, 169
Indiana General Assembly, 166
Indianapolis, 168
Indianapolis, Indiana, 165, 166
Inflation, 135
Insanity defense, 106
Internet Archive, 182
Ira Harris, 82
Irish-American, 74
Irreligion, 61
Isaac Toucey, 157, 159
Isham Harris, 61

J. B. Lippincott & Co., 124
J. Donald Cameron, 100, 102
JP Morgan Chase & Co., 123
JPMorgan Chase, 123
JSTOR, 113
Jacksonian Democracy, 43
Jacksonville, Florida, 111
Jacob Johnson (father of Andrew Johnson), 62
Jacob Thompson, 165
James Buchanan, 3, 14, 100, 104, 106, 128
James C. Jones, 61
James D. Fessenden, 132
James Deering Fessenden, 132
James Ford Rhodes, 69, 178
James G. Birney, 117
James G. Blaine, 57
James G. Randall, 49
James Garfield, 57, 154
James Harlan, 170
James Harlan (senator), 74, 169
James K. Polk, 11, 159
James M. McPherson, 48
James Madison, 38
James S. Wiley, 53
James Speed, 37, 73, 139, **144**
James W. Bradbury, 127
James W. Grimes, 72, 130
James Woodson Bates, 140
January Uprising, 88
Jay Cooke, 135
Jay Cooke & Company, 119
Jay Tolson, 179
Jefferson County, Kentucky, 5, 144
Jefferson Davis, 19, 66
Jeremiah S. Black, 81, 104
Jimmy Carter, 178
Joel Aldrich Matteson, 14
John Adams Dix, 82, 115
John Archibald Campbell, 166
John B. Henderson, 72, 130
John Bell (Tennessee politician), 18
John C. Breckinridge, 18, 53, 65
John C. Frémont, 22, 27, 86, 148
John Catron, 74
John D. Winters, 163
John Henry (representative), 3
John Lattimer, 97
John M. Schofield, 104
John Merryman, 22
John Milton Niles, 159
John P. Usher, 37, 74
John Palmer Usher, 165, 166, **169**
John Pope (military officer), 24
John Purdue, 123
John Quincy Adams, 96
John Rock (abolitionist), 122
John Schofield, 73
John Sherman (politician), 116, 153
John Speed, 145
John T. Stuart, 9
John Van Zandt, 117
John Walker (Indiana), 166
John Wilkes Booth, 5, 39, 66, 89
Joint Committee on Reconstruction, 128, 130
Jones v. Van Zandt, 117
Joseph Cotten, 91
Joseph Gurney Cannon, 169
Joseph H. Williams, 54
Joseph Holt, 99
Joseph Hooker, 26, 56
Joseph S. Fowler, 72, 130
Joseph Story, 129

Joshua Barton, 140
Joshua Fry Speed, 145
Joshua R. Giddings, 11
Journalism, 100, 159
Journalist, 99, 158, 166
Jubal Anderson Early, 31
Judge, 116
Judicial notice, 13
Jurist, 39

Kansas-Nebraska Act, 55, 118, 129, 148
Kansas–Nebraska Act, 13
Karl Marx, 87
Kennebunk, Maine, 134, 135
Kentucky, 144, 153
Kentucky House of Representatives, 145
Kentucky Senate, 145
Kenyon College, 104, 106
Kevin Kline, 112
Know-Nothing, 100

LL.D., 131
LaRue County, Kentucky, 5
Large denominations of United States currency, 121
Laurens, South Carolina, 63
Law, 83
Lawyer, 82, 116, 127, 134, 139, 144, 148, 152, 158, 159, 166, 169
Lecompton Constitution, 14, 65, 129
Legal Tender Act, 130
Legal Tender Cases, 122
Leonard Swett, 17
Lerone Bennett, Jr., 43, 46
Levi Woodbury, 149
Lewis Powell (assassin), 89, 108
Lexington, Kentucky, 8
Liberal Republican Party (United States), 123
Liberia, 10
Liberty Party (1840s), 116, 118
Lieutenant Governor of Ohio, 116, 152
Lincoln (2012 film), 113
Lincoln Boyhood National Memorial, 44
Lincoln Home National Historic Site, 45
Lincoln Log Cabin State Historic Site, 7
Lincoln Memorial, 44
Lincoln Tomb, 45
Lincoln and Seward, 162
Lincoln at Gettysburg: The Words That Remade America, 50
Lincoln cent, 45
Lincoln, Nebraska, 44
Lincolns House Divided Speech, 15
Lincolns New Salem, 9, 45
Lincolns assassination, 170
Lincolns first inaugural address, 20, 36

Lincolns second inaugural address, 33
Lincoln–Douglas debates of 1858, 16
List of Attorneys General of Missouri, 141
List of Chief Justices, 115
List of Governors of Maine, 54
List of Governors of New York, 82
List of Governors of Ohio, 116, 152
List of Presidents of the United States, 3, 4, 60, 61
List of United States Ambassadors to Russia, 102
List of Vice Presidents of the United States, 53, 54, 60
Lorenzo Thomas, 71, 72, 112
Lot M. Morrill, 54, 127
Louis J. Weichmann, 108
Louisiana State University Press, 163
Louisville Board of Aldermen, 145
Louisville Home Guard, 144, 145
Louisville, Kentucky, 144–146
Lower East Side, 95, 96
Lucy Berry Delaney, 141
Lucy Gilmer Fry, 144
Luther Bradish, 81
Lyman Trumbull, 14, 68, 72, 130
Lyons-Seward Treaty of 1862, 87

Macon County, Illinois, 7
Madison Square Park, 92, 96
Maine, 53, 54, 56, 127, 128
Maine Attorney General, 58
Maine House of Representatives, 55, 128
Maine Republican Party, 57
Maines 6th congressional district, 53
Manhattan, 95, 96
Mark E. Neely, Jr., 48, 51
Mark Hatfield, 78
Mark Twain, 141
Marlborough, Massachusetts, 158
Martin Van Buren, 118, 159
Martin Welker, 116
Mary Surratt, 90, 108
Mary Todd Lincoln, 4, 8, 57, 108
Maryland, 140, 148
Massachusetts Bay Colony, 54
Mayor of Washington, D.C., 154
Maytown, Pennsylvania, 99, 100, 102
Medal of Honor, 158
Melancholy, 9
Methodist, 104
Mexican–American War, 11
Mexico, 74, 166
Miami University, 152, 153, 165, 166
Michael OLaughlen, 108
Middlebury College, 59
Midway Atoll, 88

Military tribunal, 108
Milk sickness, 6
Millard Fillmore, 141
Mineral County, West Virginia, 5
Minneapolis, Minnesota, 95
Mises Institute, 180
Mississippi River, 142, 161
Missouri Compromise, 13, 19, 55
Missouri House of Representatives, 141
Missouri Secretary of State, 140
Missouri Territory, 140
Mobile, Alabama, 161
Money, 135
Montgomery Blair, 37, 141, **147**, 152
Montgomery Blair High School, 150
Montgomery Clift, 149
Mordecai House, 63
Morley, Missouri, 146
Morrill Land-Grant Colleges Act, 37
Morrill Tariff, 38
Morrison Waite, 115
Mount Hope Cemetery, Bangor, 59
Mount Rushmore, 44
Myers v. United States, 71

NBC, 91
Nancy Lincoln, 5
Napoleon III, 88
Nathan A. Farwell, 127
Nathaniel P. Banks, 35
National Banking Act, 38, 135
National Register of Historic Places, 59
National Union Convention, 145
National Union Party (United States), 4, 32, 56, 61, 62, 65, 66
Native Americans in the United States, 85
Naval Historical Center, 163
Nebraska, 74
Negative capability, 44
Negro, 65
Neptune (mythology), 161
New Deal, 42
New International Encyclopedia, 133, 151
New Salem, Menard County, Illinois, 7
New York, 59, 118, 168
New York City, 92, 94, 123
New York City draft riots, 29
New York State Bar Association, 83
New York Supreme Court, 85
New York Times, 119
Newspaper, 54
Newt Gingrich, 112
Noah Brooks, 16
Noah Haynes Swayne, 39
Non-denominational Christianity, 61
Non-interventionism, 88

Norman B. Judd, 17
North Carolina, 61, 63
Northern Central Railway, 100
Norumbega, 59
Norwich University, 158, 159

Oak Hill Cemetery (Washington, D.C.), 110, 123
Ohio, 116, 152, 166
Ohio State Senate, 153
Ohio State University, 153
Ohio in the War, 154
Olive Risley Seward, 82, 83
Oliver Wendell Holmes, Jr., 31
Opposition Party (United States), 127
Oregon Territory, 11
Origins of the American Civil War, 145
Orion Clemens, 141
Orphan, 100
Orville H. Browning, 74
Oscar Apfel, 112
Otto Eisenschiml, 111
Our American Cousin, 40
Overland Campaign, 30
Oxford University Press, 125, 126

Pacific Railway Acts, 37
Panama, 88
Paris, Maine, 54, 59
Parochial school, 84
Partus sequitur ventrum, 141
Peace Conference of 1861, 20, 119
Peace Democrats, 153
Pennsylvania, 100
Pennsylvania General Assembly, 102
Perry County, Indiana, 6
Personal liberty laws, 86
Peter G. Van Winkle, 72, 130
Petersen House, 40, 45
Phi Beta Kappa, 83, 117
Philadelphia, 145
Philadelphia, Pennsylvania, 169
Philander Chase, 117
Philip Barton Key II, 106
Philip K. Dick, 112
Philip Sheridan, 31
Phineas Densmore Gurley, 40
Pittsburgh, Pennsylvania, 106
Plain Folk of the Old South, 63
Plantation, 140
Poland, 88
Political corruption, 102
Political movement, 100
Politician, 82, 99, 116, 127, 134, 139, 144, 148, 158, 166, 169
Politics of the United States, 128

Polly Berry, 141
Popular sovereignty, 16
Portland, Maine, 127, 128, 131
Postmaster, 159
Preface, **1**
President of the United States, 37, 54, 60, 61, 72, 73, 82, 100, 116, 130, 135, 145, 153, 154
President pro tempore of the United States Senate, 57
Presidential Cabinet, 135
Presidents Day (United States), 45
Prince Georges County, Maryland, 134, 136
Printer (publisher), 100
Professor, 144
Project Gutenberg, 97
Protectionism, 119
Public domain, 124, 125, 133, 137, 151
Purchase of Alaska, 74
Purdue University, 123

Quaker, 105

Racial integration, 76
Radical Republicans, 5, 62, 128, 145, 148
Railroad, 100
Raleigh, North Carolina, 61–63
Ralph Raico, 180
Rappahannock River, 26
Real estate broker, 82
Reconstruction Era of the United States, 5, 57, 61, 68, 76, 109, 149
Reference: Correspondence on excavation and opening of grave-site, 168
Regiment, 153
Reinhard H. Luthin, 48
Republican National Convention, 145, 154, 166
Republican Party (US), 148
Republican Party (United States), 4, 54, 82, 100, 104, 116, 119, 127, 134, 144, 152, 157, 165, 169
Republicanism in the United States, 13, 16, 36
Revenue Act of 1861, 38
Revenue Act of 1862, 38
Richard A. Dysart, 112
Richard Carwardine, 46
Richard Hofstadter, 48
Richard Mulligan, 91
Richmond, Virginia, 21
River Queen (steamboat), 30
Robert Anderson (Civil War), 20, 160
Robert B. Warden, 126
Robert C. Kirk, 152
Robert College, 59
Robert E. Lee, 5, 25

Robert Redford, 112
Robert Todd Lincoln, 4, 8
Robin Kelley, 48
Roger B. Taney, 15, 115, 122
Rolling Stone (magazine), 179
Roman Catholic Church, 84
Roy Basler, 45
Royalton, Vermont, 117
Rufus P. Ranney, 153
Russia, 131
Russian Empire, 74

S. S. Seward Institute, 83
Sahara (novel), 112
Saint Josephs College (Kentucky), 144
Sally Hamlin, 58
Salmon P. Chase, 16, 35, 37, 39, 66, **115**, 127, 130, 135, 141, 142, 152, 161
Salmon P. Chase College of Law, 124
Salon.com, 179
Samaná, 88
Samuel Arnold (Lincoln conspirator), 108
Samuel C. Fessenden, 132
Samuel Fessenden, 128, 132
Samuel Freeman Miller, 39
Samuel Livermore, 54
Samuel Milligan, 74
Samuel Mudd, 108, 112
Samuel Wells, 54
Sangamon County, Illinois, 7
Sangamon River, 7
Santee (Isáŋyathi or Eastern Dakota), 38
Sarah Bush Lincoln, 6
Sarah Lincoln Grigsby, 6
Schenectady, New York, 95
Scholar survey results, 5
Schuyler Colfax, 60, 145
Sean Wilentz, 76, 179
Seattle, Washington, 95
Seceded, 65
Secession, 153
Secession in the United States, 4
Second Bank of the United States, 137
Second Battle of Bull Run, 25, 132
Secondary education, 83
Secretary of the Treasury, 123, 135
Seminole War, 148
Separate Baptists, 6
Seward County, Nebraska, 95
Seward Park (Manhattan), 95
Seward Park (Seattle), 95
Seward Park Housing Corporation, 96
Seward Peninsula, 95
Seward, Alaska, 95
Seward, Illinois, 95
Seward, Kansas, 95

Seward, Minneapolis, 95
Seward, Nebraska, 95
Seward, New York, 95
Seward, William Henry, 98
Sewards Day, 90
Sewards Folly, 74, 90, 95
Sewards Success, Alaska, 95
Shenandoah Valley, 31
Shermans March to the Sea, 31
Silver Spring, Maryland, 147, 149, 150
Simon Cameron, 37, **99**, 104, 106
Sinking Spring Farm, 5
Slave, 141
Slave Power, 86, 116, 128
Slave and free states, 153
Slave state, 14
Slavery in the United States, 4, 117
Smith, Caleb Blood, 168
Smithsonian Institution, 103, 131
Sons of Liberty, 168
Sons of Union Veterans of the Civil War, 154
South Dakota, 59
Southern United States, 117
Spanish-American War, 136
Speaker of the United States House of Representatives, 57
Spoken word, 58
Spot Resolutions, 11
Spring Grove Cemetery, 123, 124
Springfield, Illinois, 8, 169
St Louis, Missouri, 148
St. Charles, Missouri, 140
St. Louis, Missouri, 139, 140
St. Paul Episcopal Cathedral, Cincinnati, 123
Stanton College Preparatory School, 111
Stanton County, Nebraska, 111
Stanton Davis Kirkham, 112
Stanton Park, 111
States rights, 63
Stephen A. Douglas, 13
Stephen Douglas, 128
Stephen E. Ambrose, 45
Stephen Emery, 54
Stephen Johnson Field, 39
Stephen T. Logan, 10
Sterling Price, 143
Steubenville, Ohio, 104, 105
Steven Spielberg, 113
Stites & Harbison, 145
Sudbury, Massachusetts, 158
Suffrage, 123
Supreme Court Historical Society, 182
Supreme Court of Illinois, 12
Supreme Court of the United States, 12, 71, 74, 106, 117, 166
Suspension during the Civil War, 22

Swing Around the Circle, 69

T. A. D. Fessenden, 132
Tad Lincoln, 4, 9
Tailor, 61
Talkeetna, Alaska, 95
Taxation in the United States, 135
Team of Rivals: The Political Genius of Abraham Lincoln, 125
Temperance movement, 128
Ten percent plan, 34
Tennessee, 60–62
Tennessee House of Representatives, 63
Tennessee Senate, 64
Tennessees 1st congressional district, 61, 64
Tenure of Office Act (1867), 62, 71, 109
Terre Haute, Indiana, 169
Texas, 90
Texas v. White, 122
Thaddeus Stevens, 34, 102
Thanksgiving (United States), 38
The Conspirator, 112
The Fessendens, 128
The Honorable, 81
The Joseph Cotten Show, 91
The Lincoln Conspiracy (book), 111
The Lincoln Conspiracy (film), 111
The Slave Power, 16
Theodore R. Davis, 70
Thirteenth Amendment to the United States Constitution, 4, 35
Thomas Dickens Arnold, 61
Thomas Eckert, 107
Thomas Green Fessenden, 132
Thomas Hart Benton (senator), 141
Thomas L. Harris, 3
Thomas Lincoln, 5
Thomas Welles, 158
Thurlow Weed, 83
Title (property), 6
Transylvania University, 144, 145
Trent Affair, 4, 23, 87
Tuberculosis, 8
Tulane University Law School, 126
Typhoid fever, 8, 65

U.S. Capitol Building, 19
U.S. Constitution, 85, 135
U.S. Court of Appeals, 126
U.S. Horse Artillery Brigade, 153
U.S. News & World Report, 179
U.S. Postmaster General, 153
U.S. Presidents on U.S. postage stamps, 77
U.S. Senate, 55
U.S. Senate Committee on Appropriations, 131
U.S. Senate Committee on Finance, 131

U.S. Senate Committee on Public Buildings and Grounds, 131
U.S. Senate Committee on the Library, 131
U.S. Senator from New York, 85
U.S. Southern states, 135
U.S. Treasury Secretary, 134
U.S. presidential election, 1852, 142
U.S. presidential election, 1860, 142
U.S. presidential election, 1868, 149
U.S. state, 128
USCGC Chase (WHEC-718), 123
USCGC McCulloch .28WAVP-386.2C WHEC-386.29, 136
USS McCulloch, 136
USS Powhatan (1850), 160
USS Welles, 162
Ulysses Grant, 73
Ulysses S. Grant, 5, 29, 60, 71, 72, 91, 109, 110, 112, 154
Union (American Civil War), 5, 82
Union College, 82, 83
Union army, 106, 153
Unitarianism, 54
United Kingdom, 74
United States, 99, 100, 127, 134, 139, 140, 144, 145, 147, 157, 158, 165, 166, 169
United States Ambassador to Russia, 100
United States Ambassador to Spain, 57
United States Army, 148
United States Army Center of Military History, 103
United States Assistant Secretary of the Interior, 169
United States Attorney General, 37, 73, 104, 106, 117, 139, 140, 142, 144
United States Cabinet, 142, 148, 161, 166, 169
United States Capitol, 59, 111
United States Chief Justice, 142
United States Coast Guard, 136
United States Coast Guard Academy, 123
United States Congress, 119, 166
United States Constitution, 117
United States Court of Claims, 74
United States Democratic Party, 99, 100, 106, 147, 149, 162
United States Department of Agriculture, 38
United States Department of War, 153
United States Department of the Navy, 160
United States Deputy Secretary of the Interior, 166
United States Electoral College, 18
United States House election, 1866, 69
United States House of Representatives, 3, 4, 53–55, 61, 128, 141, 145
United States House of Representatives elections, 1862, 26
United States Military Academy, 147, 148
United States Navy, 158
United States Note, 135
United States Postmaster General, 37, 73, 147, 148, 152
United States Republican Party, 82, 99, 100, 129, 139, 142, 145, 147, 149, 159
United States Revenue Cutter Service, 136
United States Secretary of State, 37, 57, 66, 73, 81, 82, 160
United States Secretary of War, 37, 72, 73, 99, 100, 102, 104, 105, 141, 161
United States Secretary of the Interior, 37, 74, 165, 166, 169, 170
United States Secretary of the Navy, 37, 73, 157, 158, 160
United States Secretary of the Treasury, 37, 57, 73, 115, 116, 119, 127, 128, 130, 134, 161
United States Senate, 4, 53, 54, 56, 60, 62, 70, 81, 82, 100, 110, 116, 127, 128, 141, 153
United States Senate election in New York, 1849, 85
United States Senate election in New York, 1855, 86
United States Senator, 116
United States Solicitor, 148
United States Supreme Court, 129, 135, 148
United States Whig Party, 99, 100, 128, 139, 141
United States district attorney, 148
United States district court, 74
United States five-dollar bill, 45
United States non-interventionism, 88
United States of America, 169
United States presidential election, 1848, 11
United States presidential election, 1860, 4, 54, 82, 100
United States presidential election, 1864, 5, 62
University of Alabama, 182
University of Louisville, 145
University of Maine, 59

Veazie Banks v. Fenno, 122
Vice President of the United States, 37, 53, 54, 60, 62, 65, 73, 142, 145
Vicksburg campaign, 29
Victor Talking Machine Company, 58
Vietnam War, 136
Virginia, 153
Virginia Gregg, 91
Volunteer Park (Seattle), 94, 96

W.E.B. Du Bois, 76
Wade-Davis Bill, 35

Walter Q. Gresham, 134
War Democrat, 56, 62, 65
War Democrats, 5, 32, 154
War Governors Conference, 28
War of 1812, 140
Ward Hill Lamon, 40
Washington, D.C., 95, 100, 119, 123, 136, 149
We Can Build You, 112
West Point, 143
West Virginia, 153
Western Kentucky University, 77
Westfield (village), New York, 83, 93
Wheeling Convention, 153
Whig Party (United States), 4, 9, 10, 82, 83, 118, 127, 144, 145, 152, 165, 166
White supremacist, 76
Whitelaw Reid, 154
Wikipedia:IPA for English, 4
William Alexander Graham, 142
William Allen (governor), 116
William Archibald Dunning, 78
William B. Campbell, 61
William Blackstone, 9
William Brownlow, 61
William C. Bouck, 81
William Dennison (Ohio governor), 73, 116, 147
William Dennison, Jr., 37, **152**
William Duff Armstrong, 13
William Fessenden Allen, 132
William Gannaway Brownlow, 60
William H. Seward, 16, 37, 40, 66, 73, 74, **81**, 109, 119, 129, 141, 160
William H. Seward House, 91, 93
William Henry Harrison, 178
William Henry Seward Memorial, 96
William Henry Seward, Jr., 82, 83
William Herndon (lawyer), 10
William L. Marcy, 81
William Lloyd Garrison, 117
William M. Evarts, 71, 73, 126
William Marcy, 83
William Medill, 116
William Neil Dennison, 153
William P. Fessenden, 37, 88, 109, 115, **127**, 132, 134, 160, 170
William Pitt Fessenden, 72
William R. Forstchen, 112
William Rosecrans, 25
William Tecumseh Sherman, 20, 31
William Wallace Lincoln, 4, 8
William Wirt (Attorney General), 117
Wilmot Proviso, 11, 55
Windsor, Vermont, 117
Winnebago Indians, 100
Witness tampering, 108

World War II, 136
WorldCat, 51
Worthington, Ohio, 117
Writer, 158
Wyman B. S. Moor, 54

Yale College, 158
Yosemite National Park, 38

Zachariah Chandler, 65
Zachary Taylor, 11, 85, 178

www.ingramcontent.com/pod-product-compliance
Lightning Source LLC
Chambersburg PA
CBHW071843230426
43671CB00012B/2053